Brown Plus Thirty

Perspectives on Desegregation

This book is published under grants from the Rockefeller Foundation and Carnegie Corporation of New York and funds from U.S. Department of Education, Region II Race Desegregation Assistance Center.

Library of Congress Cataloging-in-Publication Data
Main entry under title:
Brown plus thirty.

    Includes bibliographies.
    1. Discrimination in education—Law and legislation—United States—Congresses. 2. Segregation in education—United States—Congresses. I. Miller, LaMar P. II. New York University. Metropolitan Center for Educational Research, Development, and Training. III. Title: Brown plus 30.
KF4155.A2B76 1986   344.73'0798   85-62471
ISBN 0-935405-00-3   347.304798

Brown Plus Thirty

Perspectives on Desegregation

Proceedings of a Conference Commemorating the
Thirtieth Anniversary of the 1954 Supreme Court
Decision in Brown v. The Board of Education of
Topeka, Kansas, held on September 11–14, 1984

LAMAR P. MILLER, EDITOR

Metropolitan Center
for Educational Research,
Development, and Training

New York University
School of Education, Health,
Nursing, and Arts Professions

Contents

Acknowledgments

In preparing this report on *"Brown* Plus Thirty,"* we were constantly reminded of the contributions of the individuals who participated in the 1954 case and made it possible for thousands of youngsters to obtain an equal education. To those individuals we are eternally grateful.

The idea for the conference and for the publication of these proceedings grew out of the long and arduous effort to fulfill the mandate of *Brown.* The staff of the desegregation center of Metro discussed the project with the directors of other desegregation centers around the country. Despite the somber mood in the nation regarding desegregation, we agreed that because some remarkable changes have taken place in the last thirty years, there was a need to conduct the conference. The directors of the other desegregation centers provided endless encouragement and wise counsel. We are especially indebted to Charles Rankin, Charles Moody, Benjamin Turner, Gordon Foster, and Olga Duff who were profoundly influential in providing assistance.

We are similarly indebted to colleagues who served as consultants and drafted and presented papers. In particular, Robert Carter, Kenneth Clark, Linda Brown Smith, Samuel Proctor, Nelvia Brady, Willis Hawley, Eugene Reville, Constance Clayton, Norman Redlich, Beverly Cole, Nathaniel Jones, Gary Orfield, William Bradford Reynolds, Julius Chambers, Stuart Cook, Derrick Bell, Thomas Atkins, Hugh Scott, Robert Crain, Michael H. Sussman, Cora Watkins, Michael Hoge, Leonard Stevens, and my associate J. Theodore Repa. The Metro Center is indeed fortunate to have the support of the administration of the University and of the School of Education, Health, Nursing, and Arts Professions. We sincerely thank President John Brademas and Dean Robert Burnham for their support and participation in the conference.

At one time or another every member of the Metro Center staff contributed to the project. Initially, Mrs. Connie Coveney was the coordinator of the conference. Her contribution and leadership during the early planning days were crucial to the success of the project, and we were saddened and shocked by her sudden illness and subsequent death. A special word of thanks goes to Dilma Koutsakis who assumed the task of coordinating the project and performed admirably. Other staff members also made important contributions. A warm thank you to Nancy Schwartz, Barbara Riley, Sandra Delson, Debra Green, Daphne Smith, Jonathan Dunn, Earl Thomas, and Stephanie D'Ambra.

Four other people were critically important. Joan Poole and Geraldine Finnegan worked tirelessly in editing the document and checking all the loose ends with the various writers. In addition, we want to thank Cheryl Hanna for her creative work in the layout and design of the book and Ruth Davis for her meticulous proofreading of the galleys. This project could not have been completed without them and we are extremely grateful for their work.

Two major foundations were partners in this project. We are most grateful to Bruce E. Williams of the Rockefeller Foundation, who not only provided advice and encouragement but was instrumental in our receiving a generous grant from the Foundation. The Carnegie Corporation of New York also provided a generous grant for the project. We are grateful to Bernard Charles of the Carnegie Corporation for his valuable advice and assistance. We also thank Tommie Jones and the Community Relations Service of the U.S. Department of Justice for their assistance in conducting the conference.

Finally, we wish to express our profound respect to the teachers, principals, superintendents, parents, and other community people who continue to work diligently to make the desegregation process succeed in the nation's schools. Providing equal educational opportunities to all our children must not fail.

LaMar P. Miller

Editor's Preface

The 1954 Supreme Court decision in the case of *Linda Brown* v. *The Board of Education of Topeka* provided the legal basis for equal educational opportunity. The Court ruled that "In the field of public education the doctrine of 'separate but equal' has no place. Separate education facilities are inherently unequal.... We hold that the plaintiffs and others similarly situated ... are by reason of the segregation complained of, deprived of the equal protection of the laws guaranteed by the Fourteenth Amendment." (*Brown* v. *Board of Education of Topeka*, 1954.) The *Brown* decision was the result of a persistent initiative on the part of black leaders and organizations over a period of years. The early 1950s marked a turning point in the history of black America due to the emergence of black leaders such as Roy Wilkins of the NAACP, Phillip Randolph of the Brotherhood of Sleeping Car Porters, Whitney Young of the Urban League, and Reverend Dr. Martin Luther King, Jr., of the Southern Christian Leadership Conference. Their leadership was supported by the involvement of unprecedented numbers of blacks as the fight for equality became national in scope. Black parents supported by black organizations viewed the *Brown* decision as a chance for equal opportunity. Over the past thirty years, however, our nation has been reluctant to move with all deliberate speed toward equality of opportunity.

Since 1954, the force of law has been required to achieve much of the desegregation that has taken place so far. The very integrity of the three branches of government has been severely tested by the controversy over desegregation. While many of the once dual school districts in the South have converted to a non-segregated or unitary status, segregation of black students in the Northeast has increased, as has the segregation of Hispanic students in all regions of the country. Moreover, the quality of the educational experience received by minority students continues to be a major problem. Even the series of national reports that appeared in 1984 on the need for excellence and improvement in education do not address directly issues related to quality education and equality of educational opportunity.

It is against this background that the staff of the Metropolitan Center for Educational Research, Development, and Training determined that there was and is a need to examine the progress of desegregation and to think seriously about the controversial issues that will face the nation in the latter part of the 1980s and 1990s. We believe that it is important to examine past and current desegregation activities, and critical to explore the prospects for achieving equality of educational opportunity in the future.

We decided to look at these issues by conducting a two and one-half day conference called "*Brown* Plus Thirty" in the fall of 1984—thirty years after the *Brown* decision. The goal of the conference was to develop a document of proceedings that would assist federal, state, and local policymakers, educational leaders, members of the legal profession, and the community at large, in making decisions leading to equality of educational opportunity for all children.

Obviously, the key to conducting a successful conference and producing a useful manuscript was to bring together the most active and knowledgeable individuals in the field. On the advice of our sponsors and our colleagues, we believe we assembled an outstanding representative group of presenters from fields most closely associated with desegregation, such as education, law, government, and social science. Presenters and participants included (1) school superintendents, especially those in cities where major events have occurred or are occurring; (2) state education department representatives; (3) federal government representatives; (4) representatives of organizations such as the Harvard Center for Law and Education, the Legal Defense Fund, the Children's Defense Fund, the NAACP, ASPIRA, and the Urban League; (5) Desegregation Assistance Center directors; and (6) representatives of law firms involved in desegregation litigation.

In addition to the presentations, we attempted to capture the excitement of the conference through a series of ongoing discussion groups. All participants were engaged in one of three groups that focused on the major legal, educational, and social issues and controversies that emerged from the conference. The conference far exceeded our expectations and generated an excitement and interest that we believe was beneficial to all concerned.

The document that has evolved from the conference reviews the historical development and impact of the *Brown* decision on American society in general and on American education in particular; assesses the current status of desegregation activities from a legal, educational, and socio-political perspective; and recommends future policy, programs, activities, research and action for the various legal education and governmental agencies. The book presents articles by individuals who were involved in the historic case, including Linda Brown Smith, the plaintiff, Robert L. Carter, one of the attorneys who argued the case, and Kenneth B. Clark, who presented important psychological evidence.

The desegregation of public schools is still a controversial and complex issue in American society. A broad spectrum of views on the means to achieve equal educational opportunity for all children surfaced during the conference and is reflected in this report. There is, for example, a pessimistic feeling on the part of many professionals in the field that progress toward achieving desegregation has been impeded by the change in educational policy of the present Administration. There is also a continuing belief, particularly on the part of minorities, that American education is by no means free of racism. The recognition that educational excellence is not a reality for large numbers of minority children is evident throughout the book.

Despite these nagging problems, there is increasing evidence that school districts can be successful at improving the quality of education through the process of desegregating schools. Creating more effective schools that focus on excellence appears to be an emerging trend in desegregating school districts.

The blends and patterns of educational activities that should obscure former educational deficiencies and provide equal opportunities for all students require creative and committed leadership. Pressures that have led desegregating school system officials to seek excellence in their schools is a healthy development for education. However, in dealing with almost any problem that is striated by sharp emotional conflict, there are times when it is easy to stop asking questions, to relax the pressure, and to live with compromise. Our aim is to highlight the issues, to nudge our constituents, and to reaffirm the commitment made in the *Brown* decision, so that a respite does not take place. If these purposes are achieved, then the conference and these proceedings will have served a useful purpose and the Metro Center commitment to equity will have been fulfilled.

LaMar P. Miller

Executive Director

Metropolitan Center for Educational Research, Development, and Training

Prologue

Reflections on Brown After Thirty Years

LINDA BROWN SMITH

It is always a pleasure to speak to gatherings on a personal note recounting the role played by my family and twelve other families in opening the door for change in public education and other areas of society through *Brown* v. *Board of Education* (1954).

When asked to be a part of this conference and share my experiences, what immediately came to mind was an old African proverb that so clearly embraces the wisdom of our ancestors: "Because We are, I am." This holds special significance for me because of the multitude of people who were activists before *Brown* and paved the way as well as those well-known and unknown that have come after.

Since the case was initiated in the early 1950s, my life has been one extraordinary experience. It all started on a balmy day in the fall of 1950, in the quiet Kansas town of Topeka, when a mild-mannered black man took his plump seven-year-old daughter by the hand and walked briskly four blocks from their home to the all-white school and tried without success to enroll his child. The child of whom I speak was me, Linda Carol Brown, and my father, the late Reverend Oliver Leon Brown.

Black parents in Topeka felt that the day of trying to enroll their children in the school nearest to their home was long overdue. Many were the evenings when my father would arrive home to find my mother almost in tears because I would only get halfway to

the school bus stop, which was a seven-block walk from my home. I could only make half the walk because the cold would get too bitter for a small child to bear. I can still remember starting that bitter walk, and the terrible cold that would cause my tears to freeze on my face. I would return home running as fast as I could back through the busy and dangerous railroad yards of the Rock Island Railroad. Through the railroad yards was the only route I could take to reach a very busy avenue that I had to cross to catch the school bus that would carry me some two miles across town to the all-black Monroe Public School. These were the circumstances that so angered black parents.

My father pondered, "Why should my child have to cross dangerous railroad tracks and face unbearable winter weather, waiting for a badly overcrowded school bus to carry her two miles across town, when there is a school only four blocks from our home? Why must I have to spend time trying to explain to my child that she cannot go to the same school with her neighborhood playmates, who are predominately white, Indian, and Spanish American, because her skin is black?"

In the face of this discouragement he, along with twelve other parents, met with the local NAACP and its lawyer, Charles S. Scott, to make plans for each family to try and enroll their child in the white school nearest home during September 1950.

After trying enrollment and being turned down, a suit was filed in federal court in February 1951. During the following July, the three-judge panel heard testimony from my father and several other of the parents who agreed that segregated schools for blacks were unequal. I had to appear with my father in court, but unlike my father, I was not asked to take the witness stand.

The case was decided in favor of the Board of Education of Topeka and its segregated elementary schools.

In Topeka, the issue was not so much integrating public schools to improve the quality of instruction, but rather the inaccessibility of the neighborhood schools. Black people were able to live all over town, but could not send their children to the schools closest to their home. As for the quality of instruction, we have to pay our respects to the black educators of the fifties, because they set untarnished examples and expected no less than our best efforts.

During the local court battle, there was a very definite division in the black community. There were those who felt this action was long overdue and still another faction that expressed concern about upsetting the balance of things, which they feared could

LINDA BROWN SMITH is the daughter of the late Reverend Oliver Brown, the principal plaintiff in Brown v. Board of Education, *and partner in* Brown & Brown Associates, Topeka, Kansas.

lead to job loss and threats of violence.

The local school board, which somehow believed itself to be above reproach, mailed threatening letters to black teachers. The most well-known letter stated, and I quote:

Dear Miss Buchanan:

Due to the present uncertainty about enrollment next year in schools for negro children, it is not possible at this time to offer you employment for next year. If the Court should rule that segregation in the elementary grades is unconstitutional, our Board will proceed on the assumption that the majority of people in Topeka will not want to employ negro teachers next year for white children. It is necessary for me to notify you now that your services will not be needed for next year. This is in compliance with the continuing contract law [emphasis in original].

If it turns out that segregation is not terminated, there will be nothing to prevent us from negotiating a contract with you at some later date this spring. You will understand that I am sending letters of this kind to only those teachers of the negro schools who have been employed during the last year or two. It is presumed that, even though segregation should be declared unconstitutional, we would have need for some schools for negro children, and we would retain our negro teachers to teach them.

I think I understand that all of you must be under considerable strain, and I sympathize with uncertainties and inconveniences which you must experience during this period of adjustment. I believe that whatever happens, will ultimately turn out to be best for everybody concerned.

Sincerely yours,

Wendell Godwin
Superintendent of Schools

After the unsuccessful attempts in federal court, an appeal was made to the U.S. Supreme Court under the guidance of the NAACP legal staff, specifically, the Honorable Justice Thurgood Marshall. At the Supreme Court level, the case was consolidated with similar cases and argued in terms of the psychological damage brought about by segregation in public education. Experts from the psychiatric community were called in to testify as to whether segregation in fact served to break a youngster's morale and block the development of the strong positive self-concept so essential to educational progress.

My family became lost in the turmoil of the ensuing years, years that scarcely touched us. "We lived in the calm of the hurricane's eye, gazing at the storm around us and wondering how it would all end."

I don't think my father ever got discouraged. He was the type of man who really had the stamina for going ahead. But at this particular time, neither my parents nor I knew how far-reaching the suit would be.

During the next three years, while the now-famous decision was in the making, my father was called into the ministry. He received a charge in the fall of 1952, and the family moved to the northern part of the city where we became the first family of the St. Mark's African Methodist Episcopal (AME) Church. I was transferred to the all-black McKinley Elementary School in North Topeka and again faced the same situation of having to walk twice the distance it would have taken me to reach the all-white school three blocks from my home.

Time stood still as the highest court of the land pondered over *Brown* v. *Board of Education*, until an afternoon in May 1954, when I was in school, my father at work, and my mother at home doing the family ironing and listening to the radio. At 12:52 P.M., the announcement came. The Court's decision on ending segregation was unanimous. My mother was overwhelmed. On returning from school, I learned of the decision, which at that time only meant to me that my sisters wouldn't have to walk so far to school next fall. That evening there was much rejoicing in our home. I remember seeing tears of joy in the eyes of my father as he embraced us repeating "Thanks be unto God." That night the family attended a rally given by the local NAACP at the Monroe School.

The following school term was so very different, not for me, because I was never to benefit from the decision. For during the 1954 school term, I entered junior high school, which was already integrated as were all the high schools in the city.

The strange thing about the Topeka school system was that the other levels of public education, at least on the surface, appeared to be integrated. Junior and senior high school students of all races attended the same schools, sat next to one another in class, but could not participate in the same school-sponsored extracurricular activities. There were white athletic teams. There were black athletic teams. There was a prom and all-school king and queen for white students. There was a prom and all-school king and queen for black students.

During the 1930s, my mother was elected all-school queen by the black students. So there is royalty in our family.

Integration in the fall of 1954 went very smoothly; it seemed as though blacks and whites had been going to school together for years. Neither I nor my family suffered the abuse and racial strife that marked integration in the late fifties and early sixties in so many parts of the country. We were very fortunate, my father would often say. He believed very strongly that God would move people to do the right thing.

The later fifties found my family living in Springfield, Missouri, where my father held the pastorate of the Benton Avenue AME Church. At this time, newspapers and magazines began to do follow-ups on me and my family, because the significance of the Supreme Court decision that carried our name was beginning to really take hold throughout the country.

It was during this time that I inherited much of the recognition that might have gone to my father, had it not been for his untimely death in 1961 at the age of forty-two. If he had lived, I'm sure he would have become a strong civil rights activist in the movements of the sixties. Little did he know years ago that when he stepped off the witness stand, he was stepping into the pages of history.

Sometimes I wonder if we really did the nation and its children a favor by taking this case to the Supreme Court. I know that it was the right thing for my father to do then, but after nearly thirty years, we find the Court's ruling remains unfulfilled.

There is still *de facto* segregation throughout much of the United States. It is not that the schools are not equally physically equipped; the problem lies in the physical make-up of the inner city. The housing patterns are still causing predominately black schools in certain areas.

We witness everyday the problem of urban renewal: the building of low-income housing in a neighborhood that is already 90 percent black, thereby making the school of that neighborhood 99 percent black.

Opposition to school desegregation is not novel, and it will continue to exist. Continued resistance to desegregating schools is symbolic; it indicates that America was founded on principles that did not include its minority populations.

Therefore, it must be fought even by blacks convinced that the educational merit of integrated schools is overstated, misconceived, or simply untrue. For quite literally the right—whether exercised or not—of black children or any children to attend integrated public schools is a right crucial not only to the success of people, but to the survival of this country. The majority of our population is growing older, and the young families giving birth to new generations are predominately black and Hispanic. With so much at stake, we cannot afford to surrender. Our efforts may or may not be successful, but fighting for survival is never a "no-win" policy.

Mainstream America will grow increasingly dependent on educated minorities as minorities move into the jobs held by middle-class whites, according to Harold Hodgkinson, senior fellow at the Institute for Educational Leadership. It's a demographic fact of life that the number of young blacks, Hispanics, Asians, and other minorities is on the rise, and that minorities will soon be moving into an aging, predominantly white work force and helping to pay its Social Security bills. "My hope is that we will have enough sense to realize that a better education for minorities, in whatever setting they find themselves, is in the best interests not only of the minority youth, but in the direct financial, personal, and social best interests of all of us," Hodgkinson said. By 1990, Hodgkinson predicts that nine out of ten urban school students will be minority members.

I have listened to and been a part of many sessions on where we stand now and where we should go from here with regard to school desegregation.

Sometimes I sense something is missing: a dialogue on the question of what is being done in the schools that teach most of the black children in our community. As school district plans are made, how do we have meaningful input? And how does the community see that school district plans actually are carried out?

The delivery of effective education requires family and community involvement in seeing that (1) schools are staffed by skillful, dedicated teachers who respect children and believe they can and will learn with proper instruction and (2) schools develop the child's self-concept or self-image that is essential for academic success.

The family must share with the school the expectations for children. Students must be taught that education is imperative for life in America because it serves to provide a fighting chance for upward mobility for all people.

To me, the impact of *Brown* is best seen in the increasing numbers of black professionals today, as well as the growing numbers of minorities, women, and disabled persons enrolled in postsecondary institutions.

These are the people that after 1954 were able to have some degree of choice. This surely made a difference in their aspirations and achievements. I feel that so-called special populations expect to achieve to a greater degree because the *Brown* decision served to lift the stigma of not having a choice.

I recently ran across a quote in a new book by one of our black women authors, Mildred Pitts Walter, that I believe says it all (Walter, 1983): "It is not the treatment of a people that degrades them, but their acceptance of it..."

REFERENCE

Walter, M.P. (1983). *Because we are.* New York: Lothrop, Lee & Shephard Books.

Keynote Address
School Integration and the National Community

SAMUEL D. PROCTOR

Since 1960 America has come closer to becoming a nation that embraces all of its people in a society of justice and equality of opportunity for all. Women, blacks, Hispanics, Asians, the elderly, the gay community, welfare recipients, and even the prison population have all pressed their cases. They have defied exclusion, rejection, and denial and moved toward the mainstream.

In the past, one major aspect of our noncommunity was the existence of racially segregated schools in the North and South, a social habit of separating school children on the basis of color. Basically, there is no fundamental difference between racially segregated schools and racially segregated military posts, hospital wards, bars, churches, bowling alleys, fraternities, lodges, housing areas, and cemeteries. The entire society, in fact, until about 1960, was divided along racial lines, and the schools simply reflected the dual social arrangement that was taken for granted.

When I was a boy in Norfolk, Virginia, we had absolutely no contact with white people other than those for whom or under whom we worked. I had a black dentist, physician, coach, pastor, mortician, postman, groceryman, laundryman, and milkman and attended all-black schools, churches, dances, ball games, festivals, and funerals.

Of course, school segregation differed from other forms of segregation because education is compulsory, students spend many years in school, and these formative years determine the entire course of a person's life. One could say, therefore, that in very important and significant ways, for generations, the schools merely reflected the values, mores and cultural norms found in the society at large with respect to race.

When the *Brown* decision of 1954 called for the dismantling of these segregated schools, the schools were placed in contraposition to the society. *Brown* called for a level of community in America that had been unknown, unanticipated, and unaccepted in the larger society. The Court had spoken, but the glacierlike pace of change characterizing black-white relations defied the Court's orders, and the resistance since 1954 has been persistent. In 1968, three-quarters of the schools had 50 percent minority enrollment and two-thirds had over 90 percent minority enrollment. In 1980, two-thirds had 50 percent and one-third had over 90 percent. White flight from center cities and high private school enrollments have caused these numbers to remain as they are, along with sheer resistance, foot dragging, legal disobedience, and federal indulgence in regard to desegregation.

Those involved in desegregation must look far beneath the surface and pay more attention to aspects of our common life that foster racial prejudice, that permit segregated housing, and that perpetuate racial estrangement, for these are all complementary to and corollaries of school segregation. It is clear that successful school integration will be the function of a wider acceptance of racial difference throughout the society.

The sad fact is that the more vocal blacks are about inclusion in American society, the stiffer and more pervasive is the resistance of whites. It appears that whenever there were very few blacks and the level of protest against racism was tolerable to the white majority, school integration was permitted uneventfully. But wherever the number of blacks to be integrated threatened to change the status of racial separation, to penetrate the wall of social distinctions, and to portend a movement toward more complete and thorough integration throughout the society, school integration was resisted through every device at hand, including the burning of school buses. The Court had argued in 1954 that the longer school integration was denied, the more deeply entrenched racism would become. Fully aware of the strain and possible tension that could result from desegregation, the Court deliberately called for a completely novel development toward major social change, beginning with the

SAMUEL D. PROCTOR is Martin Luther King Professor Emeritus, Rutgers University and Senior Minister of the Abyssinian Baptist Church of New York City.

schools. The schools were to become the innovators in the culture, the transition agents, the intervention toward a genuine community. The Court believed that the time had come to uphold the clear mandate and spirit of the Constitution against the long-standing and deeply entrenched meanness, callous ill-will, dehumanization, and noncommunity of a racially segregated school system.

Obviously, the Court's position has not prevailed, and this fact alone reveals the sheer intransigence of the deeply imbedded racial mores and the perversion of human values that have stagnated moral purpose and earnestness in American society.

No matter how imbedded the mores may be, or how intransigent racist practices may be, the record shows that great social and political change of the magnitude called for by the *Brown* decision has taken place in the very recent past. India was led into a change of such dimension by a young lawyer who applied principles of moral force to the challenge of sending 200,000 British people home, vacating the British fleet from the ports of Bombay and Bengal, and allowing 400,000,000 colonized persons to determine their own destiny. Today, it seems incredible that for 300 years, European powers controlled all of the dark-skinned people of the world, like Tiberius Caesar's soldiers, in a remote province a long way from home, standing around Calvary supervising the crucifixion of a stranger named Jesus.

Likewise, at an earlier time, thirteen fledgling colonies defied the concept of the divine right of kings by cancelling the authority of George III and declaring that all men were created equal and were endowed not by the king or the state, but by their Creator, with certain permanent and intrinsic rights, namely: life, liberty, and the pursuit of happiness. Change is possible.

The *Brown* decision called for change in the attitudes of our entire country regarding blacks, and this process has been slow. Because the basic ingredients of a national community—mutual respect and acceptance, justice, freedom, and equality—are missing, the decision has had to depend almost entirely on the force of law for its implementation. And there are some things that the law cannot do. The law cannot compel one group to accept another as equal, to admit another into its circle of polite social relations, or to behave with kindness and civility when required to associate with another group. There are other things that the law can do and must

do, but those in charge of administering the law must be committed to the enforcement of the law and the authority of the courts. Therefore, the full and effective implementation of the *Brown* decision will require the constant, unrelenting movement toward that measure of consensus, that commitment to human values, that sense of justice, that response to professional challenge to make schools a microcosm not only of the society as it is, but a microcosm of the society as it ought to be. Whenever this movement toward greater community has accompanied the desegregation process, rare and difficult as it may be, the results have been promising! But where legal integration has taken place without the accompaniment of a growing sense of community, whites have fled, private schools have mushroomed, and the consequent indifference toward the public schools has diminished the quality of education. If, then, we wish to see integration in the schools proceed, we need to focus upon those values and practices that foster a sense of true community.

We must face the fact that movement toward an integrated society does not go very far unless we face up to the moral failures of the society and deal with them. School integration is something that ought to happen, and all ambivalence about the justification of it must be challenged and removed. It is plainly wrong by any canons to assign to persons an unearned stigma, an inferior role in society based upon color, or to allow a condition of poverty, ignorance, isolation, and deprivation, unjustly imposed, to continue to have negative and destructive consequences that go unchecked and unchallenged. What will it take to gain such a consensus in America? Whatever it costs we must pay the price in order for successful school integration to occur as a moral imperative.

There is in this society a stubborn, relentless resistance to the alteration of long-standing practices based upon racial stereotypes. It is embarrassing to observe the naive expectations of persons of enormous good will who are oblivious to the extent and pervasiveness of racism in America. The Nixon and Reagan forces discovered this reality and proceeded to exploit it nationwide, North and South, in universities, labor unions, and churches.

John Rawls, in his book *A Theory of Justice* (1974), summarized the clearest and most widely acknowledged understanding of what the claims of justice really are. The first understanding must be that none of us has what he or she deserves. Each of us was bequeathed an economic,

social, and cultural incubator completely undeserved and unearned that has had an awful lot to do with where we have ended up. Those with the most fortunate sponsorship began, at the "original position," ahead of the scratch line. Those with the worst began behind the scratch line.

Now, by what rule or principle should the society behave in such a way as to sustain and enhance the position of those who inherited—without deserving it—the most privileged position, thereby denying those with the least an opportunity to overcome their deficit? By whose authority is anyone granted the absolute right to secure outcomes and benefits ahead of others, when it is so clear that no one worked for or earned his or her position at the scratch line? Of course, outcomes will always differ for obvious reasons, but inequality of opportunity, impediments, undeserved weights, and arbitrary restraints should be removed. This position is so palpably self-evident that in order for one to deny it, one simply must be arrogant, loud, violent, and given to the law of the jungle, regardless of what one's own cultural bias may be. People are being given undeserved starting points in life. The atmosphere that would promote school integration is quite different.

The kind of community that would allow, encourage, support, and embrace school integration is one that would be sensitive to the moral imperative of Immanuel Kant, Amos of Tekoa, and Jesus of Galilee, namely: Whatever it is that you wish for yourself, be willing, anxious, and eager to grant to others. And the details on how, when, how much, by whose hands, and in what manner can always be arrived at if the heart is willing in the first place.

Next, school teachers and administrators have an obligation to create a microcosm in the schools that manifests the best that we know. Insofar as we are able, we must keep those intractable social determinants and economic predictors of academic achievement from pulling and tugging at the school door! And, inside the school's walls, an environment will be created and enjoyed that frees teacher and pupil from the prophecies made by the computers. This environment will be conditioned by an atmosphere of mutual helpfulness, respect for all persons and expectancy of the best, encouraging each student and teacher to become a part of a miniature world for six hours that behaves differently, a world that invites everyone to rise to the full potential of his or her capacities, no matter what the rumors have predicted about native intelligence or the inexorability of social determinants. The school itself will then become a catalyst, generating that kind of moral fermentation that creates the attitudes and understanding conducive to the emergence of genuine community now and a more enriched community in the future.

What I suggest here goes beyond mere exhortation and rhetoric. It has to do with skilled teachers acquiring the empathy to learn the details and lacunae of their students' world, to understand their vernacular, their thought coinage, their metaphors, and their cosmic outlook. It means constructing the curriculum on what is known, felt, and understood by the students, then teaching them what they need to master in order to become full and self-reliant participants in a free society.

So, the creation of the microcosm in the schools that will generate a sense of community is more than a matter of moral resolve; it is a professional challenge to produce those dramatic "for instances" that demonstrate that racist assumptions are wrong and that racial prejudice is ignorance and tribalism. Such professionalism will create the catalyst that is required.

Ultimately, however, the implementation of the *Brown* decision is a power question. It is a moral issue; it is a professional challenge. But, in the final analysis, all of the foot dragging, circumvention, and word games about "excellence" and "accountability" and "save our schools" resolve into a simple power question: Who can cause it to happen and who can prevent it?

If the political party in power came to power with the wide support of racists and radical right-wing resisters who have a loyalty to the old order that ignored the claims of justice with respect to blacks, then such a party will install an attorney general, a commissioner of education, and a budget director who will turn their backs on the moral arguments, cut off funds for professional services, and erect one barrier after another to integration. They will encourage private, "Christian" schools; advocate vouchers to provide funds for the middle class to abandon the public schools; allow cities to become filled with boarded up buildings, alcoholics, the chronically and desperately poor, slum landlords, and violent schools; fight for tax benefits for those who wish to build a private school system; and make integration a moot issue, with no one to integrate.

On the other hand, if the party in power believes in justice and fairness, if it supports the Constitution and obeys the law, it will not only require integration *de jure* but will work for that consensus toward a community that embraces justice and personal fulfillment and will foster integration *de facto* as well.

Power does corrupt. Absolute power indeed does corrupt absolutely. Lord Acton could have added further that nothing comes to pass without power, and the only remaining question is the extent of good will in the hearts of those with the power.

REFERENCES

Brown v. Board of Education of Topeka, 347 U.S. 483 (1954).

Rawls, J. (1974). *A theory of justice*. Cambridge: Harvard University Press.

PART I

The Present Status of Public School Desegregation

A Personal View of the Background and Developments Since the Brown Decision

KENNETH B. CLARK

When I was asked a couple of months ago if I would participate in this conference, I was at a low ebb in my life. I had to deal with the problem of not being with my wife, Mamie Clark, who passed away about a year ago. Whenever I talk about *Brown*, I start by making clear my dedication to that wonderful human being who made it possible for me to be involved in the work with lawyers and the NAACP on the *Brown* decision. What is generally not known is that the research quoted in the 1954 Supreme Court *Brown* decision was not initiated by me. The whole question of the effect of racial segregation on personality development of Negro children was Mamie's master thesis research. When I saw her thesis, I said, "Mamie, you need help here," in the usual male chauvinist manner. "I'm going to take this over for you." She said, "No. We're going to collaborate." So when anyone ever introduces me or writes about me and my contribution to *Brown* if I'm around I usually correct them by saying, "Mamie and Kenneth Clark." I saw the importance of what she was studying. When she became pregnant, I took over the field research while she took time at home to find out what I was doing in the field. After each trip, we discussed the results.

I would like to talk about the historical antecedents of *Brown*. Going over my notes for this presentation, I recalled my work with Thurgood Marshall and Bob Carter and my preparation for the role of social scientist in seeking to overthrow the precedent of separate but equal. We met frequently, sometimes around the clock. The lawyers were trying to find out what, if anything, the social scientists could contribute in overturning that precedent. Bob Carter argued very strenuously with some of his colleagues that the only way he could be sure of increasing the chances for overturning *Plessy* v. *Ferguson* (1896) was to demonstrate that segregation inflicted crippling damage on human beings and thereby violated the Fourteenth Amendment. When Bob came to talk with me about this, he said, "Kenneth, we know that we cannot demonstrate physical damage, and the courts are used to having inequities of this sort demonstrated in terms called "damages that are concrete and observable." We must demonstrate, if possible, psychological damage, damage to the insides—the personality—of human beings." I went up to Columbia University and I talked with Otto Klineberg. He told me, "You and Mamie are doing the kind of research that is somehow related to the psychological damage of social injustice." I really wanted to help, but I did not know whether the research that Mamie and I had done was relevant to what Bob Carter, Thurgood Marshall, and the other lawyers had in mind. However, I had a monograph that I had prepared for the 1950 Mid-century White House Conference on Chil-dren and Youth (Clark, 1950). That monograph summarizes all of the available research on the effects of prejudice, discrimination, and segregation on American children. I gave them this monograph to read. I thought that if it was at all relevant to what the lawyers had in mind in demonstrating damage, then maybe we could help. Bob took the monograph and in about two weeks he came back and he said, "Kenneth, this is so relevant and so appropriate, it is as if it were prepared for us." He asked us to help. We were to bring together social scientists to be expert witnesses at the trials of some of the cases they were handling and to help the lawyers become very accurate in the presentation of the psychological damages that segregation imposes on human beings. This was the only way they were going to be able to convince the courts to overturn *Plessy* v. *Ferguson*.

Getting involved with *Brown* was the turning point in our lives. Mamie and I wanted more children, but we didn't have them because of *Brown*. Our whole

KENNETH B. CLARK is Distinguished Professor Emeritus of Psychology, City College of the City University of New York; member, New York State Board of Regents; founder with his late wife Mamie of the Northside Center for Child Development; and President, Clark, Phipps, Clark & Harris. Dr. Clark was instrumental in preparing the Social Science Statement in the Brown *case.*

perspective of the meaning of life was changed, and everytime I see Bob Carter now, I remind him that he took me out of the purely academic sphere. Before my involvement with the *Brown* cases, I wanted to stay in pure research and to investigate the neurophysiological basis of social problems. I never did get around to that work.

I recall that in discussion with the lawyers, I would accuse them of talking like social scientists and they'd accuse me of pretending that I was a lawyer. We couldn't stop exchanging roles except in court, where Thurgood, Bob, and others in preparing us for our role as expert witnesses insisted that we had to present our facts on the basis of our research, not on the basis of the advocacy, which was their role. And I would argue that they were moving into my social science territory. At the end when we got the positive decision on *Brown* in 1954, I promised Thurgood that I'd give him an honorary degree in social psychology. Many years later when I was elected to the Board of Regents, we tried to award him an honorary degree. By that time, he was a Justice of the U.S. Supreme Court, and he refused the degree on the grounds that he wanted to remain objective.

What were the legal antecedents to *Brown*? The *Brown* case did not come out of nowhere to be everywhere. *Brown* was preceded by at least a hundred years of legal struggle. I'm not an expert in legal history, so I will start arbitrarily with one case that was a legal antecedent to *Brown*: The *Dred Scott* decision of 1857. That was probably the earliest attempt to use the federal courts as a vehicle to attain racial justice for Negroes in America. (In 1857, I believe we were called either Negroes or "nigras.") The *Dred Scott* decision, however, reinforced the inferior status of the Negro people through the judicial doctrine that the Negro had no rights that the white man was bound to respect. This was stated definitively and categorically in *Dred Scott*.

I consider the *Plessy* v. *Ferguson* decision in 1896 a more sophisticated continuation of *Dred Scott*. There was some progress beyond *Dred Scott*, but *Plessy* left unchanged the social and judicial perceptions of the Negro as different from other American citizens. The doctrine of separate but equal, which was enunciated in the *Plessy* decision, must have been, and seems still to be, predicated on the assumption that in spite of the Emancipation Proclamation, in spite of rather strong civil rights legislation passed

by Congress, Negroes were to be treated separately. In spite of the Thirteenth, Fourteenth, and Fifteenth Amendments, *Plessy* indicated that the Negro American was still being viewed by the judicial system as a socially and politically inferior human being. *Plessy*, in a more sophisticated way than *Dred Scott*, gave judicial sanction to the second-class citizenship status of black Americans.

This insistence on the inferior status of the Negro citizen implicit in the *Plessy* decision cannot be considered to be inadvertent in view of the rather strong dissent by Justice Harlan. Justice Harlan's dissent to the *Plessy* decision could be considered a model for Chief Justice Warren's 1954 *Brown* decision. Both said essentially the same thing: You cannot separate Negroes on the basis of race or color without indicating that you consider them inferior and thereby questioning their humanity and violating the Constitution of the United States. In attacking the *Plessy* decision, Justice Harlan spelled out quite clearly that the doctrine of separate but equal could only be sustained on a racist basis and that the Court in propounding the doctrine was restating in more palatable form the *Dred Scott* decision.

The history of the civil rights legislation in state and federal courts up to the *Brown* decision of 1954 has to be considered in terms of this basic question: How is the Negro to be perceived and treated in relation to the treatment of other human beings within the framework of American democracy? The underlying problem was that the Negro was regarded—and the judicial decisions before the 1940s reinforced that perspective—as semi-human or, in some subtle or not so subtle way, as subhuman. Not only as different, but different and inferior. The common denominator of *Dred Scott* and *Plessy* and almost all court decisions up to *Brown* was that the Negro was seen in some way as special and apparently unworthy of the rights that white-American citizens, and even the most recent immigrants to this nation, possessed. Unlike other groups of Americans, Negroes always had to seek and attain their rights through litigation or legislation. Other Americans had attained their rights through application of the U.S. Constitution. Indeed, what Negroes were required to do to seek the judicial determination of their rights was itself indicative of the basic racial reality of the society in which they lived and which we hoped that *Brown* would have removed. Unfortunately, it does not seem to have

done this yet.

Given this analysis, the *Brown* decision of 1954 represents an ongoing attempt to use the judicial system to remove once and for all the special and inferior categories to which Negroes have been relegated, and apparently continue to be relegated. It was an attempt at least to ensure (and this is the best that we could have hoped for before the past three or four years) that governmental power, and particularly the power of the judiciary, would cease to function as an agent in reinforcing the Negro's second-class status.

There is this constant struggle before the federal courts (more so than before the other branches of our federal government) to remove governmental, judicial, and executive powers as instruments in reinforcing the second-class status of black Americans. We thought that with the *Brown* decision and its legislative aftermaths, we had stopped the executive branch of government from reinforcing the second-class status of black Americans. If one takes a good look at the record of the Reagan Administration, one sees that the power of the executive branch is being consistently used to effect a functional repeal of the *Brown* decision. The Justice Department, specifically and ironically the Civil Rights Division of the Justice Department, has gone before the federal courts to roll back the gains that we have added to the civil rights struggle since it started with the historic *Brown* decision and the Civil Rights Act of 1964. It is now being argued by the present Justice Department that the Court decisions and the civil rights laws that were designed to remedy past racial discrimination must now be used to block such remedies. This is one of the worst problems facing black Americans today. How can one combat this Orwellian view that the power of justice should be used to perpetrate injustice?

It is a fact that the legal–historical background of *Brown* is to be seen in the series of cases brought before the U.S. Supreme Court in the late 1930s, 1940s, and 1950s. The decision handed down in those cases indicated that *Brown* would be inevitable. In this regard, it was the *McLaurin* v. *Oklahoma State Regents* case of 1950 that sought to attack the constitutionality of segregation per se. This is not generally known, and I certainly did not know it until I started working with the lawyers at the NAACP, that they really wanted to deal with the basic issue of the unconstitutionality of segregation without regard to the alleged equality. The precedents of *Plessy* prevailed. The lawyers of the NAACP in presenting their arguments attempted to outflank the rationale of *Plessy* v. *Ferguson*. However, the Court decisions in these earlier cases were still based on the *Plessy* v. *Ferguson* separate but equal doctrine. One should add, however, that the standards of equality set by the Court in these cases were increasingly higher in each case. This made it become increasingly clear that to continue to segregate blacks would become economically difficult if not impossible. To maintain separate educational facilities at the higher and professional educational levels would drain the already limited economic power of an economically limited section of the country. These decisions, in spite of their retention of the *Plessy* doctrine and the fact that they were narrowly drawn in their specific restrictions, required that the lawyers of the NAACP attempt to outflank *Plessy* in terms of individual cases. The narrowly drawn and restricted decisions that the Court handed down on these professional law school and graduate cases did not address the larger issue of the constitutionality of racial segregation in general, or racial segregation in elementary and secondary levels of education.

Given these facts, the NAACP decided to take head-on the issue of the apparent effect of racial segregation itself without regard to the equality of the facilities. They had to confront the *Plessy* doctrine directly, and they had to fight it at the level of elementary and secondary schools or they would be in court ad infinitum. It must have been assumed by those who planned these cases that in view of the increasing erosion of a biracial system of education on graduate and professional school levels, attacks on segregation per se would be more likely to succeed if they were initially directed at segregation in state-supported educational facilities at all levels, including elementary and secondary schools. It must have been further assumed that such a legal attack was useless unless a Court decision was obtained concerning the unconstitutionality of segregated schools per se. Short of this, the *Plessy* doctrine, probably on a more sophisticated level, would prevail. I remember reading in some black newspapers criticism of the NAACP's attempt to appeal *Plessy*. These newspapers felt that "gains" were being made under *Plessy* and that if we lost, we would perpetuate laws requiring and permitting racial segregation in all other aspects of American life.

I suppose that one of the reasons the NAACP lawyers decided to continue their

attacks on *Plessy*, in spite of the risks, was the language that came from a pre-Warren Court—the Vinson Court—that dealt with the *McLaurin* decision. In 1950, in the important *McLaurin* v. *Oklahoma State Regents* decision, the Vinson Court gave a signal or message, a subtle and (to use my psychologist's jargon) subliminal point that they saw the time had come to attack segregation per se. Here is some language from that *McLaurin* decision of 1950. You recall that McLaurin was admitted to the law school of the University of Oklahoma under the *Plessy* doctrine. But the faculty, regents, and administrators of that law school decided that they would obey the letter of *Plessy* by admitting him but would violate the spirit of that law by separating him from other students: he had a separate place in the library, a separate place in the cafeteria, and he was isolated in the classrooms. Being an optimist, I often wondered whether the decision makers at the University of Oklahoma didn't do that deliberately in order to get the case before the Court. I just can't believe that people in the academic field could have been so cruel as to do this kind of thing to another human being unless there was a hidden agenda, namely, that they wanted the Court to say, "You can't do this." Whether or not the motivation was positive, the Vinson Court said the following: "The Regents in keeping McLaurin apart from the other students, handicapped him in his pursuit of effective graduate instruction. Such restrictions impair and inhibit his ability to study, to engage in discussion and exchange views with other students, thereby impairing his ability to learn his profession." The *McLaurin* decision went further and—I repeat—tended to suggest to the lawyers of the NAACP that this kind of cruel separation could impair the ability of a graduate student to study, to learn, and to evaluate. An important part of the educational process was the ability of the indivdual to integrate and communicate with others freely. This I believe opened up the opportunity for lawyers to attack segregation at other educational levels.

I have some observations on the trial level of *Briggs* v. *Eliot* (1954), which was the first of the school segregation cases that came to trial in Charlestown, South Carolina. It was the late Justice J. Waitis Waring who sent the lawyers back to prepare their case and return to the federal courts in South Carolina to challenge *Plessy*. The NAACP lawyers sought to challenge *Plessy* rather than to end segregation within *Plessy* in South Carolina. The

first of the cases that we approached from the perspective of the damage of segregation without regard to alleged equality was the *Briggs* v. *Eliot* case. It was argued before a three-judge court in Charleston, South Carolina, on May 30, 1951.

We went through four cases at the state level: *Briggs* v. *Eliot* (1952) in South Carolina, *Davis* v. *Country School Board of Prince Edward County* (1952) in Virginia, *Brown* v. *Board of Education* in Kansas, and *Belton* v. *Gebhart* (1953) in Delaware. (This Delaware case was the only case that the plaintiffs won at the trial level.) The only one of these four cases on the state level that I did not testify in was the one in Kansas, the *Brown* case.

My involvement in these cases reinforced my persistent belief that blacks in America had to pursue this ongoing struggle for their basic and simple rights of citizenship. They had to seek adjudication of these rights and have them constantly tested in the courts. There is no question that the *Brown* decision was a historical one. The Warren Court said to the nation, we're tired of having to test over and over again whether the Constitution of the United States is color blind. It was just a repetition of what Justice Harlan said in his eloquent dissent in the *Plessy* decision in 1896. Some of us were naive enough to believe that *Brown* was the end of the struggle for racial justice. But it wasn't.

Racism in American democracy continues. Some cosmetic changes have been made, but it grieves me to tell you that more children, in absolute numbers and by percentage, are in racially segregated schools in New York City, in New York State, and in other northern urban areas than there were in 1954 at the time of *Brown*. The center of gravity of the struggle for racial justice in the United States has in fact moved from the southern states, where it was easy for us to have allies in the fight against the more flagrant form of racism, to northern urban communities. Now our earlier allies are our smiling, sophisticated adversaries. Our research demonstrated the deep psychological and educational damage that occurs when children are arbitrarily excluded, segregated, and restricted. Our findings remain as true now, thirty years after *Brown*, as they were when we presented our "Social Science Statement" (*Brown* v. *Board of Education*, 1954) to the Supreme Court. This is as true in northern *de facto* segregated schools as it was in southern *de jure* segregated schools. We now know this to be a fact—but we have gotten tired. We now act as if these children are expendable. We apparently are suffering from battle fatigue. We accept segregated schools in northern urban centers on the grounds that they are not *de jure*; but they are *de facto* segregated schools, and unfortunately we do not yet have the litigation that will help us make very clear that *de facto* segregation is as damaging as *de jure* segregation.

I wish that it was possible for me to bring a more positive or optimistic message at the conclusion of this look into the dark and sketchy history of racial litigation in the United States. It would be dishonest, untrue to myself, and condescending to you if I were to tell you that I am not depressed that thirty years after *Brown,* Linda Brown is still struggling to obtain justice for her child.

Thirty years after *Brown,* I must accept the fact that my wife left this earth despondent at seeing that damage to children is being knowingly and silently accepted by a nation that claims to be democratic. Thirty years after *Brown,* I feel a sense of hopelessness, rather than optimism, because the underlying theme of *Plessy* and the explicit statements of *Dred Scott* persist. The majority of Americans still believe in and vote on the assumption that blacks are not worthy of the respect, and the acceptance of their humanity, which our democracy provides to others.

REFERENCES

Belton v. Gebhart, 91A. 2d 137 (1953).

Briggs v. Eliot, 103 F. Supp. 920 (1952).

Brown v. Board of Education of Topeka, 347 U.S. 483 (1954). (*See also,* Appendix to Appellants' Briefs—The effects of segregation and consequences of desegregation: A social science statement.)

Clark K. (1950). *Effect of prejudice and discrimination on personality development.* (Report for Mid-century White House Conference on Children and Youth). Washington, DC: Children's Bureau, Federal Security Agency.

Davis v. County School Board of Prince Edward County, 347 U.S. 483 (1952).

Dred Scott v. Sanford, 19 Howard 393 (1857).

McLaurin v. Oklahoma State Regents, 339 U.S. 637 (1950).

Plessy v. Ferguson, 163 U.S. 537 (1896).

An NAACP Perspective on the Status of Public School Desegregation

BEVERLY P. COLE

Thirty years after *Brown*, the Reagan Administration's philosophy has encouraged many school districts to retrench on their school desegregation efforts.

Taking their cues from this Administration, instead of fine tuning desegregation plans to make them more equitable, school districts have been using this opportunity to return to the neighborhood school concept. Blacks, who have usually borne the burden of desegregation efforts, are being told by the school districts that they should forego the long rides and return to their neighborhood schools where the school districts will now consider enhancing their programs. However, for blacks this is an empty gesture since busing would have to continue in many areas because most schools in the black communities have been closed.

The former U.S. Commission on Civil Rights accurately summarized the Reagan Administration's school desegregation policies by stating (U.S. Commission on Civil Rights, 1982) that they "reflect an unparalleled assault on the mandate of *Brown*...(which if left unchecked) threatens to halt and in some cases reverse the progress that has been made in desegregating the Nation's public schools."

Today, formidable barriers to equal educational opportunity are being established at all levels of government in all parts of the nation. The Justice Department has unequivocally abandoned court-ordered busing as a remedy for unconstitutional school segregation despite the 1971 decision in *Swann* v. *Charlotte-Mecklenberg Board of Education*, which made it clear that busing is an acceptable tool for ending racial isolation in the public schools. The U.S. Commission on Civil Rights (1981) further stated that "desegregation plans cannot be limited to the walk-in school."

In several major cases, the Justice Department has switched sides because of the busing issue and has offered its services to those school districts that wanted cases reopened for the purpose of reversing busing orders.

The emphasis of this Administration is supposedly on voluntary options for desegregation. Yet, in Seattle where local school authorities voluntarily implemented a school desegregation plan and a state referendum forbade it, the Reagan Administration, despite its pronounced support for local control of education and the authority of school districts to chart their own course, supported the referendum seeking to end Seattle's voluntary desegregation efforts. Fortunately, the Supreme Court ruled against the state and the Justice Department.

One could go on enumerating the attempts by this Administration to turn back the clock on school desegregation. But, in spite of formidable obstacles and resistance, progress has been made. Unfortunately, the failures have been so widely publicized and the victories so little noted.

A recently released study by the National Education Association (NEA), entitled *Three Cities That Are Making Desegregation Work*, reports on the status of desegregation in three urban school systems: Charlotte, North Carolina; Austin, Texas; and Seattle, Washington. This study was conducted by an eight-member inquiry panel, of which the director of education for the NAACP was a member along with Arthur Fleming, former chairman of the U.S. Commission of Civil Rights, and Meyer Weinberg, editor of *Integrated Education*. Hearings were held in each of the three cities. School and city officials, teachers, students, parents, businesspeople, and other community leaders testified about the desegregation process. Although this study was qualitative in nature, the findings corroborated the quantitative findings of researchers such as Bob Crain, Willis Hawley, and Gary Orfield. Some of the NEA's findings were as follows (National Education Association, 1984):

■ When asked about the advantages of desegregation, many of those testifying spoke of the need for public schools to prepare students to deal with the kind of diversity they would encounter in the world after school.

BEVERLY P. COLE is Director of Education, National Association for the Advancement of Colored People.

- There is increased public support for community needs and a heightened sense of civic pride. School bond issues have been passed by a large margin. In Charlotte, North Carolina, an airport bond issue passed with the help of blacks because they felt they had a greater stake in the community. In addition, residents are proud that the city overcame its resistance to desegregation and complied with the law.

- Because of a successful desegregation program in the schools, a positive climate for integration has been developed. The schools have brought people together in a way that no other institution could have done. Blacks serve on more boards, committees, and commissions. Charlotte, a city with a twenty-five percent black population, elected its first black mayor.

- There is more parental involvement in the public schools than ever before. The involvement started with the turmoil of the early stages of desegregation, but now it serves as a positive force for the purpose of monitoring and enhancing the schools' programs. For the first time, politically influential white parents have an interest in schools in predominantly minority neighborhoods because their children have been assigned there.

- Progress in the desegregation of housing has resulted from pupil assignment plans. White parents are less inclined to flee, while black parents are exposed to more choices. The cooperation of the realty companies in not steering prospective tenants to neighborhoods according to race is very important in this process.

- The achievement scores for all children have improved, with black and Hispanic students making progress toward closing the gap between themselves and their white counterparts.

- The educational reforms and innovations initiated by the desegregation process have resulted in the improvement of education for all children. The white students have learned that the customs and values of their culture are not the sole customs and values of a pluralistic society, while the black youngsters have learned that they can compete in the wider world. In addition, problems needing resolution were exposed that had not been dealt with or even acknowledged prior to desegregation.

- There have been deliberate attempts to eliminate inequities in building facilities and educational resources.

This study indicated that the desegregation process had not been easy. In most cases, minorities bore the brunt of the desegregation process: Black schools were often closed, black students were bused a longer distance from home, and a disproportionate number of black students were transported. However, no one expressed a desire to return to the way it was before desegregation.

In Charlotte, North Carolina, a retired principal was asked if he thought black students in the community would be better off in a segregated system, considering the losses the students experienced in the closure of black schools. He answered, no, and enumerated the things which had been lacking or inadequate in the black schools prior to desegregation (NEA, 1984):

...no pencils, no shades, no projectors, no filmstrip machines, not enough crayons, desks were not appropriate for children's sizes, overcrowded classrooms...you name it...The basic tools for learning. Black teachers and principals had to get out and have barbecues, fish fries...and were not even exposed to what a standardized classroom was like in terms of class size, class climate, and conditions and materials to work with!

Julius Chambers, the legal counsel for the plaintiffs in *Swann* v. *Charlotte-Mecklenburg*, was asked to give his opinion of some efforts to improve the quality of schools without desegregation. His response (J. Chambers, personal notes) was one of skepticism: "Voluntarily no one will come up with a plan that will ensure equal educational opportunities...In the implementation of the plans somehow black schools still end up underfunded. But more importantly, students will not get the kind of exposure that is needed to make America great, for education affects the total person and the total community." Federal Judge James McMillan made the same point when he stated (NEA, 1984), "Segregation produces inferior education, and it makes little difference whether the school is hot and decrepit or modern and air-conditioned. It is painfully apparent that quality education cannot live in a segregated school, segregation itself is the greatest barrier to quality education."

The progress of desegregation and the *Brown* mandate can best be epitomized by the statement of a white Austin student who admitted to the NEA panel that she had boycotted classes and participated in "Hell no, we won't go" rallies. She stated (NEA, 1984): "At the beginning of my senior year, I looked back and I thought about all the kids that had gone to junior high with me and...had transferred to private schools...or had just moved...And I looked at them and I realized how much they had lost because I had such a learning experience at Johnston...I learned to meet everyone...I feel that I have kind of grown as a person into adulthood."

The younger students are living examples of human relations at work. Their silence eloquently answers the question: "Is desegregation working?" Visitors to the various schools often asked of the little ones, "How are you getting along with your classmates?" The students would invariably look in a perplexed manner, not knowing what the inquirer was talking about, for this was the only life they knew.

Even in these "successful" cities, the process of moving from desegregation to integration is not complete. The NEA report discusses in detail the problems and challenges that remain. These second-generation problems are even more critical after desegregation is accomplished:

- There are disproportionately higher suspension and expulsion rates for black and Hispanic students.

- Dropout rates are higher for black and Hispanic students than for whites.

- Segregated classrooms exist within desegregated schools. The majority of white students are in the gifted and talented classes, and the majority of black students are in the remedial and lower track classes or in the special education classes.

- Although the gap in the achievement test scores between minority and white students has narrowed since desegregation, it still exists.

- Some extracurricular activities have only white participants.

We all must make a concerted effort to finish the uncompleted task of guaranteeing all children in this nation an equal chance to receive a quality, integrated education that will equip them to survive in this pluralistic, technological society. Progress has been made, but there is so much more to be done. In the words of Beatrice Thompson, a black television reporter from Charlotte (NEA, 1984): "...This cake ain't finished baking yet. It's started to rise, but it's not finished."

REFERENCES

Brown v. Board of Education of Topeka, 347 U.S. 483 (1954)

National Education Association. (1984, May). *Three cities that are making desegregation work* (pp. 73–75; 97–98). NEA, Washington, DC. *Id*. at pp. 19, 20, 28, 72, 94, 95.

Swann v. Charlotte-Mecklenburg Board of Education, 402 U.S. 1 (1971).

U.S. Commission on Civil Rights. (1981, November). *With all deliberate speed: 1954–19??* (Clearinghouse Publication 69, p. 15). Washington, DC: U.S. Government Printing Office.

U.S. Commission on Civil Rights. (1982, December). *Statement of the United States Commission on Civil Rights* (Clearinghouse Publication 76, p. 32). Washington, DC: U.S. Government Printing Office.

Brown Thirty Years Later: The Chicago Story

NELVIA M. BRADY

INTRODUCTION

This year commemorates the thirtieth anniversary of the *Brown* v. *Board of Education* (1954) decision, which ruled that separate educational facilities are "inherently unequal." It is ironic for me personally because in 1954 I became a kindergartner at a public inner-city school in one of the most segregated cities in the nation: Chicago. The school I entered was called "desegregated." The irony is that thirty years later, I am responsible for managing the implementation of Chicago's "new" Desegregation Plan, which began its fourth year in the fall of 1984!

During the thirty years since the *Brown* decision was rendered, and indeed since I became familiar with the Chicago Public Schools, the meaning of this decision has changed as it is translated into the practical tasks of desegregating a large midwestern urban school system. The *Brown* decision (1955), known as *Brown II,* established a standard for the implementation of school desegregation that required school systems to demonstrate "good faith" in desegregating themselves "with all deliberate speed."

The *Brown II* decision was considered a clear victory. However, in the past three decades, "with all deliberate speed" has come to mean "speed without motion." Segregation is still with us under freedom-of-choice plans, transfer programs, school closings, tuition grants, and other aid to segregated schools. The Chicago story provides an illustrative example of how these decisions are interpreted in 1984.

Affecting this continual reinterpretation of the meaning of *Brown* are numerous other desegregation court cases, including *Milliken* v. *Bradley* (1974) in Detroit, *Morgan* v. *Kerrigan* (1975) in Boston, and *U.S.* v. *Board of Education of Chicago* (1983). Litigation has been combined with legislation, most significantly in the Civil Rights Act of 1964, which was once a principal weapon of the federal government in the struggle to end school segregation. This act was intended in part to ensure that states and municipalities followed the *Brown* decision and that school boards acted affirmatively in remedying segregation. Title IV authorized federal assistance to aid desegregation, and Title VI forbade recipients of federal financial or technical assistance from practicing discrimination on the basis of race, color, or national origin. Other litigation and legislative efforts have been made to thwart desegregation, particularly since 1977. These include efforts to limit court-imposed busing as a desegregation remedy, to prevent the use of withholding of federal funds based on desegregation, the elimination of the Emergency School Aid Act (ESAA), and the *Bakke* decision (*Regents of the University of California* v. *Bakke,* 1978). Indeed, since 1981, the Civil Rights Division has not filed a single desegregation suit, and it has refused to appeal cases.

THE CHICAGO STORY

Chicago, like other large urban school districts, has been affected by these changes as well as by its own history of racially segregated neighborhoods, ethnically divided communities, legally restricted housing for blacks, and entrenched political machinery. During the last twenty-five to thirty years, Chicago somehow managed to avoid any serious efforts to desegregate its schools.

In 1961, black parents sued the Chicago Board of Education charging racial segregation of students (*Webb* v. *Chicago Board of Education,* 1961). In 1963, charges were dismissed against the board with the proviso that it survey the Chicago school system for racial segregation in student assignment patterns. As a consequence of the suit, an advisory panel chaired by Philip Hauser of the University of Chicago released a report in 1964 stating that there appeared to be racial segregation in the schools of Chicago. In 1965, the U.S. Office of Education threatened to withhold federal funds from Chicago Public Schools because of noncompliance with Title VI of the Civil Rights Act of 1964. In 1976,

NELVIA M. BRADY is Associate Superintendent, Chicago Public Schools.

Superintendent Redmond acknowledged that there was both student and faculty segregation in the Chicago Public Schools, and he developed several possible scenarios for remedying the situation. The Chicago Board of Education submitted several reports (the Hauser Report, the Redmond Report, the Havighurst Report, among others) in response to a 1971 request by the Illinois Office of the Superintendent of Public Instruction. This office requested that the Chicago Public Schools submit reports in accordance with *Rules Establishing Requirements and Procedures for the Elimination and Prevention of Racial Segregation in Schools* (State of Illinois Board of Education, 1976) for the period from 1963 through 1971. The application for Emergency School Aid Act (ESAA) funding was rejected in 1973 because of Chicago's noncompliance with Title VI of the Civil Rights Act of 1964.

Finally, in 1976, after reviewing the Chicago Public Schools' progress toward the elimination of student segregation, the Illinois Office of Education concluded that Chicago's efforts were unsatisfactory and they recommended that a comprehensive plan be developed. They placed the Chicago Public Schools on probationary recognition status. The Chicago Board of Education adopted a resolution in 1977 to develop and implement a comprehensive Equal Educational Opportunity (Student Desegregation) Plan by the spring of 1978 and to initiate the first phase of the plan in September 1978. Probationary status continued and was extended to March 15, 1978. "Access to Excellence," a modest student assignment initiative, was developed and adopted, but probationary status continued. In 1979, the Department of Health, Education, and Welfare (HEW) Office for Civil Rights announced its preliminary finding of continued deliberate segregation of students by the Chicago Board of Education. The board's ESAA application was again refused in 1979, and the board was ordered to develop an acceptable plan by October 15, 1979. David Tatel, Director of the Office for Civil Rights, provided the Board of Education with several options for their consideration, but these were rejected by the superintendent as unworkable.

In October 1979, the Chicago case was referred to the U.S. Department of Justice for possible prosecution. Between November 1979 and January 1980, one of many financial crises erupted. The superintendent resigned, along with two top financial officers and the board president,

and legislation was passed establishing the School Finance Authority and the position of Chief Financial Officer, and dismissing all sitting board members. In addition to its internal cataclysms, the Chicago Board of Education was informed by the Justice Department that it was guilty of unlawful segregation of students on the basis of race and was invited to enter into negotiations under threat of suit.

Not until this time in 1980 did the Chicago board appear to become aware of the "with all deliberate speed" requirement of *Brown II.* Pressure became substantial enough to begin to cause changes. The Chicago story provides a case example of the present status of public school desegregation and how it works in large urban school districts.

Negotiations held during the summer of 1980 between the Department of Justice and the Chicago Board of Education resulted in a Consent Decree filed in U.S. District Court for the Northern District of Illinois on September 24, 1980 (*U.S.* v. *Board of Education of Chicago,* 1980). The Consent Decree acknowledged the existence of substantial racial isolation in Chicago schools but set aside the issue of responsibility. In turn, the board committed itself to developing and implementing a systemwide plan to remedy the present effects of past segregation of black and Hispanic students. The Consent Decree required a plan that would include four major focal points. The first called for the creation of "the greatest practicable number of desegregated schools, taking into account all the circumstances of Chicago." The second objective called for the provision of "educational and related programs for any black and Hispanic schools remaining segregated." The third objective included making necessary changes in the school system to remedy institutional barriers to equity. Finally, the fourth objective focused on the obligation of both the Chicago Board of Education and the United States of America to "find and provide every available form of financial resources adequate for implementation of the Desegregation Plan."

Working under the leadership of Dr. Robert L. Green, national experts planned and later developed a Desegregation Plan consisting of three major components. The first and most significant of these was a focus on improvement of education in black and Hispanic schools through the implementation of the Chicago Effective Schools Project. The model for this project is based on the belief that all students can learn whatever the schools identify as desirable

behavioral outcomes. The overall basis for the project model is the result of school effects research (Edmonds, 1979). In the Chicago Public Schools, the school planning committee is responsible for the development of an Effective Schools Plan that addresses six broad areas; school leadership; instructional emphasis; school climate; staff development; parental involvement and support; and assessment of student progress. The intervention strategy begins with a comprehensive local school needs assessment designed to gather information on eleven basic dimensions and then translate that information into support expectations and long-term goals coupled with annual action plans. The Chicago Effective Schools Project is currently being fully implemented in 107 of the most challenging black and Hispanic schools. In addition, the plan has introduced changes throughout the school system in test procedures, special education, affirmative action, bilingual education, discipline, staff development, and other areas.

The second element of the plan consisted of a Student Assignment Component that set forth a variety of programs designed to encourage student diversity and to establish the greatest practicable number of desegregated schools in a manner that would not cause resegregation. This element of the plan makes use of a variety of methods and techniques that rely heavily on voluntary participation in 44 full-site magnet schools, over 150 magnet programs within schools, and a citywide voluntary transfer program. Magnet schools and programs offer specialized curricula, organizational structures, and teaching techniques in an attempt to educate as many students as possible in a racially diverse environment. The Chicago Public Schools have operated selective magnet-type vocational and technical schools for decades, but during the past decade the system has established highly innovative magnet schools, including the Disney Elementary School, the Metro High School, the Hyde Park Career Academy, and the Whitney Young Magnet High School. These schools aid in slowing flight from the city, but more importantly, their creation is part of a comprehensive desegregation plan that helps to improve existing inner-city schools and to reverse the trend toward deterioration of neighborhoods throughout the city (Campbell & Levine, 1977). Currently, over 185,000 students attend desegregated schools, including magnet schools and programs, in a system that is continuing to decline in white enrollment. As of this writing, 33 percent (132 schools) are defined as desegregated in a school system that is only 14.7 percent white.

The final element of the Desegregation Plan consisted of a fiscal component that addressed the Board of Education's promise to provide adequate financial support for the plan's implementation. The board's 1983–84 desegregation budget, which included a one-time 20 million dollar congressional appropriation, totaled 87 million dollars, providing over 2,000 staff positions and equipment, supplies, and other services to support the desegregation effort. Currently, the board is involved in litigation against the United States in an effort to gain compliance with the Consent Decree provision, which both the board and the government seek, and to secure resources adequate to implement the plan. The cost of implementing the plan during the 1984–85 school year has been estimated at approximately 103 million dollars. The United States position in this litigation, according to Judge Milton Shadur (*U.S.* v. *Board of Education of Chicago*, 1984, Shadur, J., opinion), has been to "stonewall." He said that "what the United States says before this Court is that the promise of the United States is worthless." He found the United States guilty of "stubborn noncompliance" and said that it "seeks to flout that principle (that the President is above the law) as well as its contractual undertakings under the Consent Decree." The current Administration has slowed down progress in the fiscal component area. While praising the plan during its inception, the Administration has not seen fit to meet its commitment to assist in funding. School prayer, tuition vouchers, and sending educators into space are considered more important by this Administration.

Unlike many plans developed earlier in the course of school desegregation history, the Chicago Student Desegregation Plan has attempted to address three dimensions of equality of educational opportunity: (1) equity of access at the district, school, and classroom level; (2) equity of process, by assuring equal treatment of students as they go through the system; and (3) equity of outcome, by assuring that minority students' achievements are adequate for full participation at each grade and in the larger society (Moody, 1981–82). The implementation strategy, and indeed the Desegregation Plan itself, took into consideration the realities of urban school systems in the 1980s. These realities are stark when examined in the context of the *Brown* decision.

Two desegregation realities have affected the Chicago Student Desegregation Plan. Let me briefly highlight these.

The first reality documented in the *Racial/Ethnic Survey of Students* (Chicago Public Schools, 1984), is that the Chicago Public Schools are 60.6 percent black and 21.9 percent Hispanic, with a continuously declining population. This has been the trend in school systems all over the country. In the ten largest school districts in the country, minority students constitute an average of 68 percent of the school population (Ravitch, 1978). Our largest cities have fewer white students with whom to desegregate. Cities have become increasingly populated by minorities and public school populations, even more so since 1954. In 1979, Washington, D.C., schools were 96.5 percent nonwhite, Atlanta's schools 89 percent nonwhite, Detroit's 83 percent, and San Francisco's 77 percent (Friedman, 1979). With a minority population of over 80 percent in the Chicago Public Schools, equal educational opportunity cannot mean merely that a black child must have access to a white child in order to receive equity. The Chicago Student Desegregation Plan is *not* designed to ensure that every black and Hispanic child has a personal association with white children as a criterion of equal educational opportunity. Indeed, many minority members, myself among them, are offended by the implication that education for minorities, indeed their intellectual development, depends on interaction with whites. The plan stresses the need for multicultural experiences, but it is realistic. It attempts to provide programs and policy initiatives that will institutionalize equal educational opportunity and at the same time improve the quality of education in every school and for every child.

A second significant aspect of our desegregation reality in Chicago is related to the notion that attendance in all-minortity schools "affects the hearts and minds of the children in a way never likely to be undone" (*Brown* v. *Board of Education*, 1954). Within the context of the American societal value system, segregation has a significant negative impact on those who are segregated. We also recognize how deliberate and legal isolation of minorities in separate school facilities has defined those schools and indeed those students as inferior and has treated them as such. Desegregation often leads to dramatic changes. For example, the U.S. Commission on Civil Rights (1982) found that

school desegregation results in improvement in achievement for minority students. Beyond taking every possible step to desegregate the Chicago Public Schools, our approach has been to vindicate the constitutional right to equal protection by addressing the *treatment* of minority schools and minority students. An all-minority school education would not be nearly so disturbing if minority children were learning at the same rates and levels as white pupils and receiving the same quality of instruction in the same kind of setting, with an equal number of qualified staff members and with equal resources.

If this were so, there would be no justifiable rationale for rushing to remove black students from good black schools to attend low-achieving white schools. In any case, the system should provide the option to move. However, the real issue is quality. Beyond student assignment, the Chicago Student Desegregation Plan attempts to address process and outcome inequities that occur systematically in minority schools.

The real issue addressed by *Brown I* and, to a different degree, by *Brown II*, regarding assignment of black and white students to the same school, was not just a matter of a white child and a black child sitting in physical proximity. The issue was access to quality resources. The *Brown* decision recognized that mixing students of different races was probably the best way to ensure that quality resources were distributed equitably. However, that was in the South in 1954. It is no longer 1954. Nor is the issue of desegregation primarily applicable to predominantly white southern school districts. Considering the problems of northern school districts in 1984, the mixture of races in itself cannot ensure the equitable distribution of resources.

Chicago continues to have over 370 racially identifiable schools, but this does not mean that these schools must receive inferior treatment or indeed that they are stigmatized. Indeed, the Chicago Student Desegregation Plan mandates improvement of racially identifiable schools. Some integrationists have earned their reputations by going to any length to place black children in schools where they will be in the minority. Many so-called integrationists have used the alleged pursuit of equality for black and minority students as an excuse for and a means of reaffirming their view of white superiority. It is curious to note that white integrationists always propose desegregation in circumstances where white children are in the majority. Indeed, some integrationists pursue desegregation with such a vengeance that one cannot help but question whether or not they are afraid to have anyone discover than an all-black urban school can effectively teach all of the children who attend.

Indeed, I have often considered that we are close to moving intra-district busing and metropolitan busing to perhaps interstate rail (not to be confused with the underground railroad). However, it is not the predominance of black students that causes negative results for racially identifiable schools. It is the institutional malfeasance that so frequently exists when a school attains a black or minority identity. The school attains a stigma and is systematically accorded less than equal status. It is this *institutional* treatment that the Chicago Student Desegregation Plan attempts to address. These two realities—that the Chicago Public Schools are predominantly minority and that minority schools can be quality schools—differ substantially from the reality present in 1954. If Chicago is in any way representative of other large urban areas, then these realities exist in many other cities.

SUMMARY

This brief discussion has attempted to accomplish three objectives: (1) to present the Chicago desegregation story as an example of desegregation in the 1980s; (2) to highlight the kinds of school desegregation issues that affect desegregation in the 1980s; and (3) to address the different contexts within which desegregation operates as they relate to the *Brown* decision. The obvious question that remains is whether school desegregation is worth major efforts in the future. Perhaps our time would be better spent pursuing improvements in educational efforts despite the racial composition of school enrollments. In an article entitled "Facing Educational Facts" (1983–1984), Derrick Bell commented that "the sad truth of a great deal of the school desegregation that has occurred is that placing blacks and whites in the same schools does not, as we had hoped, ensure equal educational opportunity for black children." Perhaps it is time, three decades after *Brown I*, to reassess our efforts.

The real message here is that we must do more than continue to focus on research and to write dissertations about the problems of all-black schools and predominantly black or minority school systems. The reason why we have done little to desegregate urban schools is because desegrega-

tion has been personally and socially unacceptable to the larger white community. This is portrayed poignantly by the current Administration's purposeful retreat from desegregation support and the "devastating downward spiral" (Reid, 1983) that now follows *Brown*, thirty years later. Those who are most concerned about improving and increasing the degree of cross-cultural and interracial interaction in the schools—an appropriate goal—should focus their attention and their demands for change on the root of the problem, not on its victims. The root of the problem is the generic "white community" and its supporting political structure. This is where the solution should be sought.

Part of the answer implied by the Chicago Student Desegregation Plan lies in a redefinition of desegregation. In a traditional and limited sense, desegregation has meant the mandatory mixing of certain numbers of white, black, and Hispanic pupils in all schools. This should be abandoned as the primary, and in many instances, the sole objective. Racial balance, as an isolated goal, must be rejected as the definition of desegregation. Instead, we must obliterate the conditions that create unequal treatment and unequal outcomes for minority students in urban areas. Indeed, it is these circumstances that any desegregation plan must change if we are to apply *Brown* to the practical tasks of desegregating large urban school systems in the 1980s.

REFERENCES

Bell, D. (1983–1984, December–January). Facing educational facts: A respectful response to Kenneth Clark. *Educational Leadership*, 86–87.

Brown v. Board of Education of Topeka, 347 U.S. 483 (1954).

Brown v. Board of Education of Topeka, 349 U.S. 294 (1955).

Campbell, C., & Levine, D. U. (1977). Whitney Young Magnet School of Chicago and urban renewal. In D.U. Levine & R.J. Havighurst (Eds.), *The Future of Big-City Schools* (pp. 139–149). Berkeley, CA: McCutchan Publishing Corp.

Chicago Public Schools. (1984, October 31). Racial/ethnic survey of students.

Edmonds, R. (1979). A discussion of the literature and issues related to effective schooling. *6*, CEMREL, Inc. Newsletter.

Friedman, M. (1979). School integration today: The case for new definitions. In M. Friedman, R. Meltzer, & C. Miller (Eds.), *New Perspectives on School Integration* (pp. 1–22). Philadelphia: Fortress Press.

Milliken v. Bradley, 418 U.S. 717 (1974).

Moody, C. (1981–82, Winter). *Progress*. Washington, DC: Education Commission of the States, p. 14.

Morgan v. Kerrigan, 401 F. Supp. 216 (1975).

Ravitch, D. (1978). The white flight controversy. *The Public Interest*, 145–147.

Regents of the University of California v. Bakke, 438 U.S. 265, 407 (1978).

Reid, H. O. (1983). State of the art: The law and education since 1954. *Journal of Negro Education*, *52* (3) 234–249.

State Board of Education, State of Illinois. (1976, February). *Rules prescribed by the State Board of Education establishing requirements for the elimination and prevention of racial segregation in schools*. Illinois: Author.

U.S. v. Board of Education of Chicago, 717 F. 2d 378 (Consent Decree, September 24, 1980). *Id*. at 4, 12.

U.S. v. Board of Education of Chicago, 717 F. 2d 378 (7th Cir. 1983).

U.S. v. Board of Education of Chicago, 80 C 5124 (June 8, 1984, Opinion of Judge M. Shadur).

U.S. Commission on Civil Rights. (1982, December). *Statement of the United States Commission on Civil Rights* (Clearinghouse Publication 76). Washington, DC: U.S. Government Printing Office.

Webb v. Chicago Board of Education, 223 F. Supp. 466 (N.D. Ill.) (1961).

School Desegregation Patterns in the States, Large Cities, and Metropolitan Areas— 1968–1980:

A Report to the Subcommittee on Civil and Constitutional Rights of the Committee on the Judiciary of the U.S. House of Representatives

GARY ORFIELD

INTRODUCTION

Since the fall of 1981, the House Subcommittee on Civil and Constitutional Rights has been conducting extensive hearings and studies of school desegregation in the United States. Chairman Don Edwards requested that the Department of Education supply the subcommittee with primary data on the levels of segregation of black and Hispanic public school students. These data, covering the period from 1968 —when systematic federal data were first collected—to the 1980-81 school year, were provided in the form of printouts prepared by the DBS Corporation for the Education Department. Chairman Edwards then requested that the Joint Center for Political Studies analyze the data and report to the committee on their implications.

This report is the second part of the center's response to that request. The first part was a report submitted to the committee in September 1982. It analyzed the broad national and regional trends in the desegregation of black and Hispanic students. It showed that the southern and border states led the nation in desegregation of black students, that segregation of

black students was increasing in the Northeast, and that there has been a serious increase in the segregation of Hispanic students in all regions of the United States.

This second report focuses in on states, metropolitan areas, and large cities. It shows substantial variation among these areas, indicating that the general changes are not simply products of particular legal or historical patterns affecting regions. This variation makes it possible to consider the likely effects of various types of desegregation plans on the extent and durability of desegregation.

The 1980 city data and much of the state data in this report are here released for the first time. And this is the first time that any federal racial data for schools on a metropolitan level have ever been released.

TRENDS IN THE STATES

American states differ greatly in their racial compositions, population trends, and levels of school segregation. In some states, virtually all black and Hispanic students attend well-integrated schools, with no discernible trends toward segregation. In others, segregation of black and

Hispanic students is intense and rising.

In about a third of the states, there is no possibility of significant additional busing for desegregation in the near future, because there is no significant school segregation. Some states that had very substantial segregation problems have made remarkable progress in desegregation within a very few years. Much of the remaining segregation is located in a few large industrial states.

There were 20 states in 1980 with more than three-fourths of the black students in majority-white schools. Most of these states had very few students in segregated schools. In the case of Hispanic students, who are highly concentrated in a few parts of the country, the great majority of the states had little serious segregation in 1980. In 29 states, less than a fourth of the Hispanic students were in predominantly minority schools.

GARY ORFIELD is Professor of Political Science, University of Chicago.

This report was prepared by Professor Orfield for the Joint Center for Political Studies.

These statistics show that in major regions of the United States, there are no serious segregation problems at this point, either because there are few minority children at all or because states already have desegregation policies that have eliminated most segregation. Although the issue is commonly discussed as a national policy problem, contemporary segregation is actually most severe in a relatively small number of states. Within those states, the large-scale segregation often exists in one or a handful of metropolitan areas.

The problem is that many of the states with serious segregation remaining are those with the largest percentage of minority children. Most black students attend schools in just nine states: New York, Texas, Illinois, California, Georgia, Florida, North Carolina, Louisiana, and Michigan. Unfortunately, Illinois, New York, Michigan, and New Jersey head the list in segregation of blacks, and a number of the other states rank close behind. Among those states with the largest black enrollments, only Florida and North Carolina rank high in the achievement of desegregation, for reasons that will be discussed later.

Hispanic students are even more highly concentrated in certain areas. A substantial majority of all Hispanic pupils in the United States attend schools in California and Texas. Most others live in New York, New Mexico, Illinois, Florida, and Arizona. The growth in Hispanic enrollment is most rapid in the same areas.

New York is by far the most segregated state for Hispanic students. In California, Illinois, and Florida, Hispanic segregation is increasing rapidly, and in Texas, an already severe segregation problem is slowly becoming more intense. The existing trends in the states most important for Hispanics show that segregated education is likely to continue expanding.

BLACKS AND THE SOUTHERN AND BORDER STATES

The 17 southern and border states have shown the most dramatic changes since the Supreme Court ruled out "freedom of choice" desegregation in 1968 and approved the use of busing in 1971. The dramatic changes over the entire region, however, do not tell the whole story. Among these states, which are subject to the same general legal requirements, desegregation has occurred in very diverse ways and has had strikingly different results. Increases in the percentages of black students attending majority-white schools ranged from 0 to 41 percent during the period studied. Three of the states today have more than nine-tenths of their black students in integrated schools, one state has more than three-fourths of its black children in predominantly minority schools, and five others have about two-thirds of their black pupils in such schools.

The largest increases in integration have taken place in Delaware, Kentucky, and Florida, each of which had begun to desegregate at the beginning of the period and made decisive increases in integration during the seventies. The increases are clearly related to the county-wide city-suburban busing plans implemented in many Florida districts in 1971 and the similar plans imposed in metropolitan Wilmington and Louisville by federal court orders later in the decade. At the other end of the spectrum, with the lowest gains and continuing high levels of segregation, are several states and the District of Columbia, in which very large numbers of black students attend separate central-city district schools that enroll relatively few white students and have limited desegregation plans or none at all.

Recent Resegregation in Some States

Among the southern and border states, three have shown some significant *increases* in the percentages of black students in intensely segregated schools since 1974. From 1974 to 1980, the percentages of black students in schools that were 90 to 100 percent minority rose 9.4 percentage points in Tennessee, 5.0 percentage points in Florida, and 4.3 percentage points in Mississippi. These changes indicate the need to update desegregation plans periodically to deal with the growth of segregated residential patterns if the accomplishments of the last generation are to be consolidated.

Changes in Segregation of Black Students in the North and West

Most of the massive changes in racial segregation since the sixties have been in the southern and border states. Many northern and western states have very small black populations. Among those in which at least 5 percent of the students are black, only nine have had substantial changes in black segregation patterns—Colorado, Indiana, Kansas, Nebraska, Nevada, New Jersey, New York, Ohio, and Wisconsin. Schools in New York and New Jersey have become substantially more segregated. These states, along with other industrial states where school desegregation has not changed substantially, have the most segregated schools in the United States.

The four states with the most segregated schools for blacks in the United States, according to the three measures used in this study (percentage of black students in predominantly minority schools, percentage of black students in 90 to 100 percent minority schools, and percentage of whites in the class of a typical black student), are Illinois, Michigan, New York, and New Jersey. Also included among the top ten in each of the three measures are Pennsylvania, California, Mississippi, and Louisiana. Missouri and Texas are among the most segregated on two of the measures. Thus, the four states with the most segregated schools, and two others among the top ten (California and Pennsylvania) are outside the southern and border state area. None of these highly segregated northern and western states is among the ten states with the highest black percentages in total state enrollment. The southern states, with considerably higher proportions of blacks to desegregate, have less segregated school systems.

Outside the South, the states with the largest gains in desegregation are those in which black students are concentrated in one or a few urban centers *and* where there have been major court orders requiring urban desegregation. In Nebraska, the Omaha court order ended most segregated education in the state; in Wisconsin, most blacks live in Milwaukee, and a court-ordered desegregation process emphasizing magnet schools significantly reduced segregation; Ohio has been the scene of very active litigation and major court orders in Cleveland, Columbus, and Dayton, as well as a voluntary plan in Cincinnati. Blacks in Nevada are concentrated in the Las Vegas area, where a metropolitan plan was implemented; Denver was the location of the first Supreme Court busing plan affecting a nonsouthern school district; and Indiana has had major court-ordered desegregation in Indianapolis.

In New Jersey and New York, the only states where black segregation has increased significantly, there have been some successful efforts to desegregate small cities and the suburbs of large cities, but there have been no significant desegregation plans in the largest cities.

Segregation has increased primarily because of the rapid declines in whites in the central-city school districts and the steady spread of ghettos and barrios to cover more and more of the central cities.

Changes in the Segregation of Hispanic Students

The trends in desegregation of black students are full of complexities and cross currents, and there have been vast increases in desegregation in some areas. In contrast, the pattern for Hispanic students is overwhelmingly toward greater segregation. Between 1968 and 1980, a great deal of effort went into desegregating black children, but very little attention was paid to the increasing segregation of the rapidly growing Hispanic communities. Hispanic settlement is highly regional, and Hispanic school enrollment has become very large in certain states. With the exception of Colorado, these states all show increasing segregation.

The changes are particularly important in the three states that educate 69 percent of Hispanic public school students—California, Texas, and New York. By all three measures used in this report (percentage of Hispanic students in predominantly minority schools, percentage of Hispanic students in 90 to 100 percent minority schools, and percentage of whites in the class of a typical Hispanic student), New York is the most segregated state in the nation, and Texas, which educates more than a fourth of Hispanic children in the United States, is the second most segregated. California is experiencing very rapid increases in the segregation of its Hispanic students.

The most dramatic increases in segregation of Hispanic students between 1970 and 1980 took place in California, Illinois, and Florida. Texas and New York were already highly segregated and became modestly more segregated during this period. Only two states, Colorado and Wyoming, had significant declines in segregation. In Colorado, this was probably due to the school desegregation order in Denver, the largest city in the state, which has more Chicano than black students. Wyoming, an energy boom state, had a large in-migration of white families.

The fact that the Hispanic enrollment is growing in states with high and increasing segregation suggests that the problem will become even more severe. Although there was a sharp decline in national public school enrollment in the seventies, California and Texas each had an increase of

nearly 300,000 Hispanic students. Data for 1982 from Los Angeles suggest that the number of Hispanic students is still growing.

The changes mean that Hispanic children growing up in the 1980s will face quite different school situations than those growing up a decade or more earlier. In California, Florida, and Illinois, for example, the typical Hispanic student in 1970 was in a one-half white school; by 1980, he was in a two-thirds minority school. Hispanic students are more and more likely to find themselves in schools with large numbers of the poor, the non-English speaking, and other minorities.

THE CITIES AND SEGREGATION

Although it is useful and interesting to compare regions and states, many of the decisions that determine educational integration take place within individual school districts or metropolitan areas. And what happens in one large city can affect more minority children than what happens in several small states.

Furthermore, because of residential segregation, minority families are often extraordinarily dependent on one or a handful of urban school districts within a state. Outside the South, both blacks and Hispanics are overwhelmingly urban residents, principally of central cities within large metropolitan areas. And as minority dependence on these districts has grown, white enrollments have declined.

Another reason for examining the big cities before turning our attention to entire metropolitan areas is that, since the late sixties, they have been at the center of most of the conflict over desegregation. Far-reaching progress against rural and small-town segregation had been achieved by that time, and many small cities were in the process of peaceful desegregation. Since then, the political history of busing and school desegregation has revolved around big cities: Charlotte, Detroit, Richmond, Dayton, Columbus, Los Angeles, Denver, Cleveland, Seattle, and others. Cases in these cities have been the focus of Supreme Court decisions and civil rights efforts.

Sweeping conclusions about the feasibility and success of school desegregation have been drawn from community battles over implementation and the conflicting claims of school officials and various advocates about the results in their own cities. The decline of white enrollment in certain big cities after court-ordered deseg-

regation, for example, has often been cited as proof that busing cannot work as a remedy and in fact has the long-term consequence of increasing racial separation.

Thus, to gain a better perspective on the issues raised, it is very important to review overall changes in the demographics of central-city school systems. The data permit some simple comparisons among city school districts of approximately similar size that have followed radically different desegregation policies, or no such policies at all. The data also permit examination of the different experiences of central-city-only school districts and districts that include both the central city and the suburbs.

Some of the most general patterns of big-city changes in school district composition are evident in Table 9*. The districts listed in that table serve almost 25 percent of the nation's black and Hispanic children but only 2 percent of white children.

Between 1968, when the systematic collection of national data began, and 1980, there was a clear and steady increase in the predominance of the minority student population in the largest city school systems. This trend held regardless of the region of the country or whether there was a school desegregation plan within the city schools. Six of the ten largest districts were more than half minority by 1968, but none was as much as two-thirds minority. By 1980, all had more than two-thirds minority students, and most had at least three-fourths minority students. Interestingly, the change in racial composition was most rapid in several sunbelt cities: Los Angeles, Houston, Dallas, and Miami.

A closer look at big-city school districts that serve only the central-city portion of the metropolitan area shows a striking nationwide pattern of nonwhite majorities. Of the fifty school districts listed in Table 10, two-thirds had nonwhite majorities by 1980, and half of the remainder were rapidly moving in that direction. In other words, only about a sixth of these cities had reasonably secure white majorities. These were generally younger cities that included areas which would be considered suburbs elsewhere or cities in states with few minority residents.

White Enrollment Decline in the Largest Districts

The percentage of whites in central-city school districts has been declining for

---

We have included only Tables 9, 10 and 17 from the original article. For complete tables, contact the Joint Center for Political Studies.

decades. Although in recent years most attention has been focused on the decline of white enrollments following busing orders, statistics show that the proportions of whites in the largest districts in the United States—whether they have central-city or county-wide school systems—have been declining for twelve years. Virtually all large districts, regardless of whether they are desegregated or include both the city and the suburbs, have declining percentages of white enrollment. Indeed, because of the more rapid natural growth of minorities, the total national percentage of whites enrolled in schools—private as well as public—is gradually declining.

There have been large declines in white enrollment percentages, both in systems with purely voluntary desegregation plans, such as Houston and San Diego, and in those with mandatory busing plans, such as Detroit and Memphis. A number of the districts that have become overwhelmingly minority were well on the way to this transition long before desegregation began. Desegregation plans may have varied the rate of change, but not the basic direction of change (see Table 10).

What does make a difference, according to these figures, is the scope of the district. In the five largest central-city-only school districts, white enrollment percentages dropped sharply during this period. In the largest metropolitan districts, declines in white enrollment were less than half as large, despite the fact that most metropolitan districts were under far-reaching orders to bus for desegregation. What appears to be centrally important is not the student assignment plan, but the degree to which the school district encompassed the housing market area and thus made flight impractical. A number of the largest southern metropolitan areas were also still receiving a substantial net migration of whites, which aided stable desegregation.

Increases in Percent Black

The data on increases in black enrollment percentages in large districts are difficult to summarize and interpret. In contrast to the popular view, not all of the biggest increases in black enrollment occurred in inner cities, and not all of the inner-city areas experienced rapid growth in the percentage of black enrollment. Some large central-city school districts have been experiencing declines in the *numbers* of black students in recent years; the *percentages* of black students have increased only because whites are leaving the city more

rapidly than blacks and blacks have more children, on the average, than whites. Some of the most rapid changes were in suburbs rather than cities. In a number of cities, the large increases in minority enrollment have been for Hispanic rather than black children.

The largest changes were in the city of Atlanta and two of its suburban counties; Prince George's County, outside Washington, D.C.; Detroit; Gary; Birmingham; Milwaukee; Memphis; and Flint, Michigan. Black enrollment in each of these jurisdictions increased by more than 20 percent. Atlanta, Detroit, Memphis, and Gary were overwhelmingly black school districts and were continuing to change. Detroit and Memphis had busing orders; Gary did not. Atlanta and its suburbs experienced rapid changes in spite of a political bargain that strictly limited busing in the hope of achieving stability. Prince George's County, Maryland, adjacent to a Washington, D.C., ghetto area, began a rapid racial change in the late sixties and had a major busing order in 1972. In Memphis, where a busing plan was resisted bitterly and a parallel "segregation academy" system of fundamentalist white schools was created, black enrollment increased by 21 percentage points between 1968 and 1980. Milwaukee, which has a moderately smaller school system, implemented a nationally acclaimed desegregation policy that relied on voluntary transfers to magnet schools without substantial resistance. The number of blacks in Milwaukee increased by 22 percentage points.

The cities and large metropolitan districts where the proportion of blacks increased less than 10 percent from 1968 to 1980 have very different compositions. The list includes some of the nation's largest urban school systems—New York, Los Angeles, Chicago, and Philadelphia. It includes Denver, the first northern school district ordered to implement busing by the Supreme Court. And it includes areas with the largest metropolitan busing plans in the United States—Tampa, Louisville, Las Vegas, Jacksonville, West Palm Beach, and St. Petersburg. Most of these areas had substantial migration of white families from the frostbelt.

Some districts had either no growth or declines in their black enrollment percentages, including San Francisco, Newark, and the southwestern cities of San Antonio, Tucson, and Corpus Christi. San Francisco, which probably has the nation's most diverse student population, was one of the first cities outside the South to implement

busing for desegregation, but the black proportion did not rise.

The statistics show that busing had only a modest and perhaps temporary effect on enrollment changes. The effects seem to be strongest in initial phases of busing in those central cities with large minority enrollments that are surrounded by white suburbs that are not included in the busing plan. The data also show that there are more basic influences on enrollment trends that operate strongly on the demography of cities regardless of whether there is a school desegregation plan. The data also show that in many communities with little or no increases in the numbers of blacks, Hispanic enrollment is increasing as white enrollment falls.

Hispanic Enrollment in the Large Districts

The increases in the enrollment of Hispanic children in the nation's largest school districts, one of the most important trends from 1968 to 1980, was one of the major reasons for the national increases in Hispanic segregation. In Los Angeles, the Hispanic enrollment had increased from 20 percent in 1968 to 49 percent by 1982. A similar change occurred in Dade County, Miami. In Chicago, the proportion of Hispanic students more than doubled, reaching 20 percent as Hispanic children replaced whites. A very similar change took place in Dallas, and even more growth, from 13 percent to 28 percent, occurred in Houston, which was the largest city in the South by 1980. Majority Hispanic districts, including El Paso, San Antonio, and Corpus Christi, experienced rapid increases in the Hispanic share of their total enrollment. Some older industrial cities that have become secondary migration centers for Hispanics experienced sharp increases from what had been very low percentages of Hispanic students. Boston, for example, had an increase from 3 percent in 1968 to 14 percent in 1980. Newark's Hispanic enrollment had increased to 20 percent by 1980 and Jersey City's to 29 percent.

One of the major contrasts between statistics for blacks and Hispanics is that there are many more major school districts with virtually no Hispanic children. At this point, the Hispanic population is still far more geographically concentrated than blacks or non-Hispanic whites. Most Hispanic school children are in California or Texas. The 1980 Census showed that close to half of the nation's Hispanic population was in ten metropolitan areas, three of which are part of the Los Angeles urban complex.

The enrollment trends show the emergence of some overwhelmingly Hispanic school districts and the development, in a number of the nation's largest urban areas, of major school districts with two large and different minority populations. In some of these districts, the whites are already the third largest group of students and are rapidly losing ground. Urban educators in some cities must now deal with the problems of two major segregated and unequal minority communities. Black and Hispanic children, who may have very little contact with whites, face the need to work out relationships with each other. (In a few cities, very rapidly growing Asian immigrant settlements are introducing still further complexities.) As settlement patterns continue to develop, the list of large school districts confronting these challenges is likely to grow.

The Trends and the Future of Big-City Education

The issues of segregation and equality for minority students have been on the agenda of big-city educators for a generation, but the statistics in this report show that little progress has been achieved and that most segregation remains in the large cities. In fact, the large-city school systems are now predominantly minority. The trends in the schools generally foretell trends in the cities as a whole and in the labor force and electorate. The trends show that race relations will be a central issue in tomorrow's cities of unprecedented racial diversity and separation.

There are signs, also, that the changes that emerged in the big cities during the post-World War II period are now beginning to have large impacts on some suburban districts as well. Not only will many central-city school officials be forced to deal with another major minority group, but some suburban school districts that have always been all-white will confront sweeping changes.

The data on the largest districts point again to the importance of closely examining metropolitan area-wide desegregation plans, which diverge from the prevailing big-city patterns in fundamental respects. Metropolitan school systems have the highest levels of integration and the greatest stability. Given the present composition of the large central-city districts and their well-established patterns of change, metropolitan approaches offer the only alternative

for a growing list of cities like Washington, D.C., Atlanta, and Newark, where integration is impossible and where middle-class minority families are rapidly following whites out of the city. Segregation by race is supplemented by segregation by class and intensified by the political boundaries that separate the segments of the population. Recent sharp cuts in federal and state aid to big-city school districts have weakened the major mechanism that had been developed to deal with some of the consequences of racial and socioeconomic transformations of central-city education.

Desegregation Levels in the Largest Systems

During the seventies, there were dramatic changes in the racial composition of schools in many central cities as a result of major demographic changes and a variety of desegregation plans. Among the largest urban districts, there have been widely varying changes in the average percentages of whites in the schools attended by the typical black student, ranging from an increase in white students of 72 percentage points to a decline of 19 percentage points. The changes depend on the residential patterns of the metropolitan area and the nature of the school desegregation plan adopted. In general, the greatest increases in integration of black students were in the big-city districts that include much of what would elsewhere be called surburbia within their boundaries and that have sweeping busing orders. The declines in desegregation have been in central-city districts where there is either no desegregation plan or where an earlier plan was eroded by demographic changes.

A closer look at the demography of the larger districts of the southern and border states, almost all of which have desegregation orders or plans, shows the differential impact of the demographic changes on different sorts of school districts. The desegregation plans limited to central cities faced the same patterns of demographic change that affected cities across the nation. White enrollment, and thus the possibility of continuing integration, was far more stable in the county-wide districts with city-suburban busing than it was in the central-city-only districts without any significant mandatory desegregation (including Houston, New Orleans, and Baltimore). The next section shows that integration levels are much higher in these stable metropolitan areas with county-wide school systems.

Black children in Washington, D.C., attend the most segregated big-city schools in the United States. The school system is 94 percent black and only 3.4 percent white, and thus significant desegregation within the system is impossible. Eighty-three percent of the district's minority children were in schools where the white enrollment was 1 percent or less. Only one D.C. minority student in 200 was in a school that was as much as half white. The only large cities that came close to this level of segregation were Newark, Atlanta, and Chicago. The nation's capital had a predominantly black enrollment even when its schools were still segregated by law, and it is subject to the problems of separate and suburban districts more absolutely than other cities, because of its unique status outside any state.

Hispanic Enrollment in the Big Cities

Hispanic enrollment is rapidly becoming more important in the nation's largest school districts. In five of the 50 largest central-city school districts, Hispanic students were the largest single racial group by 1980: San Antonio Independent (74 percent), Corpus Christi (65 percent), El Paso (67 percent), Dade County (Miami) (38 percent), and Los Angeles. In Los Angeles, which has the nation's second largest school district, the 1982–83 enrollment was 49 percent Hispanic, and the percentage of Hispanics is rapidly increasing.

The Hispanic enrollment (and the much smaller Asian enrollment) is growing much faster than the black or white enrollments nationally and in many school districts. Many big-city systems have had declining white enrollments for years and recent drops in black enrollments as well. Migration, differential birth rates and age structures of the population, and continued white suburbanization all point toward a continuation of the pattern. In a number of large districts where blacks remain the dominant group, Hispanics are likely to overtake whites as the second largest group. In Chicago, for example, Latinos now comprise 20.4 percent of the enrollment, and as of fall 1982, there were only 16.3 percent whites.

Metropolitan Desegregation Patterns

The basic unit of analysis for social trends in the United States is the metropolitan area. When one speaks of the Chicago economy, the Los Angeles housing market, the Atlanta power structure, the Houston transportation problem, or the pollution problem of any major city in the United States, the entire metropolitan area is being considered, not merely the central city. Most Americans live within metropolitan complexes, but most of the urban dwellers live outside the central cities. In a few areas, this is true for minority residents as well. We routinely receive data on metropolitan housing and job statistics and many other kinds of information simply because this is the basic unit of analysis for understanding many issues in American society. The federal government, however, has never released data comparing metropolitan areas on school desegregation problems and progress. We know that most remaining segregation is concentrated within big districts inside metropolitan areas. This makes it very important to compare the results in areas which have taken quite different approaches to desegregation.

The future of integration for currently segregated minority families will be determined largely by decisions about the future of schools and housing in large metropolitan areas. In Illinois, for example, more than two-thirds of all the black and Latino students in the state attend the Chicago public schools, which are among the nation's most segregated. Only about one-sixteenth of the whites in the state, however, attend Chicago schools. What happens within the school system in the Chicago metropolitan area will affect more minority families than anything else that can be done in the state. In fact, there are very few entire states that have as many black and Latino students as this one metropolitan area.

Although the federal government has periodically released data for central cities, it has not produced comparative statistics for metropolitan areas. In fact, its data collection system, which is set up to look at individual districts only for civil rights enforcement purposes, requires production of data from central cities, but often omits many individual suburbs, particularly suburbs that have few minority students. The data collected are particularly inadequate for metropolitan areas with highly fragmented educational systems that include many small suburban districts. This pattern characterizes the older urban centers in the East and Midwest—areas that are often the centers of segregation in what are now the nation's most segregated states.

These problems with the federal data system mean that we lack basic knowledge about segregation trends in some of our most important urban communities. And since the federal statistics are the only statistics collected nationally and serve as the basis for research and policy debate as well as civil rights activities, this is a very serious problem indeed. Using the current statistics, it is not possible, for example, to say anything about segregation trends in such vast urban areas as metropolitan New York or Chicago.

This report uses the federal data to assess and compare metropolitan desegregation trends in those areas where the information collected by the Department of Education is at least minimally adequate, which tend to be the less fragmented metropolitan communities of the South and West. Because so few large northern metropolitan areas can be analyzed, this study provides only a comparative analysis of metropolitan desegregation trends in the South and West.

The only metropolitan areas that can be studied are those on which the U.S. Department of Education has racial data for *most* of the students. To find out which areas these are, the 1980-81 Education Department data were compared with the total metropolitan public school enrollments through a special tabulation by the National Center for Educational Statistics, which had total enrollments, but not racial data, for all districts from the previous school year. This report includes data only for those metropolitan areas, Standard Metropolitan Statistical Areas (SMSAs), in which the Education Department data are estimated to cover at least 70 percent of the total enrollment. Because the sample has always counted a considerably higher proportion of minority than white children, these statistics offer very strong coverage of minority children's experiences in terms of desegregation.

In order to avoid problems that could arise from reporting those measures of segregation which are highly sensitive to the percentage of white students counted, only one measure of segregation is used in this portion of the report. That measure, the exposure index, shows the percentages of white students in the schools attended by the typical black or Hispanic student in the metropolitan area. Since the sample includes the great majority of blacks and Hispanics and the schools they attend, this measure is the most reliable analysis of the existing federal data. And since desegregation policy is designed to rectify the

segregation of minority youngsters, this is a useful and powerful measure to begin a comparative analysis.

Along with other data collection problems, the federal survey sampled different districts in different years within the suburbs. But since all the samples had the common feature of greatly oversampling districts with significant minority enrollments, this is not a fatal problem for this analysis. The statistics presented here should be accepted, however, as the best possible approximations rather than exact findings.

General Findings

Metropolitan areas include very large numbers of students, and a short list of the largest metropolitan areas, in terms of total enrollments, would include a very significant fraction of all students in the United States. In the 1980–81 school year, for example, more than a sixth of U.S. students went to schools in metropolitan New York, Los Angeles, Chicago, Detroit, Philadelphia, and Washington, D.C. All of these metropolitan areas had small white minorities and large numbers of segregated nonwhite children in their central-city school districts. None had a desegregation plan crossing city–suburban boundary lines; several had no significant desegregation at all. None of the ten largest metropolitan areas had substantially desegregated public schools. Forty-two entire states have smaller enrollments than metropolitan New York, or metropolitan Los Angeles, or metropolitan Chicago. Obviously, progress toward desegregation or regression toward segregation in these large metropolitan regions and their smaller counterparts in other states deserves the most careful analysis.

There are extraordinary differences among metropolitan areas, even among those of relatively similar size and racial composition in the same region, and sometimes even in the same state. In some, there have been virtually no segregated schools for more than a decade, in others, there are very few integrated schools and hundreds of black, white, and Hispanic schools. Some entire urban communities have had little experience with segregation and now have an entire generation of students who have known integration as the norm. In others, racial isolation operates on a large scale and is more intense than it was a generation ago. According to research by Diana Pearce at Catholic University, those metropolitan areas in which schools have been desegregated are now experiencing considerably more housing integration than those which retained segregated schools. According to research by Robert Crain of Johns Hopkins University and Rita Mahard of the University of Michigan, city–suburban plans produce dramatically greater educational gains for black students than central-city-only plans. If the very wide differences among urban areas continue and further research confirms the broad impacts of these different approaches, the future may be one of widely divergent metropolitan societies with very different kinds of race relations.

Metropolitan Areas in the Southern and Border States

The southern and border state area is most interesting for analysis of metropolitan trends for several reasons. First, the data are most complete, and it is possible to look at trends in most large metropolitan areas. Second, it is the only region that has had a considerable number of metropolitan areas with region-wide desegregation for a number of years. Third, in the South, many suburbs as well as central cities have significant minority populations and some kind of desegregation plan. Fourth, almost all the metropolitan areas, unlike many in the North, have a substantial minority population. Fifth, the southern states include a number of the most important sunbelt cities, whose development will do much to influence race relations in the United States for decades to come. Unlike older and declining metropolitan areas, these rapidly growing communities still have many fundamental choices to make about the educational and residential patterns of their metropolitan regions.

It is important to note one source of possible confusion before looking at the data on southern metropolitan areas. A number of the same metropolitan areas were discussed in the analysis of big cities. In that section, however, the data were limited to single districts. Although some of these large districts were county-wide and happen to include most students in the metropolitan area, many included only the central city or part of the suburban ring, and none were larger than a single county. This section, in contrast, combines data from all the individual school districts surveyed within Standard Metropolitan Statistical Areas (SMSAs) as defined by the Bureau of the Census. Typically, each SMSA includes a central city and the adjacent counties that have experienced significant suburbanization. (Los Angeles is a major exception; the Census Bureau limits its SMSA to Los Angeles County and breaks its outlying suburban ring into several other SMSAs.) Many SMSAs include several counties and large numbers of independent school districts. Thus, even though the name of the central city is used in the text and tables of this section to identify the metropolitan area, the statistics refer to very different units of analysis from those in the preceding section.

Among the large southern and border state metropolitan areas for which we have adequate data, the racial composition of the schools attended by the typical black student ranges from a low of less than one-fifth white enrollment in the Miami and New Orleans SMSAs to more than two-thirds white enrollment in the Tampa, Louisville, and Wilmington SMSAs. In the relatively small number of large SMSAs with at least 5 percent Hispanic population, the range is more narrow. Hispanic students have the most contact with whites in the Austin and West Palm Beach districts and the least in the heavily Hispanic Texas SMSAs of McAllen, El Paso, and San Antonio.

The largest increases in desegregation for black students occurred in Louisville, Tampa, Wilmington, and Oklahoma City. The largest increase in segregation was in Miami. Among Hispanic students, the only substantial increase in metropolitan desegregation in an area with more than 5 percent Hispanics was in Austin, and the largest declines in the percentages of whites were in metropolitan Miami and Houston.

The relationship between desegregation policy and actual level of desegregation accomplished is obvious. All of the areas with the highest levels of desegregation for blacks have extensive city–suburban busing orders, and two of the leaders in change during the seventies have had court orders forcing merger and desegregation of previously independent city and suburban school systems (Louisville and Wilmington). The major reduction in segregation for Hispanics came in Austin, which recently implemented a major desegregation order—one of the few major busing orders with an explicit goal of desegregating Hispanics. If one compares Richmond, where the federal courts rejected city–suburban desegregation, with metropolitan areas that have city–suburban plans, the differences are clearly apparent. In metropolitan Richmond, in spite of desegregation plans within separate parts of the metropolitan area, the typical black

student is in a school that is almost three-fourths black, and the level of integration dropped from 1970 to 1980. In Atlanta, where the Supreme Court recently rejected a city–suburban plan, black students are even more segregated than in Richmond, and segregation also increased slightly during the seventies. One need only compare those figures with data from major southern and border districts that have metropolitan plans to note the striking differences in results. Metropolitan school desegregation orders have had a pronounced and lasting impact on segregation.

Desegregation orders limited to central cities have been highly successful only in cases where a central city contains much of the metropolitan population and a relatively high percentage of white students. For example, in Austin and Oklahoma City, the two cities where orders limited to the central city had the most impact, as of 1980, more than half of the students were white in contrast to many other, largely minority big-city districts in the region.

One of the important developments in the South, which is evident in these data, but has not received serious attention previously, is the emergence of some metropolitan areas where a majority of all of the public school students are from "minority" groups. Memphis and New Orleans, for example, have black majorities even on a metropolitan basis. Most of the metropolitan areas of South Texas have Hispanic majorities. Some major metropolitan areas outside the South either have or are moving toward nonwhite majorities. In a few metropolitan areas, particularly those near the Mexican border in Texas, even the most far-reaching metropolitan plan would leave many minority students in predominantly minority schools. There is a need for serious thought about what the goals of desegregation should be in such a setting, and how its progress should be measured. These questions will become increasingly important as some of the major metropolitan areas in California and elsewhere become predominantly minority in public school enrollment. For the time being, it is important to note that the statistics on segregation in some metropolitan regions reflect not merely a failure to develop desegregation policies but also some extraordinary demographic obstacles to full integration.

Overall the metropolitan trends in the South are strongly related to different kinds of desegregation plans. City–suburban plans and plans in predominantly white big-city districts have produced high levels of desegregation, which have remained high even years after the court order. In large SMSAs with predominantly minority central-city school districts, there has been much less progress in integration for minority children, whether or not there has been a desegregation plan. There has been little progress in desegregating Hispanic students on a metropolitan basis anywhere in the region, with the single exception of Austin.

Metropolitan Segregation and Desegregation in the West

The West, the only other region where the data permit some comparative analyses of the large SMSAs, is different from the southern and border areas in key respects. Its dominant minority is Hispanic, not black. Western Hispanics are rapidly becoming more segregated, in contrast to the large increases in desegregation for southern blacks. California dominates the region's statistics in a way not true for any southern state, thus California's metropolitan areas are of decisive importance for the region's black and Hispanic populations, which are both very highly urbanized.

Among the large metropolitan areas surveyed, only the Denver SMSA had a decline in segregation of both black and Hispanic students during the 1970s. Denver, which was ordered to desegregate as the result of the Supreme Court's first busing decision outside the South in 1973, has a plan designed to desegregate both groups.

The largest increases in the percentages of whites in the schools of the typical black student during the 1970s were in Las Vegas (up 14.5 percent) and Denver (up 10.2 percent). The Las Vegas (Clark County) desegregation plan is the only large metropolitan plan in the West. Most of the western metropolitan areas did, however, modestly reduce segregation of black students during the decade. One reason for the progress was the much smaller black enrollment percentages in many western metropolitan areas than in their counterparts in the South and the older industrial states.

Segregation of Hispanics increased in all of the SMSAs listed in Table 17, except in Denver and Tucson, where there were slight gains in integration. Denver and Tucson both had school desegregation orders.

The most dramatic declines in the percentages of whites in the schools of the typical Hispanic student occurred in the urban corridor of Southern California (San Diego, Orange, and Los Angeles counties), where there was massive Chicano migration. The typical metropolitan Los Angeles student had been in a 45 percent white school in 1970 but was in a 78 percent minority school by 1980. In Orange and San Diego counties, where the Hispanic percentages were much lower, the typical Hispanic student was in a school that was more than 66 percent white in 1970 but in a predominantly minority school by 1980. Los Angeles had a limited school desegregation plan, but the mandatory portions were dismantled in 1981. San Diego had a small voluntary plan limited to the central city. There were no court orders in Orange County.

Most of the major urban centers of California and the Pacific Northwest are experiencing not only substantial growth of Hispanic population but also large increases in the number of Asian children. Indeed, the San Francisco school district has far more Asian than black, white, or Latino students. When these migration trends are combined with the region's low white birth rate and the residential segregation of blacks and Hispanics, it is not difficult to understand the growing likelihood that, in the absence of strong and effective desegregation policies, minority children will find themselves in schools with few whites.

In fact, not only are minority children, except Asians, highly segregated from whites, but there is a substantial tendency for each of the minorities in these cosmopolitan cities to be segregated from each other as well. The San Francisco desegregation plan aims at creating multi-ethnic schools, and civil rights lawyers in Los Angeles urged a plan that would have a similar goal. Obviously, these will be important questions in metropolitan areas where a substantial majority of the school children will be from an assortment of minority groups.

In a number of the western metropolitan areas where segregation was addressed through a plan limited to the central city, the segregation trends produced by continuing white suburbanization, neighborhood resegregation, and continuing in-migration of minority families are gradually diminishing the level of integration for minority children. This is apparent now, for example, in Sacramento. In the long run, these forces will raise the question of city–suburban desegregation in the West if substantial integration is to be maintained.

In most instances, the western metro-politan regions studied here have shown significant progress in reducing the segregation of blacks, the region's second largest minority. However, Hispanics, the largest group of minority students, have become substantially more segregated. In the West, unlike the South, desegregation orders are far from universal even within central cities, and city–suburban desegregation on a large scale exists only in Las Vegas, an area that has levels of integration comparable to the highest in the South. The region's demographic trends foretell increasing segregation of minority children and increasing difficulties in holding on to the achievements of the past generation in those SMSAs with city-only plans and large minority enrollments. Perhaps the leaders of urban education in the West should examine the experiences of metropolitan areas in the South.

Conclusions and Recommendations

The first report of this project, submitted to the House Subcommittee on Civil and Constitutional Rights in September 1982, showed the major progress that was achieved in southern desegregation from 1968 to 1980 and suggested that the difference between that record and the much slower change in the North was due in part to the much stronger enforcement of civil rights policies in the southern and border states. An important finding was the clear evidence of increasing segregation of Hispanic children in all parts of the United States. By changing from a broad regional overview to a more focused look at states, metropolitan areas, and big urban districts, this report allows some interpretation of the reasons for the extremely wide variation among different states and urban areas in the same region. The analysis strongly suggests that the key problems of segregation facing the nation are in the cities, and that the central reasons for success in reducing segregation drastically in some states and metropolitan areas have been implementation of desegregation plans on a city–suburban basis or on a citywide basis in the small minority of big-city school districts that still retain white majorities and serve a large fraction of the metropolitan population.

The findings of this project, I believe, support the following recommendations:

1. Racial data on all school districts in metropolitan areas should be regularly collected and released.

Even with the cooperation of the Department of Education, it has been impossible to do any serious analysis of segregation trends in the largest urban areas of the eastern and midwestern states where segregation is most intense. It is impossible to develop good research and policy analysis without such basic data.

2. The implications of increasing segregation of Hispanic students and the impact on Hispanics of various forms of desegregation should be seriously investigated.

   Extremely little governmental or scholarly attention has been devoted to the rapid increase in the segregation of this very large and expanding minority group. If the consequences turn out to be anything like those produced by segregation of black education, this neglect may be similar to the failure of northern educators to address questions of ghetto education throughout its formative period in the early twentieth century. Certainly we should begin as soon as possible to evaluate the consequences and the possible remedies.

3. City–suburban desegregation plans should be encouraged and supported.

   Since the enactment of the 1964 Civil Rights Act there has been no positive action by Congress to encourage or require desegregation, except for the financial aid granted by the Emergency School Aid Act, which was repealed in 1981. Congress should reinstate that important program, which funded educational and training components of desegregation plans but not busing. It should offer special assistance for voluntary or court-ordered city–suburban desegregation.

4. Housing desegregation policy should be strengthened.

   One of the clear implications of statistics showing increases in segregation in areas without strong busing policies is that policies intended to diminish residential segregation are not working. Strengthening the very weak Federal Fair Housing Law, developing policies in support of integrated neighborhoods, and requiring administration of housing programs in a way that contributes to rather than undermines school integration could provide real support for school desegregation while taking some of the burdens of change off the courts and local educators.

Table 9. Decline in enrollment of white students in selected large-city school districts, 1968–1980.

City	Decline in number of white students	Percentage decline in number of whites
New York City	213,675	45.7
Los Angeles	222,522	63.4
Chicago	136,213	62.1
Philadelphia	45,096	41.2
Detroit	90,331	77.8
Houston	82,288	62.8
Dallas	58,929	60.2
Baltimore	38,830	58.0
Memphis	31,831	54.6
San Diego*	37,209	37.9
Washington, D.C.	4,957	59.9
Milwaukee	55,350	58.2
New Orleans	24,608	71.0
Cleveland	43,946	66.3
Atlanta	36,420	85.7
Boston	40,819	63.3
Denver	37,188	58.7

*Only predominantly white school district on list.

Table 17. Segregation of Hispanic students in selected western metropolitan areas with enrollments over 50,000 and more than 10 percent Hispanic, 1970–1980.

Metropolitan Area	Percentage of whites in school of typical Hispanic student		Change in percentage points, 1970–1980
	1970	1980	
Los Angeles	44.9	21.8	−23.1
Albuquerque	39.2	36.3	−2.9
Tucson	38.2	38.3	.1
Fresno	49.0	39.3	−9.7
San Francisco–Oakland	61.5	44.6	−16.9
San Diego	67.4	45.2	−22.2
Anaheim–Santa Ana–Garden Grove	72.8	48.7	−24.1
Phoenix	50.8	50.1	− .7
Riverside	63.1	54.5	−8.6
Denver	55.6	55.8	.2
Sacramento	70.0	56.5	−13.5
Modesto	78.5	62.0	−16.5
Vallejo–Fairfield–Napa	78.5	66.8	−11.7
Las Vegas	81.9	70.6	−11.3
Colorado Springs	72.0	71.7	− .3

Table 10. Total enrollment and racial composition of the 50 largest central-city school districts, 1980.

District	Total enrollment	% black	% white	% Hispanic	% Asian
1. New York	931,193	39%	26%	31%	4%
2. Los Angeles	538,038	23%	24%	45%	7%
3. Chicago	445,269	60%	19%	19%	2%
4. Miami (Dade Co.)*	232,951	30%	32%	38%	1%
5. Philadelphia	224,152	63%	29%	7%	1%
6. Detroit	211,886	86%	12%	2%	0%
7. Houston	194,060	45%	25%	28%	2%
8. Baltimore	129,979	78%	21%	0%	0%
9. Dallas	129,305	49%	30%	19%	1%
10. Memphis	110,113	75%	24%	0%	0%
11. San Diego	109,793	15%	56%	18%	11%
12. Washington	104,907	93%	4%	2%	1%
13. Milwaukee	87,826	46%	45%	6%	1%
14. New Orleans	85,707	84%	12%	1%	3%
15. Cleveland	80,074	67%	28%	4%	1%
16. Albuquerque	78,051	3%	53%	39%	1%
17. Columbus	73,094	39%	59%	0%	1%
18. Atlanta	72,295	91%	8%	0%	0%
19. Boston	67,366	46%	35%	14%	5%
20. Fort Worth	66,170	37%	44%	18%	1%
21. Indianapolis	65,958	50%	49%	0%	0%
22. Denver	64,274	23%	41%	32%	3%
23. St. Louis	61,474	79%	21%	0%	0%
24. El Paso	61,285	4%	28%	67%	1%
25. San Antonio	60,695	15%	11%	74%	0%
26. Newark	59,658	70%	9%	20%	0%
27. San Francisco	59,385	27%	17%	16%	40%
28. Tucson	55,654	5%	62%	29%	2%
29. Austin	55,369	19%	53%	27%	1%
30. Cincinnati	53,632	57%	42%	0%	0%
31. Portland	52,868	14%	76%	2%	7%
32. Tulsa	49,454	23%	69%	1%	1%
33. Seattle	49,156	22%	56%	4%	15%
34. Oakland	48,863	66%	14%	10%	9%
35. Buffalo	48,236	47%	47%	4%	0%
36. Fresno	47,770	12%	54%	31%	3%
37. Birmingham	46,523	76%	24%	0%	0%
38. Pittsburgh	46,239	50%	49%	0%	1%
39. Toledo	45,488	33%	62%	4%	1%
40. Wichita	44,921	19%	72%	4%	3%
41. Omaha	44,719	25%	70%	2%	1%
42. Minneapolis	42,797	21%	69%	1%	4%
43. Oklahoma City	41,185	35%	55%	4%	2%
44. Sacramento	39,873	22%	46%	17%	13%
45. Akron	38,926	35%	64%	0%	0%
46. Kansas City	38,279	67%	28%	4%	1%
47. Norfolk	37,471	58%	39%	1%	3%
48. Corpus Christi	37,383	6%	28%	65%	0%
49. St. Paul	37,051	13%	74%	5%	6%
50. Ft. Wayne	34,716	20%	77%	2%	1%

*For the purposes of this table, Dade County is considered as the central city of the South Florida urban complex.

The Research on the Effects of School Desegregation:
Real-Estate Prices, College Degrees, and Miscellaneous Other Things

ROBERT L. CRAIN

In the last thirty years, desegregation has played a critical role in black educational progress. Understanding the outcome of the 1954 *Brown* v. *Board of Education* decision by the Warren Court requires analyzing more than the effects of desegregation on how well children learn to read and write. The ability to read and write is important, but how children are socialized to become the next generation of adults is even more crucial. School desegregation is the most significant change in the schools in the past thirty years—more important than the open classroom or new math. This paper presents what social scientists have learned in last thirty years about the effects of integration of our nation's schools.

School desegregation is a very powerful tool for altering our society. But we have used it only half-heartedly, leaving vast numbers of schools segregated. This is in part because black and white intellectuals in this society are quite ambivalent about busing. In addition, the nation as a whole has never been totally committed to desegregation and has had to be pushed by court decisions to integrate its schools. It seems this ambivalence and lack of commitment are due to more than just lethargy. At some level, perhaps, Americans really don't want desegregation to work, and when it does, we then don't want to believe it works.

How much do social scientists actually know about desegregation? Is there substantial statistical evidence documenting desegregation effects, or is most of the talk

concerning desegregation obscured by fancy academic jargon and meaningless phrases? After all, it wasn't too long ago that every southern senator who needed quick applause could whip out his regular speech about the Supreme Court paying attention to all those left-wing sociologists and college professors. And the *Brown* decision did throw around a great deal of fancy social–psychological language:

Does segregation of children in public schools solely on the basis of race, even though the physical facilities and other "tangible" factors may be equal, deprive the children of the minority group of equal educational opportunities? We believe that it does...to separate them from others of similar age and qualifications solely because of their race generates a feeling of inferiority as to their status in the community that may affect their hearts and minds in a way unlikely ever to be undone...the policy of separating the races is usually interpreted as denoting the inferiority of the negro group. A sense of inferiority affects the motivation of a child to learn. Segregation with the sanction of law therefore has a tendency to retard the educational and mental development of negro children and to deprive them of some of the benefits they would receive in a racially integrated school system...(Brown, 1954; also quoted in Clark, 1955).

The decision went on to say that these findings are "amply supported by modern psychological knowledge" (Clark, 1955). The Supreme Court seemed to be promising that if we only desegregated schools, the mental health of minority children would improve and they would learn more. Do black students learn more in desegregated schools? I don't think this is the most important question, but it is the one most often asked, so let me deal with it first. The first and most critical point is that the education of black students has improved a great deal in the past two decades. The National Assessment of Educational Progress (NAEP), a national testing program designed to measure the educational achievement of the American population, found ten years ago that black students' scores in the South were going up (National Assessment of Educational Progress, 1981). More recently the NAEP found that black students' scores in the entire nation were going up as well (NAEP, 1983). How much have they gone up? In the 1960s, when the first national testing was done, the typical black student scored about three grade levels below the average white student. The average black tenth grader could read and compute about as well as the average white seventh grader. In the next ten years, about a third of that gap between white scores and black scores was erased (Burton and

ROBERT L. CRAIN is at the Center for Organization of Schools, Johns Hopkins University.

Jones, 1982; Jones, 1984).

That is a very big change. Not all of this improvement has hit the colleges yet because many of the students who took these tests haven't finished high school. When they do, we will find that the number of black students who score above 1,000 on the Scholastic Aptitude Test (SAT) will have increased by 50 percent.

Can we give desegregation credit for any of this improvement in black scores? The answer is *yes*. Social scientists have argued for a long time about whether desegregation raises black test scores. In part, this was just prejudiced left-wing scientists arguing with prejudiced right-wing scientists; and partly it was because there was little reliable data—before 1968, the federal government didn't want to offend Congress by supporting research on desegregation. Nevertheless, enough research has finally been done to settle the issue. My colleagues and I located a hundred studies that had been done in nearly as many different cities on what happened to black test scores after desegregation. What we found was quite consistent with what the National Assessment had shown. Black students typically gained about one grade almost immediately after entering desegregated schools (Crain & Mahard, 1983).

Some of the research is technically very good. There is really only one perfect way to do this sort of research, and that is to do it the way research is done in medicine: pretend that children are laboratory mice, divide them randomly into two groups, and then desegregate one group and not the other. Unfortunately, there are usually ethical or legal reasons why this method is not possible.

There are exceptions; there are five different studies where it was possible to perform such an experiment. In all five cases, the desegregated students started out with the same test scores as the segregated students, but finished the experiment scoring considerably higher. I don't think anyone can argue with these research results. (For a more complete discussion, see Crain & Mahard, 1983.)

Higher black test scores are one benefit of desegregation. What are the drawbacks? One of the most frequently talked about disadvantages is the notion that white student performance is pulled down by desegregation. Though there has been a plethora of research on this issue, nothing has demonstrated this deleterious effect. The interesting query here is *why*. If black students benefit somehow from going to

school with white students, who are generally better students than they are, why don't the white students suffer when they have to go to school with black students, who generally are worse students than they are? It appears that black and white students are affected only indirectly by the quality of their classmates. More specifically, it seems likely that when white students enroll in a predominantly black school, the teacher raises the pace of the class to what he or she would expect of a class of middle-class students. The white students learn the same amount of material they would in the school they came from, and the black students learn more because the class is paced faster. But when blacks come into a white classroom, the teacher does not slow down for them. Black students do not receive direct academic benefits from going to school with whites but rather from the increased classroom pace and the stiffer competition.

There are, however, psychological drawbacks associated with desegregation. Increased classroom pace and stiffer competition can result in black students learning more, but getting lower grades; blacks who move from a segregated school to a desegregated school may experience a loss of self-esteem. This may be simply because there is something uncomfortable about associating with people who are different than you are. Milton Rosenberg has shown that white Catholic students in Protestant neighborhoods have lower self-esteem and white Protestants who live in Catholic neighborhoods have lower self-esteem. Perhaps simply being in the minority is enough to put some dents in adolescent armor. It may also be a simple matter of the size of the fish and the size of the pond. Typically, black students who transfer to a desegregated school will see their grades go down, simply because they are unaccustomed to the competition. A working-class white student whose family moves to the suburbs would have the same experience (Rosenberg, 1965).

The danger here is obviously not the lower grades, but the perception of failure. Segregated children who previously thought of themselves as "special", compared to their peers, now realize that they are only "ordinary." This ordinariness then transfers itself to a feeling of mediocrity, a feeling of being a black lost among whites. These perceptions can then become self-fulfilling.

Fortunately, there exists a factor attenuating this loss of self-esteem. Self-confidence increases in those children who attend desegregated schools. Though they may

realize that they are only small fish in a big pond, these children grow acclimated to their larger pond. Coleman et al. (1966) found that blacks in desegregated schools score higher on psychological scales that test their internal control of the environment than do those in segregated schools. This suggests that desegregated students are less fatalistic about their lives; they feel they can control their own future. This makes sense; there are more opportunities in a larger pond. Students who go to school with whites can learn from personal experience that whites are not omnipotent and that blacks who attempt to compete with whites can do so successfully.

How painful is it for blacks and whites to attend school together? The answer seems to be *not very*. Even in the deep South, whites in high schools don't seem upset that they go to school with blacks. Blacks in high school have more difficulty, probably because they are usually in the minority; but even they do not seem to have serious problems.

In 1972 the National Center for Education Statistics surveyed high school seniors across the nation. Examination of black students' responses in predominantly white high schools, compared to those in segregated schools, revealed two problems. Blacks in desegregated schools were more likely to claim both that the courses were too hard for them and that their teachers did not think they were very good students. The differences were not large; on a scale from 0 to 10, the black students in segregated schools said their teachers rated them about 7½, and those in predominantly white schools said their teachers rated them about 7. The survey found that the more black teachers in the school, the higher the grades of the black students and the more likely they were to go to college (Crain & Mahard, 1978). The precise cause is unknown. Do the students work harder because of the presence of black role models? Do white teachers discriminate against black students or do black teachers discriminate in their favor? Whatever the answer, desegregated schools work better if they have more black teachers. Beyond that, there was no other indication that black students were particularly unhappy in these schools. They seemed to know that they were making a trade-off. The school wasn't as pleasant a place to be with all these white students around, but at the same time, they were going to a better school and one that was providing them with a better education. They can't have been too unhappy, because the evidence indicates that black students in desegregated schools are less likely to drop out of high school than those who go to segregated schools (Crain et al., 1986).

The decline in Scholastic Aptitude Test (SAT) scores in the 1960s and 1970s cannot be attributed to desegregation. Too much has been said linking lower SAT scores to misguided social goals and accusing desegregationists of putting social progress before educational priorities. It is not difficult to prove that there is no correlation between desegregation and the decline in SAT scores. The SAT scores did decline for about fifteen years, but they bottomed out in the 1980s and have recently turned upward. The American test-score watchers have been predicting this upturn for some time from their observation of students' scores on National Assessment of Educational Progress (NAEP) tests. In 1972 the NAEP found nine-year-olds scoring higher in their ability to read than nine-year-olds had previously, and in 1976 the NAEP found that thirteen-year-olds were doing slightly better on the standardized tests that they administered (Burton & Jones, 1982). The nine-year-olds in 1972, the thirteen-year-olds in 1976, and the high school seniors in 1981 are all the same group of students, of course. The children born in 1963 are slightly brighter in school than those born in 1962, thus reversing a long trend; for each year from 1949 to 1962, each successive group of newborn children had done slightly worse in school than the ones born a year earlier. Maybe the schools had gotten progressively worse. If so, it doesn't have much to do with desegregation because the schools were segregated during most of that downhill trend.

A cause-and-effect relationship between desegregation and SAT scores is probably less plausible than a relationship between nuclear bomb testing and test scores. A statistical analysis of SAT scores, for instance, shows that the birth dates of test takers who had declining test scores from 1967 to 1980 corresponded perfectly with the period when there was atmospheric testing of nuclear weapons around the world: 1949 to 1962. Nuclear fallout contains an isotope, iodine 131, which causes brain damage in mice. Fallout could have caused a slight amount of damage to newborn infants and have lowered the average SAT scores of this generation (Sternglass & Bell, 1983).

If the purpose of the school is to transform children into functioning adults,

then we want schools to produce people who can survive in the adult world—and that means a good deal more than simply scoring high on a test. One of the most important predictors of adult success is simply the years of school completed. Though everyone knows, or at least has heard of, people who are bright or plucky enough to drop out of high school or college and still make millions, most drop-outs don't quit in order to make a lot of money; they are just too lazy, too confused, too busy doing drugs or getting pregnant.

Another question we must ask is the following: If you had two black students with the same test scores, would the one from a segregated school leave school earlier? Here the evidence is persuasive. In the North, black students who attend segregated schools are not only less likely to finish high school, they are less likely to finish college. And this is not just because their segregated high school education is poor academic preparation for college. More important, the segregated high school provides poor social preparation. College is a painful experience for most students. For black students, the normal pain and stress are greatly magnified if the students find themselves dumped into a predominantly white environment for the first time in their lives.

I teach at a small university that has less than 200 black undergraduates. I asked two black undergraduates how black students with segregated schooling fared in the college. They could only name a single student who had come to college from a segregated school and that student had quit at the end of the first year. National data tell the same story. The National Longitudinal Survey of the high school class of 1972 found that a black student from a northern segregated high school was only 55 percent as likely to succeed in college as a black from the same family background who had come out of a desegregated high school (Crain & Mahard, 1978). In the study I am now doing of black students who grew up in the Hartford, Connecticut, ghetto and were permitted to transfer to suburban schools, the bused students were considerably more likely to finish high school and, if they went to college, considerably more likely to get a degree. When asked about their college experience, the students from desegregated backgrounds were less likely to complain that they were victims of discrimination in college (Crain et al., 1986). Some of my cynical friends would say that students from a desegregated school have been discriminated against so much in

school that by the time they reach college they have become oblivious to it. Perhaps, but students who come from segregated schools sometimes act in college as if they were walking through a cemetery, seeing the spectre of discrimination in every disturbing shadow. A friend who ran a black studies program at SUNY-Buffalo said that many black undergraduates from segregated schools collapsed the first time things went badly. They would either decide that they weren't smart enough to compete against whites or that the whole school was racist and they didn't have a chance.

Completing high school or college is just the first step in a successful career. Students must set their sights on good jobs, get the jobs, and perform well after they get them. Research shows that desegregated schools can help blacks accomplish all three of these things. Black students in desegregated schools have higher job aspirations. Blacks in desegregated schools not only have higher employment aspirations (Dawkins, 1982), their occupational hopes are more logically connected to their educational performance and their specialized training. In other words, there is less blue-skying when asked what they intend to do; they aspire to good jobs, but to those particular good jobs they have the best chance of getting (Braddock, Crain, & McPartland, 1984).

Blacks from desegregated schools are also more likely to know where to look for jobs. For a large number of us, the way to find a good job is to heed the old saying, "It ain't what you know, but who you know."

You get a job by being first in line with the right recommendations. A good deal of research shows that you can use friends and, more importantly, acquaintances, to find out about that good job. Women professionals, as they've tried to move ahead in the corporate world, have coined a flashy verb—networking. The black from a desegregated school has a different network that, because it is biracial, contains a lot more knowledge about the good jobs that usually only whites know about.

Black students benefit in another way from desegregated schools. White employers, even if they are not openly prejudiced, look with some puzzlement at ghetto blacks. They don't know how to evaluate someone whose background is completely different from their own. They are more comfortable when a black job applicant can produce a résumé that says, "I have been over on your side of the tracks and I have letters of reference signed by white people." I have just completed a study that demonstrates this principle. I surveyed employers by randomly offering a description of a prospective employee to the employers and asking them how they would go about deciding whether to hire the applicant. Without the employers' knowledge, we simultaneously randomly varied the kind of employee they reviewed. Those who were given a description of a black who had graduated from an inner-city school reacted more negatively than those who were given a similar description of a candidate who had graduated from "a suburban high school with a good reputation." When they saw the words suburban school, they suddenly wanted to see the student's grades, and school references became more valuable (Crain, 1984).

Finally, blacks from segregated schools have trouble working because it is more difficult for them to relate to whites. Jomills Braddock, at the Center for the Social Organization of Schools, has published a series of papers on what he calls the perpetuation of segregation. Blacks from segregated schools tend to work in segregated work groups; those who have white supervisors complain about them more than blacks from desegregated schools do (Braddock, Crain, & McPartland, 1984).

We know a good bit about the effect of desegregation on black student attitudes, but less about the impact of desegregated schooling upon white students' attitudes toward minorities. One can safely assume that white students' attitudes toward minorities are strongly affected by their school experiences. There is good reason to believe that white students will be less prejudiced if they attend desegregated schools. Racial tensions exist in desegregated schools, and black students are on the average not as good students as whites, so some analysts worry that whites will carry away more negative impressions of blacks after going to school with them than they would if they had attended a segregated school. It seems more likely that if whites develop friends and contacts among blacks, they will be less prejudiced. Distance and naiveté create prejudice. If one desegregates early in the elementary grades before racial tensions develop, significant ties between the young may develop. Further, some evidence shows that white military veterans are more willing to live in integrated neighborhoods, perhaps because of their interracial experiences in the military (Becker, 1979).

At this point, I have gotten a good distance away from the simple notion that desegregated schooling is something that affects children. I have argued that deseg-regated schools affect children but the effects do not wear off when those children grow up; their school experience remains part of them for the rest of their lives. Now let me go one step further. The school is an institution in a society made up of a variety of institutions. Does school desegregation affect the other institutions of the society? This has always been the most fundamental question. In 1932, when the National Association for the Advancement of Colored People (NAACP) decided to make school segregation a high priority (Kluger, 1975), it was not primarily interested in test scores. Rather, it saw the segregated school system as the keystone in a whole edifice of segregated institutions and believed that if that keystone could be removed, the whole structure would tumble. This was one of the most accurate predictions any group of lawyers ever made. Ten years after the 1954 Supreme Court decision, the South was undergoing a revolution unlike anything since Reconstruction. There are more black elected officials now than there were black voters then. As soon as one gets used to the idea of meeting a black sheriff in the southernmost cotton town in Mississippi, one is even more surprised to find George Wallace earnestly shaking hands in search of the black vote.

School integration is not going to work the same kind of revolution in the North, but it is having some interesting effects. One of the least noticed, but perhaps most important aspects of integration is the way real-estate markets operate in cities with desegregated schools. In the long run, of course, blacks from desegregated schools will be more likely to live in desegregated housing because they are more comfortable in desegregated settings. Young blacks who go to suburban schools in Hartford are more likely to take apartments in mixed neighborhoods. It is, however, the immediate effects of desegregation that I would like to focus on.

A few years ago, I studied school segregation controversies in northern cities and was surprised to find that the most determined and effective advocates of desegregation were often the black and white residents in integrated neighborhoods. In each case, the neighborhood group was working to stabilize its area and discovered that the schools were its worst problem. To understand this, one needs to know only one fact about patterns of residential choice. Families move when they have small children and are looking for a school. In every big city in the United States, one can find formerly white neighborhoods where black families are moving in with their small children in search of a better education. Typically, the white families living there are older and have few school-age children, so the school "tips" prematurely. By the time the neighborhood is half black and half white, the school is virtually all black, simply because the families who are moving in have school-age children while the families who are already there do not. The families moving in are black; the families who are already there are white. But if the school is identifiably black, no new white families will move into the neighborhood.

Those families, black and white, who are trying to prevent the neighborhood from becoming all black, seize upon school desegregation as a solution to their problems. School desegregation disperses black and white children over the entire city. The integrated neighborhood's school has the same racial make-up as schools in white neighborhoods, so it won't keep buyers away. Fair desegregation plans are drawn in such a way that regardless of location, a white family will experience the same amount of desegregation. Whites can no longer use the racial mix of the schools as a way of deciding which neighborhood is best. Diana Pearce has shown that in metropolitan areas where schools are desegregated, real-estate agents no longer use the name of the local elementary school as an enticement to white buyers (Pearce, 1981). Karl Taeuber has computed indices measuring the amount of segregation in housing in American cities in 1980, and it turns out that cities with desegregated schools are desegregating their housing at three times the rate of cities whose schools remain segregated (Pearce, Crain, Farley & Taeuber, 1984). This is not as impressive as it first sounds, since three times a little progress is still only a little progress, but it is significant. If school desegregation is a lever that could bring about the residential integration of American cities, then we might still see the end of the urban crisis someday.

The religious war in Northern Ireland is made much more difficult by the segregation of the city into Protestant and Catholic neighborhoods. The same is true about racial conflict in the United States. If a spaceship from Mars landed here, I suppose the Martian anthropologists would be most mystified by the willingness of Americans to kill themselves smoking cigarettes. Once they got used to that peculiar suicidal tendency, they would marvel at our willingness to tolerate continual racial warfare. When they took their spaceship home and described how there were large areas in each city where most of the black population were required to live, the audience back on Mars would ask whether there were high wire fences and guard posts to keep blacks from escaping. The anthropologists would say no, they don't do it that way. Instead, they surround the area in which blacks are required to live with a sort of no-man's-land where young members of the imprisoned group attack, rob, and terrorize members of the group that is imprisoning them.

We live in a society with one of the highest rates of violent crime in the world, but we are unwilling to admit that a great deal of that crime is of racial origin. When I talk about crime being racially based, I am not speaking merely of interracial crime. Much of the intraracial crime that makes life miserable for so many blacks is also rooted in racial inequality and racial segregation. One study found a sharp decline in black violence against other blacks during the time that the civil rights movement was most active (Solomon, Walker, O'Connor, & Fishman, 1965). (The researchers used emergency room admissions for their data.) One could hypothesize that civil rights activity created communal solidarity, which strengthened the bonds of the community and prevented violence. Someone with a psychoanalytical bent would argue that black aggression was being directed constructively toward the source of oppression, white racism, and therefore did not need to be deflected onto inappropriate victims.

Crime is not the only thing wrong with the ghetto. There are bad landlords, rats, and the high price of medicines at the local drugstore. There are also some brutal facts about real-estate values. If two veterans had returned from the Second World War, one black and one white, and used their veterans' benefits to buy homes, the white would probably have bought a tract house in a new suburb. The black would probably have bought his house in one of the more attractive neighborhoods where blacks lived in the city. Today, that suburban house (with some sweat equity in the form of a garage and a playroom in the basement) might be worth anywhere from 50,000 to 100,000 dollars. In Baltimore, the row house that the black veteran bought in a once nice neighborhood would probably be worth between 5,000 and 20,000 dollars. One cannot point to the culprit who robbed that black home buyer of anywhere from 30,000 to 95,000 dollars in equity. It's just the way

the system works. One of the major reasons why the black veteran lost money on his house was because some of his black neighbors made the neighborhood uninhabitable. The sociologist Lee Rainwater wrote in 1970 that whites created a world in which blacks were miserable. In an attempt to vent their misery, blacks often became self-destructive or expressed aggression, sometimes toward whites but more often toward other blacks, in the form of violence, theft, sexual exploitation, and child desertion. Whites remain largely unaware that they are ultimately responsible for the blacks' unhappy situation, in part because whites delude themselves, but also because the system they have created is so complicated they cannot understand it. "White cupidity creates structural conditions highly inimical to basic social adaption (low income availability, poor education, poor services, stigmatization) to which Negroes adapt by social and personal responses which serve to sustain the individual in his punishing world but also generate aggressiveness toward the self and others which results in suffering directly inflicted by Negroes on themselves and on others" (Rainwater, 1970).

I said earlier that the problem with school desegregation was the halfhearted way we enforce it. Perhaps the sheer complexity of segregation makes it difficult for us to press wholeheartedly for its elimination. Maybe we shouldn't complain too loudly; we are certainly better off than the English, who still provide Catholic and Protestant public schools in Northern Ireland. We have desegregated the schools in nearly every city where there is a white majority. White citizens seem to accept desegregation reasonably well as long as the schools remain predominantly white. One would think that since the nation is 85 percent white, desegregation would not be a serious problem; but half the black population is enclosed in a few dozen cities that have public schools with black majorities. These cities are surrounded by a white noose of suburban housing, and the only solution is to force the merger of the city and suburban school populations. Only a few suits to consolidate city and suburban schools have been brought, and the Supreme Court has ordered mergers in only two large areas: Wilmington, Delaware, and Louisville, Kentucky. If you try to imagine the residents of Bryn Mawr being ordered to send their children to school in South Philadelphia, you can imagine why it is difficult to persuade the Supreme Court to order desegregation. A compromise

strategy would be simply to require the suburbs to accept minority students who voluntarily transfer from the city. This could provide quality desegregated schooling to tens of thousands of black and Hispanic students in a city like Philadelphia. But even this scenario is a pipe dream. Philadelphia's black students will probably never get the chance to go to school in the suburbs. There is simply too much opposition to desegregation.

A colleague of mine once said that one couldn't consider school desegregation a controversial issue among whites because a controversy requires disagreement, and whites all agree that they hate desegregation. According to surveys, most whites believe it would be a good idea if blacks and whites went to school together, but they are very strongly opposed to the idea of white children being reassigned from their neighborhood school in order to make it happen. And, of course, if you don't reassign students from their neighborhood schools, desegregation can't happen. Desegregation made sense to northern whites when it was being applied to southern schools. Everyone could understand that the poor black child whose bus went past the shiny white school in order to take him or her to a dilapidated school for Negroes had a legitimate grievance. As long as black schools had old buildings, poorly paid teachers, and old books, desegregation made sense. Now, when the Court argues that a shiny, new black school with new books and qualified teachers in the inner city won't work unless white children are bused into it, it no longer makes sense to anyone. "Why should 'my' child be subject to the sacrifice of being sent to a school in 'their' neighborhood? If their school is so bad, why make my child go to it?" Whites will accept desegregation, but only if their children go to a predominantly white school in a predominantly white neighborhood. If this sounds a little like the territorial imperative of rival gangs talking about turf, I think it is. Though white parents may be subtle in their arguments, a Boston teenager essentially argues the same message, in a language anyone could understand.

They don't live over here. We live over here. They live where they live. My dad says it isn't so different over there but it isn't as nice; they don't have lots of money. Lots of their fathers don't work so they don't have lots of money. We don't have lots of money either. Maybe that's how we're a little alike but we look different to them too, so they don't like us and we don't like them. But that's okay for two groups you know, who don't have to see each other. But when you have to see each other then you might go to war and if I have to fight in a war then I'll fight over here where my friends are, not over there where their friends are. That only makes sense. You go where you have the best chance. They beat up white kids over there so if they don't want us over there then I can't see why the government is forcing us to go there. Maybe they got kids around here who want to go there and colored kids who want to come here. If they do, then the government should let them. But if they don't want to, they shouldn't have to (Cottle, 1976).

I suppose, given enough time, one could explain to this teenager and his parents what is going on here. One could explain to him that before the First World War, the real-estate agents organized a set of restrictive covenants that created segregated neighborhoods. One could explain to him that when the poor are segregated, it is impossible to provide equality of educational opportunity. One could explain all that and, I suppose, given enough time, make him understand.

After that explanation, one would then have to go and talk to the local black leader, who very likely would have a different set of equally plausible sounding objections to school desegregation: "Why does my child have to sit next to a white child in order to learn anything? Are white children so much better that something rubs off? And why can't blacks get together and organize their own schools and do as well as anyone else? Are black-run institutions no good?"

In Delaware, the NAACP brought suit and forced a merger of the largely black schools of the city of Wilmington with the largely white schools of the surrounding suburbs. When they did so, one of the first casualties was the black superintendent of schools in Wilmington, who took the first train to Washington, D.C., to get a job with the Carter Administration. A black leader in the city of Wilmington put the question to me very bluntly: "What I don't understand is, if we won this suit, how come we lost our schools?" By *our schools* he meant schools run by a black administration. But it is important to make him stop believing that the most important thing in black education is the color of the superintendent of schools. Because as long as he believes that, the white elite will be very happy to

make a deal. In Atlanta when the city fathers were trying to avoid desegregation, they struck a deal with the local NAACP. If the NAACP stopped asking for desegregation, the schools would hire a number of blacks for top administrative posts in the school system. In *The New Yorker*, Calvin Trillin argued that the leaders of the black community were opposed to a metropolitan desegregation remedy, which would have combined Atlanta's schools with the white suburbs, because they feared that such a solution would lead to a dilution of black political power. Therefore they accepted the deal offered by the white leaders. "The settlement was reached after a few days of closed discussions in a room of the Trust Company of Georgia. It was handled the way such matters had been handled in Atlanta over the years. Trade-off and compromise and congratulations all around at the end…after the announcements of the terms, one group of black parents said the agreement amounted to trading off quality education for a few big jobs for a few big Negroes" (Trillin, 1973).

In Trillin's eyes, this was a terrible sellout. I think that his view is too harsh a judgment. It is easy to understand why most black school administrators attach little importance to desegregation, and why, for that matter, most black and white leaders do not see desegregation as a high-priority goal. First, they do not know a great deal about it. The typical educator has read little concerning desegregation. And even if he or she had, facts do not change feelings very fast. At face value, desegregation seems an unlikely way to improve schooling. Doesn't it seem bizarre to put children on buses and send them off to foreign neighborhoods? And even if that doesn't frighten you, isn't there some easier way to improve education? Why do we have to support a policy that whites are so strongly opposed to? And perhaps, most importantly, there is some feeling in our guts that, Martin Luther King notwithstanding, there is something demeaning about saying that black schools can't succeed. No self-respecting black could fail to be excited by the vision of an autonomous black community with its own leadership, proud and prosperous. We feel much better thinking about Marva Collins, the headmistress of a Chicago inner-city school, who has supposedly worked wonders, than when we think about the Wilmington Desegregation Plan. No wonder so few black school superintendents have any interest in desegregation. Why should they?

There is something very simple and

sensible about saying, let's organize black schools and put in black principals and black teachers and a black superintendent of schools and show whites what a wonderful job we can do educating our children. And it is extremely difficult for me to think of a way to go to a black school superintendent and say, "I'm sorry, but you can't do it. Not in a society where 90 percent of the votes are cast by whites and 98 percent of the money is controlled by whites. You might, if you're very lucky, transform one or two schools, but to do it everywhere? You are simply not strong enough to take insufficient resources and inadequate tax money and somehow undo all the damage that has been done to black children in the last hundred years."

I keep a biblical text on my office wall from Ecclesiastes, 1:18: For in much wisdom there is much vexation, and he who increases knowledge increases sorrow.

As I try to understand my imaginary black superintendent's feelings, I realize that understanding the positive effects of desegregation increases sorrow because it drags us unwillingly out of a world that is, however unpleasant, psychologically satisfying.

Perhaps I should really ask the Martian anthropologists to come back for a second visit, and have them call on the superintendent instead of me. I know what my Martians would say: "Why on earth are you trying to run a city by drawing a line down the middle, saying blacks have to live on one side and whites have to live on the other? Everyone back on Mars thinks that's the craziest idea they ever heard of."

REFERENCES

Becker, H.J. (1979, November). *Racially integrated neighborhoods: Do white families move in? Which ones?* (Report No. 287). Baltimore: Johns Hopkins University, Center for Social Organization of Schools.

Braddock, J., Crain, R., & McPartland, J. (1984). A long term view of school desegregation: Some recent studies of graduates as adults. *Phi Delta Kappan. 66* (4), 259–264.

Brown v. Board of Education of Topeka. 347 U.S. 483 (1954).

Burton, N. W. & Jones, L. V. (1982). Recent trends in achievement levels of black and white youth. *Educational Researcher. 11* (4), 10–17.

Clark, K. B. (1955). *Prejudice and your child.* Boston: Beacon Press, pp. 158–159.

Coleman, J. S., Campbell, E. Q., Hobson, C. J., McPartland, J., Mood, A. M., Weinfeld, F. D., & York, R. L. (1966). Equality of educational opportunity, Vol. 1. *Final Report to U.S. Office of Education, Department of Health, Education and Welfare,* Washington, D.C.

Cottle, T. J. (1976). *Busing.* Boston: Beacon University Press, p. 13.

Crain, R. (1984, May). *The quality of American high school graduates: What personnel officers say and do about it.* (Report No. 354). Baltimore: Johns Hopkins University, Center for Social Organization of Schools.

Crain, R. & Mahard, R. (1978). *The influence of high school racial composition on black college attendance and test performance.* Washington, DC: National Center for Education Statistics.

Crain, R. & Mahard, R. (1978). School racial composition and black college attendance and achievement test performance. *Sociology of Education. 51* (2), 81–100.

Crain, R. & Mahard, R. (1983). The effects of research methodology on desegregation achievement studies: A meta-analysis. *American Journal of Sociology. 83* (5), 839–885.

Crain, R., Hawes, J., Miller, R., & Peichert, J. (1986). *Finding niches: Desegregated students 15 years later.* Santa Monica, CA: The Rand Corporation.

Dawkins, M. (1982). Black students' occupational expectations: A national study of the impact of school desegregation. *Urban Education. 18,* 98–113.

Jones, L. V. (1984, November). White–black achievement differences. *American Psychologist. 39* (11), 1207–1213.

Kluger, R. (1975). *Simple Justice.* New York: Random House.

National Assessment of Educational Progress. (1981). *Three national assessments of reading: Changes in performance, 1970–80.* Denver: Educational Commission of the States.

National Assessment of Educational Progress. (1983). *The third national mathematics assessment: Results, trends, and issues.* Denver: Educational Commission of the States.

Pearce, D. M. (1981, Summer). Deciphering the dynamics of segregation: The role of schools in the housing choice process. *The Urban Review. 13* (2), 85–102.

Pearce, D. M., Crain, R. L., Farley, R., & Taeuber, K. E. (1984). *Lessons not lost: The effect of school desegregation on the rate of residential desegregation in large central cities.* (Unpublished manuscript). Catholic University Law School.

Rainwater, L. (1970). *Behind ghetto walls.* Chicago: Aldine Publishing Co., p. 4.

Rosenberg, M. (1965). *Society and the adolescent self-image.* Princeton, NJ: Princeton University Press.

Solomon, F., Walker, W., O'Connor, L., & Fishman, J. (1965). Civil rights activity and the reduction in crime among Negroes. *Archives of General Psychiatry. 12,* 227–236.

Sternglass, E. J. & Bell, S. (1983, April). Fallout and SAT scores: Evidence for cognitive damage during early infancy. *Phi Delta Kappan. 64,* 539–545.

Trillin, C. (1973, March 17). U.S. journal: Atlanta. *The New Yorker,* p. 102.

The Role of the Federal Government in School Desegregation

WM. BRADFORD REYNOLDS

The role of the federal government in public school desegregation is a subject of lasting significance, particularly so as we commemorate the thirtieth anniversary of *Brown*. All agree that the minds of our youth are a most precious resource; plainly, our future depends on the active nurturing of those minds. We could not long remain a great nation if we did not offer equal educational opportunity to all our citizens. Our doing so is both a proud legacy and a grave responsibility. On this thirtieth anniversary of *Brown*, we cannot afford to rest on past accomplishments. We must continue the search for better and more effective means of fulfilling the promise of *Brown*. We must examine the past, assess the present, and by building on our experience, plan for our future.

Before turning to the Justice Department's current school desegregation efforts, let me provide a brief history for that important discussion, so that our enforcement activity in this area can be more easily understood, from both a legal and a public policy point of view.

An appropriate starting point is the oft-quoted truism given to us by Oliver Wendell Holmes: "The life of the law has not been logic, it has been experience." It was with this wisdom that the United States Supreme Court, in *Brown* v. *Board of Education*, (1954), looked back over fifty-eight years of experience under the shameful "separate but equal" regime established by *Plessy* v. *Ferguson* (1896), and in 1954 declared that racially segregated education facilities are inherently unequal and cannot be squared with the equal protection guarantee in the Fourteenth Amendment to the U.S. Constitution.

The following year, in *Brown* v. *Board of Education* (1955), the Supreme Court ordered that the nation's dual school systems be dismantled "with all deliberate speed," pointedly observing that the purpose of fashioning a desegregation remedy is to admit students to public schools on a "racially nondiscriminatory basis."

During the period immediately following *Brown II*, resistance to the Court's decree was widespread; far more emphasis was placed on the term "deliberate" than on the direction to move with alacrity. Very few jurisdictions made any measureable progress towards desegregation. In 1968, thirteen years after *Brown II*, the Supreme Court's patience gave out. In *Green* v. *County School Board of New Kent County* (1968), the Court demanded that school officials guilty of intentional discrimination in the assignment of students to racially identifiable schools come forth with desegregation plans that "promise[ ] realistically to work, and promise[ ] realistically to work *now*" (emphasis in original).

In *Green*, however, the Supreme Court did not alter the fundamental premise established in its landmark decisions of a little over a decade earlier. Race-consciousness as a tool for assigning school children had been flatly condemned in the *Brown* opinions. It most certainly was not revived in *Green*. Rather, once again the Court reaffirmed (and in no uncertain terms) that all children in a dual school system had a personal right—a civil right, if you will—to be treated in a nondiscriminatory manner. No mention was made in *Green* of vindicating that right by resorting to some "racial balance" in the classroom. Proportional assignments of students along racial lines were nowhere recognized as a permissible desegregation tool to be employed by the courts. Instead, the equal protection ideal of nondiscrimination was to be realized in *Green*, as in the two *Brown* decisions, through a system of student assignments that did not count by race.

That is essentially how matters stood until 1971, when the Supreme Court embarked on a new remedial course in *Swann* v. *Charlotte-Mecklenburg Board of Education* (1971). The district judge in *Swann* had devised a novel and wide-ranging desegregation decree that ordered race-conscious student assignment schemes into effect, employing for the first time the techniques of mandatory busing, alteration of attendance zones, and "racial-balance" assignments of school children. At issue in

---

WM. BRADFORD REYNOLDS *is Assistant Attorney General, Civil Rights Division, United States Department of Justice.*

the Supreme Court was whether judicial reliance on such remedial devices exceeded the courts' equitable authority to redress the constitutional wrong. In upholding the district court's desegregation plan, the Court, in *Swann*, for the first time acknowledged that strict race neutrality in a remedial context may not be required where racial imbalance in the school system is directly attributable to past *de jure* (or state-enforced) segregative activities. Thus, those children who had been assigned to schools because of race (all of whom are victims of discrimination) can appropriately be reassigned under *Swann* and bused elsewhere in the system on a race-conscious basis.

The Court's opinion in *Swann* was far short of a ringing endorsement of the busing remedy. Rather, it marked a modest (indeed tentative) first judicial step down a remedial path that became far more traveled than the most avid proponents of the busing remedy had ever expected. Thus, race-conscious assignments and mandatory student transfers were seen in the early 1970s as the remedies of last resort, not first impression, to be used, if at all, only if "feasible," "workable," "effective," and "realistic." Yet, by the end of the decade, use by the lower federal courts of forced busing as the predominant desegregation tool had become almost commonplace, with little attention being paid to the practical consequence of such judicial re-ordering of our public education system.

Simply stated, the social objective of racial balance in the classroom ultimately overtook the civil rights principle of racial neutrality in student assignments that is, of course, the principle that served as the centerpiece for the Supreme Court's decisions in *Brown I* and *Brown II*.

Rather than achieving racial balance, however, the preoccupation with mandatory busing has generally produced racial isolation on a broader scale. In case after case, economically able parents have refused to permit their children to travel unnecessary distances to attend public schools, choosing instead to enroll them in private schools or to move beyond the reach of the desegregation decree. Justice Powell has commented on this phenomenon in the following terms:

The pursuit of racial balance at any cost...is without constitutional or social justification. Out of zeal to remedy one evil, courts may encourage or set the stage for other evils. By acting against one-race schools, courts may produce one-race school systems (Estes v. Metropolitan Branches of the Dallas NAACP, 1980); Powell, joined by Stewart and Rehnquist, dissenting from dismissal of certiorari as improvidently granted).

After more than a decade of court-ordered busing, the evidence is overwhelming that the effort to desegregate through wholesale reliance on race-conscious student assignment plans has failed. The damage to public education wrought by mandatory busing is evident in city after city: Boston, Cleveland, Detroit, Wilmington, Memphis, Denver, and Los Angeles are but a few of the larger and thus more celebrated examples. Nor is it difficult to understand why these failures have occurred. The flight from urban public schools contributes to the erosion of the municipal tax base, which in turn has a direct bearing on the growing inability of many school systems to provide a quality public education to their students—whether black or white. Similarly, the loss of parental support and involvement that often comes with abandonment of a neighborhood school policy has robbed many public school systems of a critical component of successful educational programs.

Tragically, those who suffer the most are the very ones that the proponents of mandatory busing intended to be the greatest beneficiaries, that is, the blacks and other minorities left within the inner-city public school systems. It is they who, from most accounts, have little to show educationally as a result of the past decade of court-imposed student assignment plans. Although findings are not absolutely conclusive in this regard, a major study released by the National Institute of Education in May 1984 strongly indicates that racial-balance desegregation remedies have been ineffective in providing a better education for minority students. As David J. Armor, a noted desegregation expert, states in the report:

...the conclusion is inescapable: the very best studies available demonstrate no significant and consistent effects of desegregation on Black achievement. There is virtually no effect whatsoever for math achievement, and for reading achievement the very best that can be said is that only a handful of grade levels from the 19 best available studies show substantial positive effects, while the large majority of grade levels show small and inconsistent effects that average out to about 0 (Armor, 1984).

Small wonder, then, that the Department

of Justice has moved away from its earlier misguided preoccupation with forced busing that has too often ill-served the desegregation command of *Brown*. The admonition of Oliver Wendell Holmes to learn from "experience" has been heard. We are today committed to the pursuit of a different remedial approach to achieve the desegregation ideal announced in *Brown*—one premised on consensus, not conflict. Our focus is no longer on the mandatory transportation feature, but rather on voluntary student-transfer techniques and expanded educational opportunities designed to attract students to the public schools, not drive them away. Our remedial program has as its centerpiece special magnet schools and other curriculum enhancement programs that provide educational incentives to all children in the system. And the choice of schools is left to each student—with a full range of transfer options—not to some preconceived assignment plan superimposed on the public school system by well-intentioned judges who misperceive racial percentages and classroom proportionality as a measurement of equal opportunity.

It is a bit too early to declare the magnet program a complete desegregation success. There are, however, a number of encouraging indicators and very few discouraging ones. The Justice Department has utilized its new remedial approach in a variety of situations: from a large metropolitan area like Chicago to a small rural school district like Port Arthur, Texas. One of the best (or at least one of the most comprehensive) magnet programs was put in place late in 1983 in Bakersfield, California. As expected, we are finding that magnet schools do indeed attract students and, when strategically placed and carefully designed, can provide the needed incentive for white and black pupils to attend the same schools by choice, not by coercion.

In fact, a recent report prepared for the Department of Education of some forty-five magnet programs in fifteen school districts provided encouraging confirmation that urban school districts can desegregate quite comprehensively by relying heavily on magnets. As that report observes: "...magnets appear to be urgently desirable. A magnet can be designed to be receptive, hospitable, safe, educative and desegregatively lawful." (Lowry & Associates, 1983).

We certainly are finding that to be the case. Indeed, the NAACP has just recently, in the Cincinnati school desegregation case (*Bronson v. Board of Education of Cincinnati,* 1976) embraced the magnet school concept as an acceptable desegregation option.

In short, the federal courts are, with increasing regularity, turning to the magnet alternative (in lieu of forced busing) to desegregate dual school systems; the most avid proponents of mandatory student assignments are beginning to rely instead on voluntary transfer measures that utilize educational enhancements as the principal incentive factor; and both houses of Congress have voiced a strong preference for accomplishing the desegregation objective through means other than forced busing. Against this backdrop, it is just a matter of time—and not much time, at that—before communities will be permitted to return the neighborhood public schools to their neighborhoods, but with sufficient flexibility in attendance requirements to ensure that all children in the system, without regard to race, color, or national origin, will be accorded the full range of educational opportunities in a desegregated school environment.

To be sure, our alternative to the forced busing approach is not without its skeptics and critics. There are those who assert that magnet schools are too expensive. The short answer is that, when compared with the costs of desegregation under the mandatory transportation remedy, it is far from clear that a well-conceived magnet plan requires significantly more money. Plainly, over time, the desegregation efforts based on magnet schools and voluntary transfer measures will prove more cost-effective than the failed policies of the past. Moreover, there are, I submit, fewer better expenditures of the taxpayers' dollars than on the public education of our children, and, if truly meaningful desegregation comes at a bit higher price than originally conceived (when the only remedial tool used was the yellow school bus), it is an added cost well worth shouldering.

I often hear the refrain that magnet schools drain the best and brightest students from the public school system, leaving it worse, not better, off, and depriving those left in the regular (nonmagnet) schools of an equal educational opportunity. This criticism can only come from those not fully familiar with the remedial program involved. Use of magnet schools has never been advanced in isolation by the Department of Justice. Rather, the desegregation plan includes not only magnets, but also minimagnets (that assist in the transition from a regular to a special curriculum), enhanced educational programs (including, as appropriate, special

tutoring in basic academic skills), and other particularized teaching devices—all designed to ensure that the command of *Brown* to afford to all school children an equal educational opportunity is realized throughout the system. We have yet to witness a situation, postulated by those who are frequently so quick to criticize, in which implementation of a comprehensive magnet program benefits but a few and is otherwise educationally draining on the system as a whole. Rather, just the opposite has proven to be the case: The program has served to *enhance* the educational environment overall while achieving desegregation of the racially identifiable schools at an encouraging rate.

That is, of course, precisely the promise of *Brown*—a promise that now appears ever closer to being fulfilled. This is not to suggest that we stop probing for even better ways to achieve stable and lasting desegregation of dual school systems. The magnet program is not perfect, and we remain open to suggestions for improvement.

One other aspect of the court-ordered busing controversy deserves mention: the question of when such judicial coercion should terminate. One of the most troublesome features of school desegregation decrees is that they rarely seem to come to an end. For reasons that have never been altogether clear, there appears to be a general reluctance among district court judges who have fashioned relief in school cases to acknowledge many years—in some cases decades—later that the terms of the decree have long since been satisfied and that it is time to return the administration of the public schools to the elected officials who sit on the school board. "Unitariness" is the term used to signify the point at which the segregated system has been dismantled. This term is used to signify the point at which the segregated (or dual) school district has become desegregated (or unitary) in accordance with the court-ordered plan.

I believe one of the most important issues for the 1980s in the field of school desegregation is when, and under what circumstances, a school district under court order is entitled to a judicial declaration of unitariness, thereby releasing it from the court's jurisdiction. That issue is squarely before the district court in Colorado, where the Denver school board in the much-celebrated *Keyes* v. *School Board of Denver* (1973) desegregation litigation is asking the court, some eight years after implementation of the court-ordered plan,

for a declaration of unitariness.

We have joined in the Denver school board's request, urging the court to measure unitariness, not in terms of rigid racial percentages or the degree of racial balance throughout the school system, but rather in terms of the school board's full and faithful compliance with the desegregation requirements imposed by the decree. If the school officials have complied with all the terms of a comprehensive desegregation plan, we argue that a declaration of unitariness should follow—even if some schools in the system, due to factors beyond the school board's control, such as demographic shifts, may never have attained (or even if attained, not continued to maintain) the precise racial percentages for student enrollment contemplated in the court-ordered plan.

It is time for the federal courts to release their hold on school districts that have long been in compliance with comprehensive desegregation decrees. Our public schools better serve the educational needs of our youth if run by those who are answerable to the electorate for the decisions made, than if left under the supervision of the judiciary beyond the time necessary to fully cure the constitutional violation. There is a growing unease among educators that, in the name of desegregation, we have in many instances surrendered to the courts the day-to-day responsibility of operating our public schools—all too often with disappointing results. I therefore anticipate that the unitariness issue will begin to be addressed with greater intensity in the months ahead.

School desegregation is as critical an issue on the civil rights agenda as any we face today. Discrimination on account of race, whether it occurs in the admissions office, the schoolyard, or the classroom, is intolerable and must be eradicated in its entirety wherever it occurs. However, we cannot lose sight of the fact that the desegregation effort affects in a most crucial way the lives, aspirations, and opportunities of our children. It serves no useful purpose to claim a racial-balance victory if in the process we have effectively destroyed—or even seriously hindered—the educational potential of an entire generation of public school students. Regrettably, the preoccupation with forced busing has left just such a legacy in too many jurisdictions.

Now, thirty years after *Brown*, the country appears to have altered its course, and returned to the ideals reflected in the *Brown* decisions, where equal education—not transportation—is the predominant theme, and where the purpose is to afford all public school students, without regard to race, color, or ethnic origin, an enhanced educational experience in a school environment free from racial discrimination. It is heartening to know that we are on course with a remedial approach that promises a full and meaningful response to the callous injustice of racial discrimination—not by imposing burdens on innocent individuals because of color, but by reaching out to *all* individuals and extending the full measure of opportunity for an enhanced education in a desegregated environment.

REFERENCES

Armor, D. J. (1984). The evidence on desegregation and black achievement. In *School desegregation and black achievement*. Washington, DC: National Institute of Education.

Bronson v. Board of Education of Cincinnati, 425 U.S. 934 (1976).

Brown v. Board of Education of Topeka, 347 U.S. 483 (1954).

Brown v. Board of Education of Topeka, 349 U.S. 294, 300–301 (1955).

Estes v. Metropolitan Branches of the Dallas NAACP, 444 U.S. 437, 450 (1980).

Green v. County School Board of New Kent County, 391 U.S. 430 (1968). *Id*. at 439.

Keyes v. School Board of Denver, 413 U.S. 189 (1973).

Lowry, J. H. & Associates. (1983). *Survey of magnet schools: Analyzing a model for quality integrated education, executive summary*. Washington, DC: ABT Associates, Inc. p. 97

Plessy v. Ferguson, 163 U.S. 537 (1896).

Swann v. Charlotte-Mecklenburg Board of Education, 402 U.S. 1 (1971). *Id*. at 31.

PART II

Quality Education, Effective Schools, and Desegregation in the 1980s and 1990s

Featured Address

Impact of Desegregation on Children in the 1980s and 1990s

NATHANIEL R. JONES

Discussing the impact of desegregation on children in the 1980s and 1990s requires gifts of prophecy that I, an isolated appellate judge, do not pretend to possess. Another problem inherent in this subject is the limitation placed on federal judges speaking out on issues under circumstances that may appear to affect their ability to decide impartially cases that are likely to come before them. Nevertheless, I agree with Senior Judge Irving Kaufman of the U.S. Court of Appeals for the Second Circuit that federal judges have a duty to speak out on matters that affect the administration of the courts.

Before looking to the 1980s and the 1990s, it is first necessary to take a backward glance. Between 1969 and 1979, when I served as NAACP general counsel, I played an active role in advancing many of the major school desegregation cases. On April 24, 1979, barely a month short of the twenty-fifth anniversary of the U.S. Supreme Court's May 17th, 1954, decision in *Brown* v. *Board of Education* (1954), NAACP attorneys joined by Drew Days III, then the Assistant Attorney General for Civil Rights, stood before the Supreme Court and argued against racial segregation in public schools. They claimed that the *Brown* mandate applied to Columbus and Dayton, Ohio, and other northern cities as much as it did to Clarendon County, South Carolina; Jackson, Mississippi; Little Rock, Arkansas; and Charlotte, North Carolina

(oral arguments in *Columbus Board of Education* v. *Penick*, 1979 and *Dayton Board of Education* v. *Brinkman*, 1977).

Although the Supreme Court had adopted this view of *Brown* in the Denver and Detroit school cases, school board lawyers had succeeded, by limiting the extent of desegregation the Court would order rather than frontally assaulting basic *Brown* principles, in drawing those decisions into question. This was significant given that the aim of the school board lawyers all along was to halt the expansion of court-ordered school desegregation. Considering that impending desegregation stopped throughout the nation in August 1978 when Justice William Rehnquist, in *Columbus Board of Education* v. *Penick* (1978) (Rehnquist in chambers), blocked implementation of a desegregation plan at the last minute, antidesegregation school boards enjoyed at least temporary success.

Assistant Attorney General Days, in his argument on behalf of the Justice Department, set forth in the *Columbus* case for the first time the Carter Administration's position on court-enforced school desegregation. Any tinkering with the legal principles that evolved under *Brown*, Days warned, would run the risk of unraveling desegregation and resegregating more than five million children in over 400 communities where desegregation plans were currently in effect. He reminded the Court that those plans were premised, as were

the Columbus and Dayton lower court decisions, on settled constitutional and remedial principles. The Carter Administration's endorsement of *Brown* and school desegregation was further bolstered by the Department of Health, Education, and Welfare decision to terminate federal funds to the Chicago school system and to the University of North Carolina because of their failure to end racial segregation in their educational systems.

At the same time in the *Columbus* case, Thomas I. Atkins, then an NAACP attorney, later its general counsel, made a brilliant argument, concluding with the plea, "send *Brown* to Columbus." He said that at no time in the last twenty-five years had *Brown* meant anything to the black children of Columbus (*Columbus Board of Education* v. *Penick*, 1979, transcript of oral argument). The Supreme Court answered Atkins with a decision that sent *Brown* not only to Columbus but to Dayton and all cities of the North. During the five years since 1979, *Brown* has consistently held firm and is now leading to an increasing number of negotiated settlements of pending school cases.

Though today's climate is much more

HONORABLE NATHANIEL R. JONES is Circuit Judge, United States Court of Appeals for the Sixth Circuit, Cincinnati, Ohio. He is a former general counsel for the National Association for the Advancement of Colored People.

conducive to settlements, it should be noted that throughout the 1970s when plaintiffs urged northern school boards to take voluntary steps to desegregate they were largely rebuffed. Occasionally, school boards would agree to desegregate provided the terms were sufficiently anemic to forestall meaningful pupil reassignment. Boards adhered to a view that busing was politically undesirable and/or legally impermissible. They argued that busing was ineffective even in face of its extensive use to maintain segregation. Plaintiffs were left with no choice but to sue. Even in instances where liability was found to exist, school officials endeavored to "strike a deal" with groups of plaintiffs that would resurrect Plessy v. Ferguson (1896) and relegate significant numbers of black pupils to judicially sanctioned segregation. On more than one occasion when this was attempted, black parents and, in some instances, white parents sought the aid of civil rights groups that intervened on their behalf or assisted them in intervening.

Within the black community there is a strong degree of skepticism and suspicion about having anyone but a federal judge dispose of school desegregation cases. Interestingly enough, in January 1984 when the Cincinnati Board of Education and the State Board of Education unanimously approved a settlement, members of the minority community began to scrutinize closely the settlement's fine print. The experience that minorities have had with school boards, even those boards that include blacks, has not been reassuring. For instance, at the time of the Cleveland desegregation suit in 1976, Reed v. Rhodes, there were three black members on the seven-member Cleveland school board, one of whom was its president. Yet, the position of the black members on desegregation was barely distinguishable from that of the white members. In the Cincinnati case, Bronson v. Cincinnati Board of Education, 1984, the same situation existed, with three blacks on the seven-member Board of Education. At the time of negotiations, as was true in Cleveland, a black served as president. In the Cincinnati case, only one of the three was perceived by the black community as having a strong pro-desegregation stance.

School boards, with or without minority members, have been skittish about settling cases once filed if the settlement would require anything more than voluntary, magnet kinds of programs. Boards continue to be absolutely resistant on the question of mandatory reassignments. If reassignment of pupils is an element of the desegregation remedy, boards prefer to go to trial and have the judge order it. The hypocrisy of the school boards' position stems from the fact that the systems they are managing already transport students all over the districts and beyond. Yet boards assert that black students are being given a quality education in their present schools, which are little more than segregated warehouses, often not even up to Plessy v. Ferguson standards. It is ironic that when desegregation comes and white pupils are to be reassigned to the schools attended predominately by blacks or Hispanics, large sums of money are made available to upgrade the formerly minority schools. This hypocrisy spawns skepticism on the part of minorities about the willingness of school systems to act positively to eliminate racial segregation and to move against the inferior segregated education to which their children are exposed.

Too often people ignore what the Supreme Court said in Brown v. Board of Education (1954): "We conclude that in the field of public education the doctrine of 'separate but equal' has no place. Separate educational facilities are inherently unequal." Another of the most profound declarations in the Supreme Court's decision in Brown was referred to in a paper presented by Dr. Stuart W. Cook (1984), University of Colorado, at a symposium entitled "Psychology and Desegregation: Views from the Bench and Research Community" at the August 1984 Convention of the American Psychological Association in Toronto. In commenting on the famous "Social Science Statement" prepared under the distinguished Dr. Kenneth Clark, and cited by the Supreme Court in 1954, Dr. Cook declared:

Some observers have seen a relation between it ("Social Science Statement") and the most famous passage from the Court's Opinion: "To separate them from others of similar age and qualifications solely because of their race generates a feeling of inferiority as to their status in the community that may affect their hearts and minds in a way unlikely ever to be undone."

Dr. Cook added:

Another passage in the Opinion bears a strong resemblance to wording in the Statement: "Segregation of white and colored children has a detrimental effect upon colored children. The impact is greater when it has the sanction of law; for the policy of separating the races is usually interpreted as denoting the inferiority of the negro group..."

While the northern cases during recent years have taught us much about the nature of the "inherent inequality" of and the stigma associated with pupil segregation, these cases also quantify—often in a measurable, tangible way—the inequality between the segregated white and segregated black schools. It was a recognition of both inequality and stigma that led the Supreme Court to hold in Milliken v. Bradley II (1977) that a federal court, in the exercise of its remedial powers, could require the State of Michigan to expend millions of dollars to support ancillary remedies in the form of such educational components of a desegregation plan as counseling programs, remedial reading, and vocational education. In so doing, the Court recognized the insidious, measurable degree to which black children in the segregated black schools were being shortchanged and noted, among other things, that attitudes of white teachers had to be changed.

I had the responsibility of making the Supreme Court argument on behalf of the black children of Detroit in Milliken II in 1977, as I did in Milliken I in 1974. In Milliken II, I was pressed by the Supreme Court justices to explain why there was a need for any ancillary remedies. In framing my response, I was mindful of the confusion in the minds of some about the scope of a remedy for school segregation. Some insisted that minorities were entitled to only physical desegregation—period. I attempted to meet that argument with the following response to the court: "The plaintiffs... insist upon, in the first instance, the desegregation of schools. [But we also] insist that some agency of the State address these secondary problems that are part of bringing about the creation of a unitary system" (oral argument in Milliken II, 1977).

In writing for the unanimous Supreme Court, Chief Justice Burger (Milliken II, 1977) adopted that position in the following language:

...pupil assignment alone does not automatically remedy the impact of previous, unlawful educational isolation; the consequences linger and can be dealt with only by independent measures.

Chief Justice Burger then added:

[W]here, as here, a constitutional violation has been found, the remedy does not "exceed" the violation if the remedy is tailored to cure the "condition *that offends the Constitution.*"

The "condition" offending the Constitution is Detroit's de jure *segregated school system, which was so pervasively and persistently segregated that the District Court found that the need for the educational components flowed directly from constitutional violation by both state and local officials. These specific educational remedies, although normally left to the discretion of the elected school board and professional educators, were deemed necessary to restore the victims of discriminatory conduct to the position they would have enjoyed in terms of education had these four components been provided in a nondiscriminatory manner in a school system free from pervasive de jure racial segregation.*

In a word, discriminatory student assignment policies can themselves manifest and breed other inequalities built into a dual system founded on racial discrimination. Federal courts need not, and cannot, close their eyes to inequalities, shown by the record, which flow from a long standing segregated system.

Since federal courts are otherwise powerless to deal with the reallocation of financial resources in school systems by virtue of *San Antonio Independent School District v. Rodriguez* (1973), the *Milliken II* decision, which sanctioned broad remedies, came to be increasingly relied upon to cure the deficits in the education of minority children after proof was offered of a *Brown* violation. *Milliken II* continues to be a valuable remedial tool after *de jure* segregation is proved.

The Supreme Court committed what many lawyers, judges, educators, and others characterize as a retreat from reality with its five-four decision in the *Milliken v. Bradley* (1974). Shortly thereafter, when the U.S. Court of Appeals for the Sixth Circuit was forced to deal with the hard results of that decision on remand, Judge George C. Edwards noted with some asperity:

I join my colleagues in the drafting and issuance of today's order because any final decision of the United States Supreme Court is the law of the land. But conscience compels me to record how deeply I disagree with the decision which we are enforcing. In Milliken v. Bradley, *the Supreme Court overruled this court and the United States District Court in Detroit by reversing a carefully*

documented finding of fact that racial desegregation in the schools of Detroit could not be accomplished within the boundaries of the Detroit school district where the school population was found to be approximately 64 percent black, with a predicted 72 percent black school population by 1975–76 and 80.7 percent by 1980–81. The decision also imbued school district boundaries in Northern states (which like Michigan, had never had school segregation laws) with a constitutional significance which neither federal nor state law had ever accorded them (Bradley v. *Milliken, 1975, Edwards, J., concurring).*

In dissenting in the first *Milliken* case, Justice William O. Douglas made the following prediction: "When we rule against the metropolitan area remedy, we take a step that will likely put the problems of the blacks and our society back to the period that antedated the 'separate but equal' regime of *Plessy* v. *Ferguson"* (Milliken v. *Bradley I,* 1974, Douglas, J., dissenting). Justice Thurgood Marshall, who also dissented, issued a rebuke which I think is worthy of note because of its prophetic tone. He wrote: "In the short run, it may seem to be the easier course to allow our great metropolitan areas to be divided up into two cities—one white, the other black—but it is a course, I predict, our people will ultimately regret," (Milliken v. *Bradley I,* 1974, Marshall, J., dissenting). Fortunately, that setback did not bring to a halt all desegregation efforts. Cases involving single districts were carried forward, although, it seems to be agreed, the remedies in many of the cases could have been more meaningful if they had extended beyond local boundaries. This can still be done provided the *Milliken*-decreed criteria are first satisfied. Even so, the legal and educational justification for metropolitan solutions to school segregation is as valid now as it was before *Milliken*.

Economic and fiscal realities may yet compel state officials to do what the Supreme Court declined to do, that is, face the spinoff problems of urban school segregation such as needless redundancy and duplication of services and programs in the urban areas of the nation. A commonsense approach calls for consolidating the numerous school districts in the metropolitan areas of our nation, for such Balkanization no longer serves a valid educational purpose, if it ever did. These Balkanized arrangements operate as barriers that divide school populations on a racial basis.

Since political lines are ignored when seeking solutions to other problems they should not be a barrier to desegregation of schools. As the plaintiffs argued in 1974, in their *Milliken I* brief:

The school districts and their boundaries were shown to be administrative conveniences. The State has not hesitated regularly to cross or alter these lines in countless instances for a variety of educational purposes. The State has been careful to preserve its ultimate authority vis-a-vis the local districts.... In Michigan, local school districts are creations of the State designed to assist in administering the State's system of public schooling.

It is doubtful that any state or local school official can realistically accept Justice Stewart's view in *Milliken I* (1974, Stewart, J., concurring), that the causes of urban segregation are "unknown and perhaps unknowable." But it is hoped that even those inclined to adhere to such a view are enlightened enough to realize that school problems are no more susceptible to complete solutions within limited political or administrative boundaries than are the problems of water and air pollution, urban transportation, or law enforcement, all of which are now being approached on a regional basis. If educational problems are considered on an interdistrict or regional basis, *Brown* and its progeny require that they be addressed in a way that ensures a reduction in the degree of segregation now existing and a maximizing of the opportunities for integration with the requisite ancillary remedies.

The elimination of "separate educational facilities," therefore, remains a national command, binding upon courts, public officials, and citizens alike. It is this command that has resulted in the dismantling of dual systems in a number of cities. But there have been serious problems along the way. For instance, minorities, painfully aware of the nature of race discrimination, are understandably resentful at being required by the courts to prove that "rain is wet" with regard to current racial segregation. They also object to bearing a disproportionate amount of the desegregation burden. They have, nevertheless, been doing so at a considerable price. Opponents of desegregation have been exploiting this unhappiness and gratuitously suggesting that a little more *Plessy* v. *Ferguson* separate-but-equal treatment is the solution to the problem. On the other hand, many white parents have objected to pupil-reassignment plans that required the transportation of their children into schools previously identified as black and perceived as inferior. That black children were locked into inferior schools did not seem very important to the majority group or to officials. In spite of the integral role transportation plays in public education, political opportunists at every level entered the picture to exploit the issue they curiously referred to as "forced busing."

Two of the most potent arguments against school desegregation, in addition to the "forced busing" issue, have recently drawn responses. One argument is the contention that school desegregation and quality education are incompatible. But as Orfield points out, desegregation, when properly implemented, can foster quality education.

Three decades have taught us a great deal about school desegregation and what would be required to produce integration in areas where segregation is still untouched and expanding. Properly done, school desegregation produces significant educational gains for black children with no negative impact on white children and at a cost that is reasonable relative to the cost of other proposed educational reforms.

It appears to have a positive effect on other very important factors in the lives of the black students—college success, initial job placement, and acceptance of residential integration as an adult. (Orfield, 1984)

The second argument is that the Constitution is color-blind and does not permit the adoption of desegregation remedies that are race-conscious. With regard to the color-blind argument, the U.S. Supreme Court has made it abundantly clear in a variety of contexts that race may be taken into account to overcome the violation of rights based upon race. No one said it better than Justice Harry Blackmun of the Supreme Court in the *Bakke* case. He wrote: "In order to get beyond racism we must first take race into account" (*Regents of the University of California* v. *Bakke*, 1978).

Clearly, the Constitution does not bar use of race to remedy racial discrimination. After all, this nation has had a long history of condoning discriminatory treatment of people based upon the color of their skins. To overcome the present effects of that history it is permissible that there be racially-based remedies. The uprooting of segregation and its vestiges is what

Brown v. *Board of Education* was all about. To those who continue to quote the late Justice John Marshall Harlan's famous dissent in *Plessy* when he said that the Constitution was color-blind, all that need be said is that Justice Harlan's views were rejected by the court majority. Had his view on color blindness prevailed in 1896, perhaps America would have long ago resolved its segregation problem.

It is now thirty years since *Brown* became the law of the land. That is a period barely more than half the judicially-blessed, separate-but-equal life of the *Plessy* decision. If allowance is made for the years of delay and obstructionism, and for the fact that *Brown* did not move North in a meaningful way until the 1970s, the nation has addressed *Brown* seriously for a period of about fifteen to twenty years. Certainly, when we consider the history prior to *Plessy*, *Brown* is entitled to a period of implementation at least as long as the fifty-eight years enjoyed by *Plessy* before its efficacy is judged. Yet there are those who are "rushing to judgment" on *Brown* and questioning school desegregation. It should be clear to any rational observer that at this point, *Brown* has already transformed the face and heart of America. Honest assessments of school desegregation lead to the conclusion that the desegregation process has had positive effects for all children, black and white. During the past thirty-year period, the spirit of *Brown* has had to endure violent resistance, strategies of avoidance and delay, confused and uncertain court decisions, severe attacks on those remedies that were proving effective, uneven governmental enforcement policies, the ambivalence and schizophrenia of legislative enactments, and numerous other hurdles. In spite of the foregoing, school desegregation moved forward and its judicial precedents are holding fast.

The state of the law and the current condition of urban America suggest that treating school desegregation problems on a metropolitan, rather than on a single district basis, remains a viable option for litigators and educators to pursue. There are enough examples around to warrant a belief in success for advocates of metropolitan or interdistrict school desegregation in major urban areas. Along with this option, however, there are opportunities for obtaining additional financial resources under the *Milliken II* precedent. Unless state educators and legislators meet these twin problems of urban school segregation and inadequate resources, courts in the 1980s and 1990s will surely be pressed by

litigants to explore school policies and practices and make judicial findings as a prelude to issuing appropriate orders.

At the beginning of this presentation, I noted Judge Kaufman's observation that judges have a duty to speak out on matters that affect judicial administration. He added that silence under some conditions is not always golden. Because people will continue to litigate for vindication of their rights, judges and litigants must be sensitive to the issues of desegregation. Contrary to those who complain about heavy court dockets, I believe that in the context of civil rights, the nation is better off when persons turn to the courts. In the 1960s we saw what happens when the judicial channels are unavailing for the resolution of grievances. The litigation process becomes better able to function when social science is meaningfully involved as it was in the 1950s when Dr. Clark, Dr. Cook, and their colleagues developed and offered their famous "Social Science Statement". I would likewise note that later, the same role was played by a group of social scientists in 1977 when the Supreme Court, in *Milliken II*, took up and decided the issue of the appropriateness of ancillary remedies as a part of pupil desegregation. In the 1980s and beyond, the courts will benefit from the research of the social sciences and other disciplines, as they grapple with the difficult, irrepressible problems of school segregation.

I came to recognize the indispensable role that educators and social scientists can play in educating judges in this very difficult area of remedy during the time I served as a litigator. Congress has now provided for the current and next President of the United States to appoint eighty-nine new district and appellate judges. Those appointed will bring to their judicial duties a variety of experiences, but I dare say that few, if any, of them will have had experience in the area of school desegregation or in shaping the kinds of sensitive remedies required in school desegregation cases. These new judges and their colleagues could benefit from the precedents of the past and will need the new perspective and fresh research which social scientists can share.

This leads me to offer the following caveat. The staggering financial costs of bringing suits by private parties and the abdication by the federal government of its commitment to vigorously enforce civil rights law may bring about a climate that will encourage dangerous recidivism. This concern is born out of the recent efforts to give tax-exempt status to segregated schools and the persistent efforts by the

Justice Department to have federal courts reconsider precedents relating to the consideration of color-based claims under the equal protection clause of the Fourteenth Amendment of the Constitution.

Desegregation will continue into the 1980s and 1990s if there is no serious orchestration of government litigation seeking to reexamine the constitutional underpinnings of *Brown* or challenge the standards of proof by which plaintiffs have been able to establish their entitlement to desegregation remedies. Desegregation could be impeded in the 1980s and 1990s if the remedial principles laid out by the Supreme Court in a long line of cases, up to and including the *Columbus* and *Dayton* cases, are altered.

The Kerner Commission's warning (National Advisory Commission on Civil Disorders, 1968) about two societies—black and white, separate and unequal—should sober those who believe that America must become a single society. Achieving such a goal will be no easy task. Justice Thurgood Marshall, in his *Milliken I* dissent, offered this perspective: "Desegregation is not and was never expected to be an easy task. Racial attitudes ingrained in our nation's childhood and adolescence are not quickly thrown aside...but just as the inconvenience of some cannot be allowed to stand in the way of the rights of others, so public opposition, no matter how strident, cannot be permitted to divert this court, from [the] enforcement of [the] constitutional principles." (*Milliken I*, 1974, Marshall J., dissenting). It remains the task, then, of leaders and molders of opinions to provide the perspective needed to reinvolve all Americans in the process of correcting an historic wrong. At the thirty-year mark, there is still a long way to go.

REFERENCES

Bradley v. Milliken, 519 F.2d 679 (6th Cir. 1975).

Bronson v. Cincinnati Board of Education, 578 F. Supp. 1091 (S.D. Ohio 1984).

Brown v. Board of Education of Topeka, 347 U.S. 483 (1954). (*See also* Appendix to Appellants' Briefs—The effects of segregation and consequences of desegregation: A social science statement).

Columbus Board of Education v. Brinkman, 443 U.S. 526 (1978).

Columbus Board of Education v. Penick, 443 U.S. 449 (1979).

Cook, S.W. (1984, August). *Participation by social scientists in litigation regarding school desegregation: Past contributions and future opportunities.* Paper presented at the convention of the American Psychological Association, Toronto.

Dayton Board of Education v. Brinkman, 443 U.S. 526 (1977).

Milliken v. Bradley, 418 U.S. 717 (1974).

Milliken v. Bradley, 433 U.S. 267 (1977).

National Advisory Commission on Civil Disorders (1968). *Kerner Commission Report.* Washington, DC: U.S. Government Printing Office.

Orfield, G. (1984, May). School desegregation: Thirty years later. Ohio: *Akron Beacon Journal.*

Plessy v. Ferguson, 163 U.S. 537 (1896).

Reed v. Rhodes, 422 F. Supp. 708 (N.D. Ohio 1976), aff'd, 662 F.2d 1219 (6th Cir. 1981), *cert. denied,* 455 U.S. 1018 (1982).

Regents of the University of California v. Bakke, 438 U.S. 265, 407 (1978).

San Antonio Independent School District v. Rodriguez, 411 U.S. 1 (1973).

Ensuring Excellence and Equity in Public Education

CONSTANCE E. CLAYTON

As I reflected on the subject of the present and future of quality education, I recalled the opening lines of Charles Dickens' *A Tale of Two Cities:* "It was the best of times. It was the worst of times."

For public education in this country, that expression of ambivalence is particularly appropriate.

Not since the launching of the Russian satellite Sputnik has there been such an intense national interest in the state of public education. Over the past eighteen months, the press has reported on one study after another pointing to urgent problems facing public education in this country today. Never before have so many of the nation's distinguished scholars and educators spoken so loudly about the quality of education. And it is certainly without precedent that public education has become so major an issue of the national political scene that both the incumbent and his opponent are compelled to articulate views and promise policies to improve the nation's elementary and secondary schools.

So, if we are to judge by standards of interest and attention paid to issues, for public education these are the best of times.

For those of us, however, who live with the problems of public education, who are saddled with aging school buildings that cannot be replaced, who have to deal with the need to pay our teachers more, even as

taxpayers revolt and tax bases erode; for those of us who are the heirs to a legacy of neglect and decay, it becomes difficult not to believe that these, in fact, are the worst of times.

But I suspect that history, as it always does, will prove us wrong. These are neither the best of times nor the worst of times. They are simply *our* times, with *our* share of problems and our share of opportunities!

As superintendent of the nation's fifth largest public school system, I see both the problems and the opportunities. And it is from the vantage point of a superintendent that I would like to address the issues of quality education, effective schools, and desegregation in the 1980s and 1990s.

I will assume that in mid-September 1984, the topic invites a status report on the present—the 1980s— and a prognosis as to the future—the 1990s.

First, I will offer a report on initiatives my administration has undertaken to ensure both excellence and equity. Second, I will share with you some questions that concern me as I seek to move from crisis management to forward planning—as I look toward the 1990s and into the twenty-first century.

I see both the problems and the opportunities of the triumvirate of issues—quality education, effective schools, and desegregation. Moreover, the problems will easily overwhelm the opportunities if in our

research, in our advocacy, and in our work, we continue to confuse means and ends. Despite their intuitive and rhetorical appeal, quality education, effective schools, and desegregation are not ends in themselves. They are means employed to enable each child to develop to his or her full potential so that he or she can function as a contributing productive member of a pluralistic democratic society. The twin objectives of this goal are to ensure excellence in our schools and equity for our children.

Unfortunately, both the concern for excellence and the concern for equity too often are early casualties of battles fought over specific issues. While I could list any number of such issues, I will mention the one that is most germane to this event— desegregation.

On a personal note, I know well and appreciate deeply how long and hard the struggle has been to achieve equal educational opportunity for our boys and girls. I understand how intransigent and unprincipled the opposition has been in the past and still is today.

We owe much to the civil rights advocates who have persevered against the odds. As a career educator and a superintendent, I also know just how important it is not to be trapped by the past—thus

CONSTANCE E. CLAYTON is Superintendent, School District of Philadelphia.

forgoing opportunities for the present and possibilities for the future.

I am concerned that some of the more avid proponents of desegregation seem unappreciative of the critical need for parental involvement and control; recognition of demographic and geographic realities; and most importantly, the urgency of the task of responding to the educational needs and concerns of our children.

Philadelphia has been no exception. A substantial amount of time during the earliest months of my superintendency was spent seeking to resolve more than ten years of litigation around the issue of desegregation. We were successful in being allowed to implement a reality-based plan that has broad support in the community and among parents and that promises to achieve the maximum feasible desegregation in the minimum practicable time. The plan was developed and set forth in five interim reports.

In the *First Interim Report,* we set out the geographic and demographic realities that had to be accounted for if a workable plan were to be developed. We also set three objectives:

1. To ensure for each child an opportunity for meaningful and beneficial cross-cultural and interracial experiences so that he or she might learn better how to function in a pluralistic society.

2. To increase the number of stably desegregated schools.

3. To address the special needs and concerns of those students who will remain in racially isolated, low achieving schools.

In the *Second Interim Report,* we articulated the principles that shape the plan:

1. Education is the paramount consideration. Any proposed policy or program must be measured by its impact on and potential for educational improvement and access to excellence.

2. If desegregation is to be the objective, integration must be the goal. Desegregation should be achieved in such a manner as to enhance the likelihood that integration will occur.

In the *Third Interim Report,* we proposed a revised definition of desegregation, noting that the new definition was more realistic since it took into account the growing Hispanic and Asian student population. That report also set out the framework for the educational improvement program.

The *Fourth Interim Report* outlined the reasons for relying on voluntary transfer rather than mandatory reassignment as the primary strategy for desegregation. In that *Fourth Interim Report,* we disclosed that two surveys—one done internally and one done by an independent survey research firm—confirmed what all the available anecdotal information on desegregation revealed:

■ What parents with children in public schools want most for their children is quality education in a safe school environment.

■ Parents want and expect to have control over where their children go to school.

■ Insofar as the Philadelphia Public Schools are concerned, a mandatory pupil reassignment policy for desegregation would accelerate both the decline in overall student enrollment and an even sharper decline in the enrollment of white students.

The *Fifth Interim Report* accompanied and outlined the modified desegregation plan which committed the school district to achieving the legally required "maximum feasible desegregation" in a context and in a manner consistent with the district's legal and moral obligation to make education its paramount concern.

This determination to achieve desegregation within the framework of our commitment to education led to a plan that was quite different from those previously adopted in other districts. In Philadelphia, desegregation is now more than just a transportation and student assignment policy. It is a comprehensive educational strategy to ensure access to excellence and equity for all students.

As with any desegregation plan, we have committed ourselves to expanding the number of desegregated school sites. If successful, the modified desegregation plan will double the number of desegregated schools over a three-year period. By so doing, we will provide vastly increased opportunities for the many parents in our city who recognize the value of a desegregated education—who want to ensure that their children are equipped to live and to function in the multiethnic, multiracial, multicultural environment of our city, our nation, and our world. But the modified desegregation plan neither started nor stopped there. It addressed both equity and excellence in concrete ways.

First, the modified plan was based on the adoption and implementation of a standardized curriculum. It had become an accepted fact that there was considerable unevenness in the quality and the quantity of instruction offered. (For example, some schools offered four sciences and some only one). This disparity, when viewed in the light of the varying levels of student achievement, raised important issues of access to excellence and equity.

As promised in the modified desegregation plan, the situation is being remedied. So that every student has access to excellence of program and instruction and in order to encourage each learner to excel, a standardized curriculum has been identified that will be in complete consonance with systemwide goals and curricular objectives. This standardization will present those essential elements of a balanced curriculum that are necessary for excellence of program, product, and performance. This past spring, a fully articulated, standardized curriculum for kindergarten through grade twelve was presented to principals, teachers, parents, students, and community members. That standardized curriculum went into effect in the fall of 1984.

The proposed systemwide emphasis on thrust for excellence requires each school to have defined learning goals that guide all instruction. High-achievement expectations with an emphasis on acceptance of responsibility for learning by staff and students must prevail.

Even as we committed ourselves to a systemwide program for access to excellence embodied in the standardized curriculum, the modified desegregation plan also recognized that equity requires a special response to special needs. There are many schools for which the standardized curriculum, while necessary, is not a sufficient response to the educational plight of their students. Consequently, a Replicating Success Project has been established for those schools that need additional support to achieve their full educational potential. The goal of the Replicating Success Project is to help these schools upgrade their programs through the replication and incorporation of instructional components that have been proven successful in similar situations.

The Replicating Success Project will conduct a needs assessment survey on each identified school. The results of this survey will be matched against an inventory of each school's existing resources and programs in an effort to ascertain whether these resources and programs can be restructured and redirected to meet each school's identified needs.

With funding from a private foundation, we have moved forward with the first major replicating success module, which draws heavily on the effective schools research. As conceived and implemented, this module is characterized by all five of the factors most commonly identified as distinguishing effective from ineffective schools:

1. Strong and effective administrative leadership in instruction and management

2. Greater emphasis on, and time devoted to, basic reading and mathematics

3. A safe and orderly school environment that allows teachers and pupils to focus their energies on academic achievement

4. A climate of expectations in which virtually all children can learn under appropriate conditions

5. The use of assessment instruments to provide continuous feedback on the effects of instruction

With replicating success, as with all our initiatives, extensive plans have been made for ensuring the meaningful involvement of the most important of our constituents—the parents who entrust their children to our care.

I have outlined this initiative in order to demonstrate that in the 1980s, quality education, effective schools, and desegregation are useful and often compatible strategies for achieving both excellence and equity.

I am by no means sanguine about the future. And as I turn toward the future, you will note that I move from examples to questions. This is intentional. I stated at the outset that my concerns about the present center on the tendency to confuse means with ends and to develop tactics and strategies not clearly connected to objectives and goals. My concern about the future is somewhat different. I am concerned that we are proceeding as if we know the answers when we might not even be asking right questions.

No thoughtful person can read the work of Dean Derrick Bell, Dr. Ron Edmunds, Professor Janet Schofield, and many others, without recognizing the fundamental importance of the questions they raise. Professor Ralph Smith of the University of Pennsylvania and consultant to the School District of Philadelphia, outlined some of these questions as follows:

The time has come to ask whether (notwithstanding its mobilizing appeal to essential truth) the desegregation para- *digm that has been the subject of a liberal consensus for these decades is now theoretically viable and operationally practicable. That fundamental question could be approached in a number of ways. One way is to explore a number of subsidiary questions of which the following is a representative, but partial, list.*

1. *What ought to be the meaning and the objective of a school desegregation strategy in school districts where, while it is clear that the racially identifiable schools result from racially identifiable neighborhoods, there is ample evidence to show that the racially identifiable neighborhoods were not caused by neighborhood schools?*

2. *How should the scope and objectives of a school desegregation strategy be defined if Hispanic, Asian, and black students are increasing and the white students decreasing both numerically and proportionately?*

   Is the conventional black/white paradigm now outmoded? What should be the legal and policy response to emergent multiethnic, multicultural and multiple-minority communities?

3. *In the absence of a metropolitan plan, at what point should a school district be considered a one-race district in which any intra-district desegregation strategy would be presumptively futile?*

   How can drawing the line at a point lower than 100 percent be justified? Can some critical minimum be established as the prerequisite degree of representation essential to embark upon a school desegregation strategy? Would the inevitable emergence of a "substantial impracticability" standard operate to exempt major urban school districts?

4. *If it is true that desegregation and integration are* sine qua non *to quality education, what are the implications for education improvement strategies in one-race districts? And if it is not true, how then can the diversion of funds from education improvement strategies be justified?*

5. *How should a school desegregation strategy be reconciled with ongoing and important program initiatives to provide appropriate assistance to children from poor families, children for whom English is a second language or children in need of special education?*

Does the dispersal of the children for desegregation purposes run counter to the "critical mass" presumed by educators and federal regulations? Should the "critical mass" approach continue as a viable predicate for eligibility? Does desegregation help or hinder the mainstreaming of children with learning and physical disabilities?

6. *If due to racially differential enrollment patterns the most practicable way to expose children of one race to others during the school day is through shared-time activities, should these activities be undertaken at the cost of time-on-task?*

   Do the benefits outweigh the costs? What measurements should be used in making such an assessment?

7. *If desegregation policy addresses equity issues as well as equality issues, what does equity mean?*

I will not presume to offer answers to the questions of Professor Smith and other critical thinkers on these issues. Nor do I think the answers are self-evident. I will say, however, that as we commemorate the thirtieth anniversary of *Brown* v. *Board of Education* (1954), they are legitimate and compelling questions to which attention must be paid.

Because these questions carry the implicit suggestion that some rethinking of prevailing priorities is in order, I know they could be viewed as heresy by many who remain committed unalterably to the current framework. However, I also know that history shows that many viewed as heretics were, in fact, tellers of truths who had the misfortune to ask hard questions or bring bad news.

As superintendent, I cannot afford the luxury of complacency. I must consider carefully the questions being raised and I must be open to real answers even if they are new and different answers. I must be cognizant of the reality that what is doable is often less than the ideal. I cannot afford to be trapped in a historical lockstep unable to respond to real concerns and real problems. I cannot afford it. Our school district cannot afford it. Our children cannot afford it.

Let me be clear. The questions we must answer are not limited to desegregation. Quality education and effective schools strategies are implicated as well. As we look toward the future, excellence, ever a subjective notion, could be even more difficult to define, perceive, and attain.

As I have overseen implementation of the

various initiatives of the School District of Philadelphia, and as I have read report after report about the current state of public education, it has become increasingly clear that there is a fundamental gap between what public education is and can do today (even under the best of circumstances) and what the public desires and what might be essential to the future. It is not clear whether the desires of our most important constituency—parents—or the demands of the future can be met within the confines of the six-hours-a-day, five-days-a-week, ten-months-a-year system we now employ.

If the public school system is asked to accept children at a younger age and to keep children for a longer day, for a longer year, summers included, and then compete with the best private schools with regard to class size and individualized instruction while continuing to be open to all, we are faced with fiscal challenges and educational opportunities quite different from those of the present.

The challenge to provide quality and equity is made more urgent by the technological revolution that is reshaping the world in which our students will live and work.

How do we meet this challenge? How do we attain the level of academic excellence demanded for success—indeed for survival—in a world of unprecedented change? Is it possible that our schools can respond to such change? Indeed, that they can help chart its direction?

In closing, let me raise a final and somewhat different set of issues. As educators, we have every reason to be concerned about issues of equity and excellence in our schools. But education does not operate in a vacuum. Excellence and equity in education might well pale in significance and be impossible to achieve if other fundamental societal inequities remain unabated: if the horizons of our children are clouded by continuing high unemployment, illiteracy, deteriorating neighborhoods, disintegrating families; if their aspirations are blunted in advance by the very real constraints of poverty and discrimination; and if their prospects for survival are dimmed by the threat of a nuclear holocaust.

As an educator, I urge more concern for distinguishing means from ends, a greater appreciation for the constraints of realities, and a greater sensitivity to the parents who entrust their children to our care. Even more, I urge redoubled efforts to ensure that the children we hope to educate will have a world in which to live and a society that allows them to aspire, to achieve, and to excel.

REFERENCE

Brown v. Board of Education of Topeka, 347 U.S. 483 (1954).

Desegregation as a Tool for Establishing Quality Education

EUGENE T. REVILLE

On April 30th, 1976, John T. Curtin, Chief Judge of the U.S. District Court, Western District of New York, issued a ruling finding the Buffalo Board of Education, the Superintendent of Schools, the Commissioner of Education, and the Board of Regents of the State of New York in violation of the "plaintiffs' Fourteenth Amendment rights to equal protection under the law by intentionally causing and maintaining a segregated school system" (*Arthur* v. *Nyquist*, 1976). Judge Curtin in his comprehensive decision cited the Board of Education as "dilatory, evasive and at times obstructionist." He described one board action, the building of a junior high school in Buffalo's inner city, as an "example of blatant segregative intent with clear segregative results." Judge Curtin later declared a systemwide violation of the rights of minority children and ordered all schools to be racially balanced using 30 to 65 percent guidelines. The Buffalo Public School System was described by the New York State Commissioner of Education as being the most segregated school system in New York, and other sources have described it as one of the most segregated in the nation. *A Buffalo Evening News* article, on August 11, 1976, depicted the woeful state of court-ordered integration in Boston, cataloging the loss of 24,000 children and the police costs in excess of 24 million dollars. To say that the people of the City of Buffalo looked to court-ordered

integration with a great deal of apprehension and even dismay is to understate the case significantly.

Yet in a court order of August 27, 1982, the same Judge Curtin called integration in Buffalo "the highly successful Buffalo model of school desegregation." He further asserted that "a key to the success of the plan is the fact that for the most part, the integration of schools has been achieved by voluntary means. Through the use of innovative educational techniques, the need for fixed assignments and mandatory busing of students has been kept to a minimum. There has been no disruption of the schools, no violence, and no massive white flight of majority students from the City. Instead, the City Schools have improved through the use of these programs, and the proportion of majority to minority students has remained steady, even as the population of the City has decreased." Subsequently, in an order on May 23, 1983, Judge Curtin stated: "Upon close scrutiny and a review of the record, and in consideration of the alternatives presented by the parties, the Court concludes that the Board has in fact achieved the maximum level of systemwide desegregation practically possible and that under these conditions, the racially identifiable status of these schools does not offend the Constitution."

The tone and tint of the judge's statements changed dramatically from 1976 to

1982 and suggested another variation of *A Tale of Two Cities*. What happened to Buffalo between April 30, 1976, and May 23, 1982, is part history, part theory, and more than a little bit miraculous.

The judge's early statements hint at the formulation of the miracle. In an order on July 9, 1976, he declared that, "First, no school integration plan is going to work unless it has the long range support of the community. It has to be something all the citizens of the city, black and white, can live with together in harmony in the years ahead."

In the same order, Judge Curtin said, "An effective and feasible plan should prevent resegregation if possible. It should have permanence if possible. The Board should make sure that we provide the students in the school system with the best education possible. Out of the mix will come not only better schools, I believe, but a better community."

Aubrey McCutcheon, an attorney with extensive experience with school desegregation in Detroit and San Francisco, was engaged by the Buffalo Board of Education. In court, while constructing a framework for Buffalo's submission of plans in response to court orders, Attorney McCutcheon asserted that no remedy would be effective unless both minority and majority children

---

EUGENE T. REVILLE is Superintendent, Buffalo Public Schools.

benefited from better education. He also insisted that if the violation acted to deprive minority children of privilege and preference then the remedy must ensure that minority children have privilege and preference. This theory, though eminently reasonable, is violated often in integration plans around the country.

Early on, the Board of Education demonstrated a determination to successfully desegregate the district's schools. Each complaint or prod from the court was fully deliberated during the process of designing new plans and in the alteration of existing plans. The board insisted on maintaining control of the desegregation case and the fate of the school system and was determined to avoid a court-imposed plan or one designed by an out-of-town expert. Each of four major phases of integration was preceded by a board-approved plan designed by the staff under the direction of the board. The board's desire for a home-grown plan was an important element in the plan's success. If the school system designed the plan, it would be compelled to defend it and implement it, if not enthusiastically, at least responsibly.

To gain the support of the community, the court ordered attorney-supervised meetings in schools affected by the court's directives. This practice was extended by the school staff in subsequent phases of desegregation. Hundreds of meetings were scheduled at centers and schools throughout the community to explain the orders of the court and to solicit suggestions. Parents, plaintiffs, administrative staff members, and teachers attended these sessions in large numbers. Although suspicion and anger were expressed during many meetings, gradually acceptance and participation became the order of the day.

With the court and plaintiffs' prodding, the Board of Education's insistence on controlling its own destiny, the attorney's theory that quality education was the key to effective desegregation, and with massive community involvement, the Buffalo plan and program for school desegregation began to evolve. The idea that the plan would not be successful unless it was designed by the community led to long, tedious, and often painful meetings with parents. The board's insistence on implementing the program as the program of the school board and on keeping educational excellence as the first priority was not new or revolutionary; still, it was not the trademark of plans implemented in other court jurisdictions.

Unlike experiences elsewhere, opposition to the Buffalo Plan faded significantly with very few voices raised against the plan. In time, previously opposed groups cooperated in making a quiet and determined effort to bring about a successful execution of the court's orders. It is the opinion of many observers of the Buffalo desegregation plan that court-ordered desegregation improved the Buffalo School System dramatically. The students' reading and mathematics scores increased significantly during the implementation years. Middle-class flight was slowed and eventually reversed. In the school year 1983–84, Buffalo was the only one of twenty-nine school districts in Erie County to show an increase in school population. This turnaround was a direct result of the popularity of the Buffalo magnet schools and early childhood center programs which were designed to be the heart of the desegregation effort. Parochial and private schools in Buffalo experienced population decreases in the face of the Buffalo Public Schools' population increase. Parents who had sought private educational settings for their children began to enroll them in the Buffalo Public Schools. The high school dropout rate was the lowest in fifteen years and attendance statistics improved with the enrollment gains. As a result of this phenomenon, the Buffalo City School District is receiving a gradually increasing share of county tax revenue, reversing the downward trend during many previous years.

During the desegregation effort, the school system solicited and received broad community support. Business, labor, government, and religious groups all worked together to support integration in Buffalo. Of special note was the cooperation of all elements of the religious community. Ministers, priests, and rabbis rode buses, stood in schoolhouse doors to welcome children, and preached sermons to assure the peaceful implementation of each phase of the program.

A well-designed public relations campaign was implemented by the board's staff. Not only did major newpapers and television stations provide free time, but administrators in the print and electronic media helped design the public relations campaign. During major phases of the desegregation effort, it was difficult to read a newspaper, watch a television program, or listen to a radio presentation without witnessing a boost for magnet schools or early childhood centers. Radio disc jockeys and television stations adopted schools and made "magnet schools" a household term

in the City of Buffalo. The "Buffalo Plan" as it was labeled in court, was truly a total community effort.

The following brief chronology of events leading up to the various court orders, and a description of the school system's responses will increase understanding of pertinent factors that affected this change.

Ten years after *Brown* v. *Board of Education* (1954) and seven years following the tragic events in Little Rock, Arkansas, Yerby Dixon and other black parents filed a complaint on behalf of their children against the Buffalo Public Schools. The suit, which was filed in September 1964 with the New York State Commissioner of Education, brought about unsuccessful attempts by Commissioner James Allen and and his successor, Commissioner Ewald Nyquist, to prod the Board of Education into action.

Commissioner Nyquist at one point stated plaintively (E. Nyquist to A. B. Gardner, letter, January 20, 1972), "Faced with the hard fact that segregation is more severe in Buffalo now than it was seven years ago, with over 20 schools more than 90% or more black and 29 schools 90% or more white, it is clear to me that only a new approach can equalize educational opportunity for the children of Buffalo."

As a matter of fact, in March 1972, the majority of an appointed board acted to receive and file a staff report on desegregation and approved a motion indicating that the board, as presently constituted, was opposed to any form of forced busing. The board called for a letter to Commissioner Nyquist to advise him of its inability to produce a plan for desegregation on April 1, 1972, as requested.

Consequently, there wasn't any major action to desegregate Buffalo's Public Schools until the district's first elected Board of Education was seated in July, 1974.

The *Arthur* v. *Nyquist* suit was filed in the U.S. District Court, Western District of New York, in June 1972 by plaintiffs including the Buffalo Branch NAACP, the Citizens Council on Human Relations (CCHR), and others. In October 1974, the court began deliberations on the case pursuant to its findings. On April 30, 1976, the Buffalo Board of Education was found guilty of deliberate segregation of its schools.

Following the first stage of remedy hearings, Phase I of the Buffalo Plan was approved and implemented in September 1976 by the City School District. Ten elementary schools (both minority and nonminority) were closed, eight other elementary schools were integrated, and two city-wide magnet schools were created. The Waterfront School, which offered an open-space education program, and the City Honors Program for the gifted contributed to the success of Phase I. Although approved by the court, Phase I was only the first step toward the comprehensive desegregation plan that was required by the school authorities.

Community involvement continued to serve as the basis of Phase II, which was implemented in September 1977. This phase provided for the creation of eight additional magnet schools, the designs for which were researched in terms of their appeal to the total community as well as their educational value.

The district's high schools were racially balanced through a combination of redistricting, recruitment of minority pupils for attendance at vocational and technical schools, the creation of four secondary magnet schools, and the phasing out of an all-female, predominantly minority vocational school. These actions combined with the Quality Integrated Education (Volunteer Transfer) Program, in operation since 1966, guaranteed that no school would enroll less than 20 percent minority children. Phase II was termed a resounding success.

In attesting to this success, Judge Curtin commented in June 1978:

...the magnet program has been successful in attracting integrated student bodies and in offering innovative educational opportunities to students attending Buffalo Public Schools...the Superintendent and his staff have made an extraordinary effort to bring the plans for Phase I and II to reality. They have managed to shift a large number of students, renovate many school facilities, and establish entire new programs for the magnet schools with a minimum of disruption. This is indeed a remarkable accomplishment.

Although significant progress had been made, a cloud loomed on the horizon. The Quality Integrated Education Program became the target of a concerted attack by the plaintiffs. The program, which provided options for minority parents, was the district's sole method of integration prior to the 1976 district court order. Its effectiveness as a desegregation tool had been marred by a recommendation in 1966 (Buffalo Board of Education Report to Commissioner of Education) that, "No white children shall be transported into non-white residential areas except by their own choice." This codicil was unanimously rejected by the new

board, but the program's usefulness was questioned and its intent was maligned by the plaintiffs. Compounding problems was an additional cloud in the form of a significant financial deficit, directly related to forming the magnet schools, which marked the beginning of fiscal problems that relentlessly plagued the court and the school board.

In an order on June 6, 1979 (*Arthur* v. *Nyquist*), the court ruled that Phases I and II were not enough to complete the desegregation process; the district was ordered to desegregate the remaining fifteen all-minority schools. The Quality Integrated Education component was to be given a limited role, leading to eventual dismantling of the program. Magnet schools had been placed in the black community to balance the burden of transportation. The Quality Integrated Education Program had served as a major tool in reducing racial isolation in schools outside of the black community.

The board's staff was again put to the task. Desegregation of the remaining racially identifiable schools provided the most difficult and perplexing problems. The staff's efforts brought about Phase III.

Phase III, implemented in September 1980, was again spurred by school closings and the addition of magnet schools. Highlighting the plan was a whole new concept of early childhood centers that provided a framework for pairing schools in the remaining racially isolated areas. The early childhood centers were attractive educational models offering full-day pre-kindergarten and kindergarten programs and using exciting early childhood instructional concepts for pre-kindergarten through second grade students. These concepts were gleaned from successful programs around the nation. Nationally validated programs offered at these sites included Talents Unlimited, Early Intervention, and Project STAMM (Systematic Teaching and Measuring Mathematics). These program components were designed to help teachers recognize and develop the talents of productive thinking, communication, and forecasting skills; to screen pupils' to determine their learning readiness; and to provide a comprehensive sequential mathematics program not offered in other district schools.

Phase III received the enthusiastic approval of the court. In an order on June 19, 1980, Judge Curtin stated:

...the proposals are based on the concept of offering parents and children an excellent educational program through

which desegregation can be accomplished. A principal part of the proposal, the new Early Childhood Centers, promises to be an excellent educational experience, attractive to all parents, and it promises to provide a new impetus in the desegregation process. I believe that giving children opportunity for an integrated learning experience at an early age is most beneficial to everyone involved.

The judge's enthusiasm for the early childhood programs was tempered by his and the Second Circuit Court of Appeals' concern about the slow pace in which Phase III was being carried out. In light of this concern, an order on January 5, 1981, required that Phase III be expedited and that the successful early childhood centers that were presently located in the black community, be paired with schools in the white community as a step toward completion of desegregation and elimination of the few remaining racially isolated schools.

The creation of fourteen academies for grades 3-8 in peripheral areas of the city enabled the Board of Education staff to extend the early childhood concept to these districts, thus providing a framework for school pairing coupled with an educational motivation. Judge Curtin decided (*Arthur* v. *Nyquist*, 1981):

...the court is convinced that the advantages to Phase IIIx* for September, 1981 exceed the reason for further delay. Primarily the Court is satisfied that this plan will maintain quality education by furthering the goal of equal educational opportunity. The school board has shown that the Early Childhood Centers and Magnet Programs can provide students with an excellent education. The pedagogical creativity and academic achievement displayed by these programs has merited the participating schools a high regard in the community and has generated some fairly long waiting lists for admission to them. The proposed academies, which are the new 3-8 grade schools, are designed to be an important supplement to the existing, largely successful educational structure. It is worth observing that on these points, there is no dispute whatsoever among the parties in this suit.

Phase IIIx ushered in fixed assignments to the largely voluntary desegregation program. The press and community had

*x means "expedited"

scrutinized the "forced busing" with some apprehension and with a great deal of interest. The plan stimulated more publicity than any of the preceding three phases, and the opening day of school in September 1981 was a media event of magnificent proportions. Though there were numerous challenges involved in implementing the plan, the opening day of school continued the calm and harmonious climate experienced at each of the previous stages of the desegregation program; the day culminated years of anxiety and accomplishment. The Buffalo community accepted, and in many ways took to its heart, court-ordered desegregation. This ended years of agony and effort. Moreover, the Buffalo theory that its plan should be homegrown with parental and community involvement and educational excellence as its goal was proven to be sound.

What of the future? Nationally, there is ample evidence of retrenchment in integration. The federal government, from the Office of Education to the Office of the President, is decidedly cool about further integration efforts. The leadership deplores "judicial activism" and must be dragged kicking and screaming to promote progress in this area. A modest reinstitution of federal support in the form of the Emergency School Aid Act for court-ordered integration was passed only after much pressure and a long costly delay. Opponents claim that desegregation has failed by citing statistics stressing resegregation and "white flight." Integrationists seem a dying breed and yet the warning about two separate nations is as cogent today as it was when it was first stated in the U.S. Report of the National Advisory Commission on Civil Disorders in 1968. Successful integration programs such as Buffalo's, however, can provide valuable lessons. With proper preparation, full involvement of the community, and a good-faith effort, integration can succeed. The goal of desegregation should be improved educational opportunity. *Brown* (1954) marked a giant step forward for equity. Despite recent setbacks, great strides have been made. With continued efforts by a concerned citizenry, the justice promised by *Brown* and subsequent desegregation rulings will eventually become a reality.

Locally, the Buffalo Public Schools are still struggling to complete the effort even with strong community acceptance. For three consecutive years, the school system has sought court assistance for proper program funding. The problem of adequate funding has plagued the schools from the inception of the case. In 1976 a disastrous teacher strike, fueled by inadequate funding, threatened Phase I of the desegregation plan. Intervention of the court was considered an alternative. As early as 1979, Judge Curtin commented, "...whatever device is approved by the Court for racially balancing the schools...it must be adequately funded. Anything less frustrates the intent of the court-ordered desegregation program and impairs its chances of success."

In frustration the school board went to the federal court in 1981 to acquire adequate funding for continuation of the integration program. A recalcitrant mayor, James Griffin, unsympathetic to the program, appealed Phase IIIx to the Supreme Court without the support of the Board of Education and was niggardly in supplying funds for the desegregation program. Buffalo has a strong mayoral system of government, and the public school district is dependent on the mayor and Common Council for funds. The mayor criticized the board's desegregation effort in his papers to the Court opposing the board's motion for more funds. Under pressure, the mayor agreed to provide 3 million dollars in a consent order. In 1982 the plaintiffs again petitioned the Court for 7.4 million dollars. Following lengthy deliberation in a heavily publicized order, Judge Curtin ordered the full 7.4 million dollars.

The Second Circuit Court of Appeals unanimously upheld Judge Curtin, noting on July 2, 1983,

...we recognize, as did Chief Curtin, that it is more costly to achieve desegregation through a plan that relies heavily on the voluntary preference of parents to send their children, white and black, to high quality schools than simply to pay for the bussing of children to distant schools. The Buffalo Board of Education deserves commendation for the course it is pursuing, and the District Court has not erred in determining that in 1982–83 it needed an additional $7.4 million to continue its progress.

An appeal to the Supreme Court by the mayor was not heard.

The Buffalo Board of Education returned to the District Court for financial relief for the 1983–84 and 1984–85 school years. The board's plight is especially disheartening in light of the singular success and acceptance of its programs.

The Buffalo problem is a microcosm of the national reluctance to fund integration efforts. The Justice Department has entered cases on the side of those opposed to adequate funding of creative efforts, including efforts most concerned with educational excellence. Thus the federal government finds itself in the anomalous position of encouraging voluntary, educationally oriented programs, but working diligently to inhibit funding of such efforts.

Inadequate funding is only part of the problem. Careful planning and conscientious implementation of programs are necessary components of successful desegregation plans. Court orders are greeted too often by outright opposition and half-hearted attempts at implementation. An exchange of information about planning is most important.

After a school system meets the requirements of the court order by racially balancing the schools, the job, in the words of the popular song, has just begun. A school system found guilty of segregating its schools undoubtedly has more than a trace of the racism that provoked the court order and that racism certainly infects the community. The entire school system must establish as a first priority the banishment of this infection. In-service training programs, biracial committees, other creative programs, and parental involvement must focus on this unfinished task. The result will be an educational experience for children that is second to none, namely, a truly integrated educational system. This goal remains part of the unfinished business of the 1980s and 1990s and as a fitting commemoration of the landmark *Brown* v. *Board of Education* decision of 1954.

REFERENCES

Arthur v. Nyquist. Civ. 325 (1972). (See also oral order, court orders, and Judge Curtin's comments: April 30, 1976; July 9, 1976; June 29, 1978; February 23, 1979; June 19, 1980; May 19, 1981; August 27, 1982; and May 23, 1983.)

Arthur v. Nyquist, U.S. Court of Appeals for the Second Circuit, No. 1037 (1983), p. 15.

Brown v. Board of Education of Topeka, 347 U.S. 483 (1954).

Buffalo Board of Education Report to Commissioner of Education. (1966, November 10). *Sixteen point plan for quality integrated education*.

National Advisory Commission on Civil Disorders (1968). *Kerner Commission Report.* Washington, D.C.: U.S. Government Printing Office.

Hard Lessons: What We Have Learned from Desegregation

WILLIS D. HAWLEY

It has been thirty years since the *Brown v. Board of Education* decision set in motion the national movement to desegregate public schools. The experience, while much more beneficial than is generally recognized, has been painful and disillusioning. What can be learned from this experience about desegregation and, more generally, about the nation? I think the lessons are hard ones in many ways. The teaching has often resulted in conflict. The learning has been slow and incomplete. And some of the things we can learn about ourselves are not pleasant to contemplate.

Different people, of course, will learn different things from these past thirty years. The most significant lessons I find in the record are the following:

- Americans, both the beneficiaries and victims of the ways power and privilege are distributed, are much more committed to and capable of sustaining social differences than we like to believe.

- Myths, perpetrated by all sides, are more influential in shaping public policy and collective action than facts and (more or less) objective analysis.

- Despite widespread support for the principle of desegregation and our national disdain for government coercion, very little desegregation will occur if voluntary choice is the primary means we use to reduce racial isolation.

- School desegregation is an effective way to achieve a more integrated society and there is no other way to achieve social integration that even approximates its real and potential efficacy.

- The notion of "separate but equal" schools is a fantasy that will not die.

- We can effectively pursue the goals of equity and excellence but to do so will require major changes in the way we organize and operate our schools.

These general lessons have a common theme: It has been and will be much harder to achieve desegregation than any advocate of desegregation would have believed a few years ago. Indeed, one might marvel at the progress that has been made given the realities just listed. But it is also clear that future successes may be even harder to achieve and, that there may be fewer people of all races willing to pay the price.

LESSON ONE: THE HIGH VALUE PLACED ON SUSTAINING SOCIAL DIFFERENCES

Of all the social policies the nation has seen developed over the last thirty years, school desegregation seems to be the one most strongly and persistently contested. The primary reason why desegregation is contested is that it has so much potential for undermining the formal and informal barriers people of different races and social classes use to protect themselves from the influence of others who do not appear to share their values and virtues. Our neighborhoods, our churches, our social groups and clubs, and even our places of work—stratified as they are by the status differences that structure interpersonal relationships—are usually homogeneous and rarely offer the opportunity for us to encounter, as equals, people who are different from us. Desegregated schools bring our children into contact with a wide range of students from different races and social classes.

I do not mean to cast stones. Desegregation often places children in settings that are unfamiliar and seemingly uncontrollable. It is a natural instinct for parents to protect their children and themselves from the unknown. Middle-class whites are not alone in their concern that school desegregation reduces the ability of parents to shape the influences that affect their children. Fears rooted in this seeming loss of control are magnified, of course, by racial stereotypes that posit differences in ambitions, mental capacity, and sexual behavior. Concerns are heightened too by the pros-

WILLIS D. HAWLEY is Dean of George Peabody College for Teachers, Vanderbilt University and Director of the University's Program in Educational Equity.

pects of interpersonal conflict and disorder, prospects that do not become less salient even if parents can be provided evidence of their statistical improbability.

The plain fact is that those who fear that desegregation will result in the sharing of the virtues and frailties of other races and classes are correct. Thus, the likelihood of successful desegregation is not always seen as promising. The possibility of unsuccessful desegregation, on the other hand, is frightening.

LESSON TWO: MYTHS, NOT EVIDENCE, SHAPE PUBLIC ACTION

The idea that myths are stronger than facts in shaping behavior is a truism rooted in observations of many social phenomena, including desegregation. However, when an emotionally charged issue such as desegregation is involved, the willingness of the general public and policymakers (including judges) to dismiss evidence they find uncomfortable is particularly great. Like the proverbial drunk who uses lampposts more for support than illumination, actors in desegregation controversies selectively sample research and experience to predict doom or overstate likely benefits. For example, in passing the Neighborhood School Act of 1982, the vast majority of United States senators supported several "Statements of Fact" that could be readily discredited (and were in pre-vote senate hearings) by empirical evidence. Among the myths contradicted by available evidence, but often cited by opponents of desegregation, are the following:

- Desegregation has caused a decline in the quality of schooling in the nation, especially for whites.

- Despite years of effort, desegregation has had little net effect in reducing racial isolation in schools.

- Desegregation is the major cause of increased segregation of residential areas.

- Forced desegregation results in inter-racial conflict and hostility.

- The best way to achieve school desegregation in the long run is to promote residential integration and increase the quality of schools in which almost all students are nonwhite.

I will not present here the evidence that these myths are largely untrue. That has been the focus of much other work (see, for example, Rossell & Hawley, 1983). What I am interested in trying to explain is why these myths—as well as those sustained by the advocates of desegregation—are so difficult to dispel. I can think of three reasons in addition to the obvious point that people generally dismiss evidence that does not support their point of view and give credence to counter-evidence even if it is anecdotal or otherwise very limited.

First, the most often advanced argument for desegregation is that it is necessary to achieve equal educational opportunity because racially separate schools are inherently and inevitably unable to provide quality education. Two seemingly logical assumptions follow from this premise: (a) it is not desirable to send white children to schools that were not good enough for nonwhites and (b) since one could not expect nonwhites to be as well educated as the whites with whom they are being integrated and since "everyone knows" that the quality of schools is heavily influenced by the average ability level of students, formerly white schools could not be as good as they were before desegregation. That the available evidence contradicts these assumptions is beside the point. Social scientists and educators have failed to explain why the quality of education in desegregated schools should be and is better for *all* children.

Second, social scientists are trained to be skeptical and tentative about their conclusions (even though not all of us are as cautious in this regard as we should be). In the world of public choice and policy-making, research must often compete with intuition and experience, even secondhand experience. This is unfair competition. Reporters and policymakers want a story, not a number of qualified conclusions. Former Senator Edmund Muskie once observed that he yearned to meet a one-handed social scientist. Moreover, the quality of research studies is often a subject that gets short shrift. Judges, for example, have been known to trash good research when it is contradicted by less valid evidence because they cannot tell the difference.

There is a third reason why evidence about the generally positive outcomes of desegregation has had little influence on public perceptions and political debates. The process of desegregation is embedded in a number of social phenomena, the dynamics and consequences of which seem to be more difficult to comprehend than is desegregation. Declining test scores and the loss of white enrollment in central cities are two of the best examples. Desegregation is often blamed for declining test scores (and if the public knows anything about public education, it is that scores have declined). In fact, test scores have risen in those areas of the country where desegregation is most pervasive. It is much more difficult to understand the effects on test scores of television, changes in high school curricula, and the growing proportions of both single-parent families and working mothers than it is to blame the apparent reduction in student achievement as the product of desegregation. Similarly, in explaining the growing proportions of nonwhites who inhabit our cities, one seldom hears of the massive loss of whites from many northern and midwestern cities that have not desegregated—as most have not, or about the dramatic growth of the nonwhite population resulting from immigration and birth rates higher than that of whites. Who knows, in this regard, that the nonwhite population of private schools was growing almost as fast as the nonwhite population of public schools in the late 1970s.

In summary, myths, not evidence, dominate the public mind when the wisdom of desegregation is being debated. And the prevailing myths will not, for reasons just suggested, readily yield to more positive information about the consequences of desegregation. Therefore, progress that could be made is mired in philosophical debates from which there seems no escape.

LESSON THREE: VOLUNTARY DESEGREGATION IS A CONTRADICTION IN TERMS

The current United States Assistant Attorney General for Civil Rights, William Bradford Reynolds, frequently announces that the Reagan Administration favors school desegregation, but believes that it can be achieved by encouraging and facilitating voluntary decisions by parents. Those who share this view are whistling Dixie. There is evidence that voluntary choice promoted by magnet schools and encouragement from public officials and other leaders can desegregate specific schools. When there are relatively few nonwhites in a community undergoing desegregation, creating magnet schools and making small boundary changes can desegregate a school system. But there is extensive evidence that desegregating a few schools by parental choice will not desegregate many school systems with more than 30 percent minority students without the threat of mandatory reassignment (see Smylie, 1983; Rossell, 1983). The most persuasive practical argument for voluntary desegregation seems to be that it will retain whites and thus, in the long run, we will end up with more interracial contact than would occur if desegregation were forced. But this argument remains speculative. Ultimately, desegregation will have to occur if the prediction is to be realized. What are the processes that will make whites more receptive to desegregation at some later time? As Smylie's (1983) comparison of voluntary and mandatory plans suggests, among districts with more than 35 percent nonwhite students, those using voluntary plans seem to experience as much white loss as districts that mandate desegregation for almost all students. Further, school desegregation clearly promotes residential integration (Pearce, Crain, & Farley, 1984) and thus reduces the need for mandatory pupil reassignments.

It would be wonderful if school desegregation could be achieved voluntarily. But readers who have learned the first two lessons described in this paper will understand why voluntary desegregation is not likely to do the job in most cities.

LESSON FOUR: SCHOOL DESEGREGATION IS THE BEST WAY WE HAVE TO ACHIEVE AN INTEGRATED SOCIETY

This lesson may be good news or bad depending on the kind of world in which one would like to live. It is a hard lesson to learn for those who seek an integrated society, because we have few options by which to achieve integration other than school desegregation. As the prospects for desegregation decline in some school districts, the hopes for an integrated society diminish accordingly. How does school desegregation foster social integration? Let me count the ways.

1. School desegregation can, when school officials make use of the opportunities presented, result in reductions in racial prejudice (Schofield and Sagar, 1983). The key role of school desegregation in promoting racial tolerance is explained by two well-documented propositions:

   a. Racial attitudes develop early in life—by age ten to twelve—and once set are difficult to alter.

   b. Reductions in prejudice occur most readily when persons of different races share common experiences through interpersonal interaction.

2. Minority students who attend desegregated schools are more likely to attend desegregated colleges (McPartland, 1982).

3. Persons who attend desegregated schools are more likely to live in desegregated neighborhoods (McPartland, 1982).

4. School desegregation fosters residential desegregation (Pearce, 1980; Hawley et al., 1983). Indeed, Pearce, Crain, and Farley (1984) have shown that between 1970 and 1980, almost all the residential desegregation in large central cities occurred where school systems were desegregated.

5. School desegregation promotes the integration of employment by fostering the upward social mobility of minorities and reducing discrimination by white employers (Trent & Braddock, 1984).

Perhaps we will find ways other than school desegregation to speed the nation's slow progress toward an integrated society. Maybe we can do it by teaching children who do not know children of other races that they should not be prejudiced. Maybe there will be enough blacks and Hispanics who will be successful despite their segregated childhood experiences so that stereotypes will crumble. But these are distant hopes sustained neither by evidence nor social theory.

LESSON FIVE: THE FALSE PROMISE OF SEPARATE BUT EQUAL SCHOOLS

White opponents of school desegregation have long endorsed the practical wisdom of separate but equal schools. Recently, increasing numbers of minority leaders and whites who had once advocated desegregation seem to be calling for a retreat from desegregation and a strengthening of minority schools. There appear to be three reasons for this change: frustration over the resistance by whites to desegregate and inequitable burdens of pupil assignment, concern about the possible loss of racial and ethnic identity among minorities in predominantly white schools, and new evidence on ways to improve the quality of inner-city schools, whether desegregated or not.

The third of these reasons leads to what

might be called the pragmatic separatist position. It is clear that today we know a lot more about how to enhance student achievement than we ever did and that significant improvements in racially isolated schools can be attained. This is encouraging news for many minority children who will, because of the population distribution in cities, inevitably attend a racially separate school. It is one thing to assert that we can do better than we have in educating children in predominantly minority schools and another to say that racially separate schools are likely to be more effective than racially desegregated schools.

To believe that we can have separate but equal schools requires the acceptance of at least two assumptions:

1. That low-achieving youngsters will learn as effectively in homogeneous schools as they will in classrooms with a greater mix of student ability

2. That the resources of the society will be allocated to minority schools not only in a nondiscriminatory way—but in ways that acknowledge that quality education for students from low-income families, for various reasons, requires more resources than quality education for children from more affluent backgrounds

I could review the evidence relating to these two assumptions, but I submit that few will wager a day's pay—much less their firstborn—on the rightness of either of them. Further, let us remember that the ability of minority students to use their education to better themselves, their families, and their communities is conditioned by the responsiveness of those who control jobs and political power and by the willingness and competence of minorities to use their knowledge and skills in settings dominated by whites.

How one comes out on tough policy decisions depends not only on one's assessment of a policy's benefit but on one's assessment of its costs. Thus, one may grant that desegregated schools can be somewhat more effective for minority youngsters and still favor separate but equal schools if one holds one or both of two other beliefs:

1. That the costs of desegregation to minority students are high—in terms of time spent on the bus and loss of self-esteem and racial identity

2. That desegregation—or integration—will follow from greater equality rather than be produced by it

Concerning the first of these beliefs, the available evidence shows that riding the bus does not in itself reduce school performance (Rossell & Hawley, 1982) and that there is little persistent effect of desegregation on the self-esteem and racial identity of minorities (Epps, 1981). The direct evidence on the psychological effects of desegregation is not clear and the consequences may be situational. But it is hard to imagine that desegregated minority students, who generally do better in school and feel more confident about participating in predominantly white settings than their segregated counterparts, sustain psychological damage as a result of their experience.

With regard to the argument that equality of condition will lead to interracial acceptance, rather than the other way around, there are at least two problems. The first of these has to do with the assumption that outstanding racially separate schools will become the rule rather than the exception. We have discussed this already. The second problem is that the assertion is ahistorical and understates both the influence of racism and its persistence. This position seems, indeed, a bit paradoxical since it is the conviction that racism is pervasive and intractable that leads some to believe in the need and inevitability of minority schools in the first place. By what known process will racism dissipate in a world where most people have little contact with persons of another race until they are old enough to go to war?

LESSON SIX: EQUITY AND EXCELLENCE WILL REQUIRE SIGNIFICANT EDUCATIONAL REFORM

The good news of this lesson is that there is no necessary trade-off between equity and educational excellence. Indeed, one without the other is a fraud. There is a large and growing amount of research that identifies practices and school characteristics that promote student achievement. Most of these practices can be implemented as well in schools that give a high priority to equity and equality as in those that do not. For example, high expectations and frequent evaluations of student performance are two of the most important things one finds in effective schools. (For an extensive review of these issues, see Hawley & Rosenholtz, 1984). But programs that focus on equity and equality do pose some special challenges for schools. The bad news of this lesson is that if these

challenges are to be met, it will be necessary to change some fundamental ways that schools function and educators behave. Let me discuss four of the most important directions that need to be taken if we are to have quality integrated schools.

Parent Involvement

Parent involvement, especially shared governance, has been at the heart of efforts to serve the educational needs of minorities and the disadvantaged better. But the political functions of parents have dominated discussions of parent involvement, especially when desegregation is the issue. These strategies are less effective than:

- Teaching parents to teach their children and monitor homework

- Home-based reinforcement programs in which parents are the allies of teachers in rewarding or denying certain behaviors

- Taking schools to parents (that is, meeting with parents in their homes or in nearby places like neighborhood schools, churches, housing complexes, or recreation centers)

Adapting to and Using Student Diversity

Most efforts to increase equal educational opportunities result in an increase in the social and racial diversity of schools and classrooms. This complicates teaching and at the same time affords opportunities to students and teachers. Arguing for heterogeneous grouping and against tracking is insufficient. Effective strategies for dealing productively with student diversity include:

- Cooperative team learning

- The use of the so-called "multiability classroom" approach

- The avoidance of competitive student evaluation schemes

- Interactive teaching rather than teacher-dominated instruction

- Peer tutoring

- Multiaged classrooms and learning groups

Ensuring the Maintenance of Order

Because advocates of equity and equality have been concerned with discrimination and are suspicious of authority, the importance of discipline in schools that are

desegregating has not always been given adequate attention. Practices that promote orderly environments include:

- Clearly articulated rules

- Consistent and aggressive enforcement of established rules

- In-school suspension programs where needed

- Environments that emphasize academic achievement for all

- Opportunities to question fairness of the rules and of their enforcement

Human Relations Programs

Attempts to foster equity and equality often incorporate some form of human relations programs. While most of these programs are not very effective, they can be; they can complement, rather than detract from, other school programs. The characteristics of effective human relations programs include the following:

- A focus on behavioral change not attitudinal change

- Interracial contact

- Concern to ensure that the "implicit" curriculum of the school, the things teachers and principals do and value, is congruent with the goals of the human relations program

- The direct confrontation of stereotypes and conflicts

- Comprehensiveness—the programs must be embodied in all school practices and policies and be so integral to other activities of the school that they are "invisible."

In developing and articulating these and other strategies to promote equity, excellence, and equality, it is important to provide clear and vivid pictures, real-life examples, models, and simple theories so that the logic of what is being proposed can be understood and accepted.

The six lessons discussed here have been hard to learn and most are difficult to accept. They tell us that the road ahead is rocky still. But we have learned much about how to do a better job in promoting the goals of desegregation, if we choose to pursue those goals. I have touched only briefly on these more positive lessons because the problem is not so much how to more effectively desegregate our schools; the problem continues to be whether we really believe in the goal. Bringing attention to some of the reasons why the quest for desegregation has been so difficult may be helpful to those who have kept the faith or who recognize that a segregated society will not only be unjust but will inevitably be wasteful and at war with itself.

Given the hard lessons of the last three decades, it may also be helpful to remember that while *Brown* initiated the process of desegregation, real momentum developed only within the last fifteen years, or less. We are only now beginning to see, in the behavior and opportunities of recent high school graduates, what the consequences of attending desegregated schools from early grades can be. The early returns are promising.

REFERENCES

Epps, E.G. (1981). Minority children: Desegregation, self-evaluation, and achievement orientation. In W.D. Hawley (ed.), *Effective school desegregation: Equity, quality and feasibility.* Beverly Hills, CA: Sage Publications.

Hawley, W.D. (Ed.) (1981). *Effective school desegregation: Equity, quality and feasibility.* Beverly Hills, CA: Sage Publications.

Hawley, W.D., Crain, R.L., Rossell, C.H., Smylie, M.A., Fernandez, R.R., Schofield, J.W., Tompkins, R., Trent, W. T., & Zlotnik, M.S. (1983). *Strategies for effective desegregation.* Lexington, MA: Lexington Books, D.C. Heath.

Hawley, W.D. & Rosenholtz, S.J. (1984, July). Good schools: What research says about improving student achievement, *Peabody Journal of Education, 61* (4) 1–177.

McPartland, J.M. (1982). *Testimony before the subcommittee on separation of powers of the committee on the judiciary*, U.S. Senate, 97th Congress, 1st Session, on Court-ordered school busing, September 30, 1981. Washington, DC: U.S. Government Printing Office.

Pearce, D.M. (1980). *Breaking down barriers: New evidence on the impact of metropolitan school desegregation on housing patterns.* Washington, DC: National Institute of Education.

Pearce, D.M., Crain, R.L., & Farley, R. (1984). *Lessons not lost: The effect of school desegregation on the rate of residential desegregation in large central cities.* Paper presented at the annual meeting of the American Educational Research Association at New Orleans.

Rossell, C.H. (1983). Desegregation plans, racial isolation, white flight and community response. In C.H. Rossell and W.D. Hawley (Eds.), *The consequences of school desegregation.* Philadelphia: Temple University Press, pp. 13-57.

Rossell, C.H. & Hawley, W.D. (1982). Policy alternatives for reducing white flight. *Educational Evaluation and Policy Analysis, 4* (2), 205-222.

Rossell, C.H. & Hawley, W.D. (Eds.) (1983). *The consequences of school desegregation.* Philadelphia: Temple University Press.

Schofield, J.W. & Sagar, H.A. (1983). Desegregation, school practices, and student race relations. In C.H. Rossell & W.D. Hawley (Eds.), *The consequences of school desegregation.* Philadelphia: Temple University Press.

Smylie, M.A. (1983). Reducing racial isolation in large school districts: The comparative effectiveness of mandatory and voluntary desegregation strategies. *Urban Education, 17,* 477-508.

Trent, W.T. & Braddock, H.J. (1984) *Desegregated schools and desegregated work.* Paper presented at the annual meeting of the American Educational Research Association, at New Orleans.

Heretical Thoughts on a Serious Occasion

DERRICK BELL

One can predict a spirited debate on the degree to which a well-integrated student body contributes to quality schooling for minority children. But all will agree that implementation of the *Brown* decisions has failed to provide the "equal educational opportunity" promised in 1954. Predictably, a major focus of this conference will be on what went wrong in the intervening decades that caused the results to fall so far short of our expectations.

A recent Joint Center for Political Studies analysis of school desegregation statistics gathered by a congressional committee indicates that during the 1980–81 school year, almost half of the black students living in the Northeast attended schools that were from 90 to 100 percent minority, and 63 percent of black students around the country attended such schools. Millions of black students in the South are enrolled in desegregated schools, but much of this desegregation had been achieved by 1972, and in recent years, the South has become slightly more segregated. In several areas, school boards are in court trying to eliminate busing and other school desegregation procedures. The Justice Department is supporting many of these attempts to undermine school desegregation plans (Orfield, 1982).

The facts are worse than the figures. The facts show intense segregation of blacks in areas of the Northeast, Midwest, Washington, D.C., Maryland, the deep South,

and California. Here large numbers of blacks live in mainly black and often poverty-level neighborhoods where the need for effective education is great and the schooling available most inadequate.

A good starting place for this inquiry is the second *Brown* decision (*Brown* v. *Board of Education*, 1955). There, as we all remember, the Supreme Court refused to grant the black petitioners' request that all segregated schools be enjoined to desegregate immediately. The Court was understandably cautious. Strong political resistance was already evident, and neither President Eisenhower nor the Congress had indicated much enthusiasm for actions that would support or enforce the Court's order. Substituting rhetoric for firmness, the Court sent the school desegregation cases back to the district courts with vague directions to desegregate the schools "with all deliberate speed" (*Brown* v. *Board of Education*, 1955).

The Court's 1955 decision has been criticized as a serious error that provided desegregation opponents time to organize a campaign that threatened secession and succeeded in delaying any meaningful compliance for at least ten years. Professor Alexander Bickel defended the Court's caution as prudence. He wrote the following (Bickel, 1964):

While the vitality of constitutional principles as reflected in specific court orders

ought, to be sure, not be allowed to yield simply because of disagreement with them, disagreement is legitimate and relevant and will, in our system, legitimately and inevitably cause delay in compliance with law laid down by the Supreme Court, and will indeed, if it persists and is widely enough shared, overturn such law.

If nothing else, the last two decades of continued resistance to school desegregation serve to validate Professor Bickel's words as more than an abject apology for the Court's lack of courage. Still, the district courts to which the *Brown* cases were returned were located in communities in which the segregated way of life was deemed very close to godliness. And the misplaced faith the Court placed in the lower courts' ability to act with a resoluteness the Supreme Court had lacked is laid out plainly in the pages of legal history. For most of us, that history is not pleasant reading.

It is a question that some here will deem heretical if not seditious, but what might have been the outcome had the Court

DERRICK BELL is Dean, University of Oregon Law School.

This contribution is based on an article, Bell, D. (1983), Learning from our losses: Is school desegregation still feasible in the 1980s? Phi Delta Kappan, 64, 572.

specifically delayed for at least five years any order requiring the dreaded "mixing of the races"? Suppose the Court had instead required the total equalization of school facilities and resources. It would have seemed cruel and unprecedented at the time, but more progress might have been made in the long run had the Court expressly deferred desegregation relief in favor of a rigid insistence that school boards equalize the facilities in black schools.

We who worked so hard for school desegregation tend to dismiss as unimportant the fact that many southern districts, hoping to undermine the attack on racial segregation, had taken substantial steps to eliminate the most obvious and odious of the disparities between black schools and white schools. School officials hastily constructed buildings and found money for new textbooks, laboratories, libraries, and gymnasiums. The equalization programs were sufficiently far-reaching that the massive Coleman Report of 1966 (Equality of Educational Opportunity) failed to find the vast differences in buildings, books, and facilities between black and white schools that researchers had expected (Jones, 1973).

Because the language in the *Brown* decision promised actual integration, we dismissed this tardy effort to put the "equal" back into "separate but equal" as offering too little and coming too late. We ignored the fact that the *Brown* precedent placed within reach the equal facilities that blacks had sought, mostly in vain, for generations. Seeking what we considered the ultimate legal right, integration, we rejected the educationally useful equal facilities.

Perhaps the advantages of better facilities would have been more apparent if the Supreme Court had ordered them at once while specifically deferring school integration. But suppose in addition to requiring the equalization of all facilities and resources, the Court in 1955 had recognized that separation of students by race facilitated the real evil of segregation: white dominance over blacks in every important aspect of life. To correct this imbalance the Supreme Court could have required that blacks be fairly represented on school boards and other policymaking bodies.

This remedy would have given blacks a real potential for participation in policymaking—a prerequisite to full equality still unattained in many predominantly black school systems. In addition, this "equal representation" rule would have helped protect the thousands of black teachers and principals who were dismissed by white-dominated school systems in the 1960s and 1970s, when school desegregation plans aimed at achieving racial balance were implemented.

Southern school districts would certainly have resisted implementation of this plan, but their defensive strategies would not have been bolstered by the emotionally charged concerns of parents that school integration would lead to interracial sex and marriage, a fear that sufficed to send so many otherwise sensible whites to the ramparts shouting, "Never."

School integration advocates will protest that a judicial approach that did not give priority to pupil desegregation would have played into segregationist strategy by making black parents satisfied with all-black schools. But since the 1780s, when the first public schools opened in Boston, black parents have urged racially separate as well as integrated schools, in their quest for effective schooling for their children.

Of course, there have always been black parents who preferred to send their children to mainly white schools either because of convenience or out of a belief that such schools would better meet their children's educational needs. These parents would have continued to push for integrated schools. Paradoxically, black schools with good academic reputations would have furthered integration by serving as magnets for some white children just as such schools do today. And, if black children had received a quality education in the court-ordered equalized schools, they would have been far better prepared for the academic and emotional challenges of school desegregation than, in fact, most were.

We know, of course, that the Supreme Court ordered neither integration nor equalization of segregated schools for a decade after the *Brown* decision. In fact, with the exception of striking down instances of total recalcitrance such as Little Rock in 1957 (*Cooper v. Aaron*, 1958), the Court's involvement in the first ten years of school desegregation after *Brown* was generally nonproductive and often counterproductive.

If civil rights groups and black parents had known in advance that the courts would refuse to order school desegregation for ten years, what might they have done? There is the possibility they would have become discouraged by the delay in student desegregation and simply done nothing until the Court was willing to act. More likely, they would have done what eventually needed to be done in each community where a desegregation decision was issued, that is, to organize parents and the community to effectively implement the court-ordered equal money and control mandates. How this might have been accomplished is revealed in the history of segregated schools.

We know that many and perhaps most black schools under the segregated system were quite bad. The unjust and racist disparities in funding almost guaranteed the inferiority of black schools. Moreover, the black schools were under the domination of white systems that not only saw no benefit in these schools becoming quality institutions, but also gained some perverse sense of satisfaction from the obviously inferior status imposed on the black schools. Thus, principals in the black schools were appointed and retained based on their ability to keep order in the black schools rather than on their ability as educators. If they managed to provide a decent learning environment, there was usually little objection as long as the learning process posed no overt threat to white dominance.

The fear by blacks that segregated schools would be inferior could and did become a self-fulfilling prophesy. W.E.B. DuBois explained the phenomenon well. He maintained that black children needed neither separate schools nor integrated schools. What they needed was a good education. He noted that even in 1935, Negroes would "fight frenziedly" to end formally segregated schools, but if the schools remained all-black, the tendency was simply to accept the idea that nothing of educational value could take place in black schools. Having lost interest, blacks, DuBois claimed, "scarcely raise a finger to see that the resultant Negro schools get a fair share of the public funds so as to have adequate equipment and housing; [and] to see that real teachers are appointed" (DuBois, 1935).

Happily, not every black community and every black school teacher and principal succumbed to the self-fulfilling prophecy of black incompetence in their schools. In far more instances than we have records to show, individual teachers rose above the inadequate resources and the stifling atmosphere in the black schools to encourage excellence, to motivate ambition, and to teach those skills and qualities of self-regard that produced scores of black success stories in the business and professional world. Some of these black schools gained reputations for quality; these were too soon forgotten when in 1954, the flood of hope for integration seemed to sweep away the heroic accomplishments of black teachers in segregated schools.

It is hard for me to accept arguments that the loss of educational techniques that worked against all odds in pre-*Brown* black schools was not a devastating one. It is even harder to imagine that such a loss would have occurred had the Supreme Court initiated the school desegregation process by demanding an immediate end to inequities in funding and facilities and a proportionate role for blacks in educational policymaking.

The scope of this loss did not become apparent until after the school desegregation process was well underway. But, even in southern districts where millions of children are attending desegregated schools, the presence of both races in the same school does not guarantee equal access to educational opportunities for black children. Even today there are few desegregated districts in which black scholastic achievement scores are equal to those of whites, and even fewer where expulsions of black students and instances of disciplinary actions against black pupils do not exceed by substantial margins expulsions and disciplining of whites. In addition to these grim facts are black children's stories of isolation, insensitivity, and outright rejection experienced in public schools that may be perfectly balanced by race, but remain dominated by whites.

Certainly, desegregated schools are not without success stories, but the number of black students who overcome the obstacles to their success represent a small dividend indeed, given the long years invested in school desegregation. The number of desegregated schools where all black children, not just the best and the brightest, are treated in accord with their needs is even smaller.

Had we, the civil rights lawyers, been more attuned to the primary goal of black parents—the effective schooling of their children—and less committed to the attainment of our ideal—racially integrated schools—we might have recognized earlier that attainment of our ideal would not, in a society still committed to white dominance, ensure that our clients and their children would gain the equal educational opportunity for which they sacrificed so much and waited so long.

But many black parents and their community leaders realized early on that there could be no effective schooling for black children without parental involvement in both the educational process and in school policymaking. Experience, often painful, taught them that true parental participation does not result from simply enrolling their children in mainly white schools, particularly if those schools are located a long bus ride away from their homes and neighborhoods.

Thus, in a number of areas, including Atlanta, St. Louis, Detroit, Milwaukee, Portland, and Dallas, blacks have rejected plans calling for more racial balance in favor of policies that in varying forms promise more control and a more equitable distribution of educational resources. In some instances, courts have recognized and encouraged educationally oriented plans. Civil rights organizations are less prone than they once were to seek court orders for racial-balance relief over the objections of local parents.

Of course, the pressures of racism may well condemn any plan to educate minority children, especially the children of the poor. And surely all black parents should have the option to send their children to mainly white schools. But given the uncertain educational outcome of exercising that option more than thirty years after *Brown*, black parents who prefer to do now what perhaps the Supreme Court should have done in 1955 ought to be encouraged and not assailed.

At least they are trying to learn from our losses. The barriers of continued white resistance, a less than supportive Supreme Court, and the growing concentration of most poorer blacks in large urban areas render ridiculous the efforts to gain meaningful compliance with *Brown* through reliance on racial-balance plans. The chances for further progress in the 1980s rest with those who have decided that the better route to educational quality may lie in those schools where black children and their parents are not treated as strangers.

REFERENCES

Bickel, A. (1964). The decade of school desegregation: Process and prospects. *Columbia Law Review, 64,* 193, 196.

Brown v. Board of Education of Topeka, 349 U.S. 294 (1955). Id. at 300.

Cooper v. Aaron, 358 U.S. 1 (1958).

DuBois, W.E.B. (1935). Does the Negro separate schools? *Journal of Negro Education, 4,* 328, 332.

Equality of Educational Opportunity. (1966). (F 55,238:38000) Washington, DC: U.S. Government Printing Office.

Jones, F.C. (1973, Fall). The inequality controversy. *Journal of Negro Education,* 537–549.

Orfield, G. (1982, October). Desegregation in the public schools, 1968-1980. *Focus, A Publication of the Joint Center for Political Studies,* pp. 4–5.

Effective Schools Through School Desegregation

HUGH J. SCOTT

There remains considerable disagreement between white and black Americans and even among black Americans as to what the permissible and effective policies and practices in the desegregation of public education are (Scott, 1983). The courts recognize that there is no universal, fail-safe answer to the complexities of school desegregation. The data bank on school desegregation is extensive, complex, and often contradictory. Research findings on the very sensitive and highly important topic of the effects of school desegregation on the academic achievement of white and black students tend to have something to support almost every point of view (Miller, 1979). There are no agnostics in school desegregation. School desegregation strategies are derived from the pervasive social beliefs and principal educational assumptions and priorities of those who exercise power in the determination of the permissible policies and practices (Kirp, 1976).

There are potential social and educational benefits to be gained by white and black students from an equitable desegregation of the public schools. Intelligently conceived and equitably implemented school desegregation strategies remain an imperative in American education. The reassignment of black students from all or mainly black schools, whether or not the reassignment requires busing, has been and still remains an effective desegregation strategy in some school districts. A racially integrated, effective school for all students in a pluralistic society is the best model for a public school, but this does not mean that it is the only acceptable model or that the presence of predominantly or all-black schools necessarily represents an infringement of a constitutional right of black students.

Sufficient school desegregation history exists to indicate that the path to equal educational opportunity and a quality education for most black students is not via the outworn and inefficacious overreliance on racial-balance remedies. Racial-balance remedies enacted in response to the *Brown* decision (1954) were never intended to make improvement in the academic performance of black students a major goal (Bell, 1981).

Today, numerically determined educational equity is not as important an issue as improving the quality of schools that black children attend and should not be the sole desegregation strategy acceptable to the courts, attorneys for plaintiffs, civil rights organizations, and parents. I challenge the unrealistic and nonproductive preoccupation with numerically determined educational equity which is part of the inevitable debate about the appropriateness of various ways and means of achieving compliance with the mandates of *Brown*. The fault lies not with the *Brown* decision but with its implementation. *Brown* is applied to desegregation strategies in a manner that virtually guarantees a lack of attention to educational quality for black students.

More black students now attend schools identified as racially isolated under *de facto* segregated practices than attended segregated schools under *de jure* segregated practices (Jones, 1979). The majority of black students now live in the large urban centers and attend schools that are predominantly minority (U.S. Commission on Civil Rights, 1977). The preeminent challenge confronting school desegregation is to use *Brown* as an instrument for making mainly minority schools more effective, rather than less nonwhite (from an interview by Scott with Ruth Love, 1981). Black Americans should not tolerate ineffective, inequitable, and obsolete desegregation strategies out of fear that to challenge them would give aid and comfort to those who believe in the separation of the races or who would turn back decades of progress in civil rights. Desegregation efforts allegedly seek to contribute to the process of black Americans securing the blessings and privileges of first-class citizenship; they cannot succeed if they impose, even temporarily, second-class status on blacks as a means to this end. Blackness is neither greater nor less than whiteness. What black Americans are prepared to

HUGH J. SCOTT is Dean, Programs in Education, Hunter College of the City University of New York.

accept and reject in terms of the permissible policies and practices in school desegregation will reveal just how deeply rooted pride and consciousness are in black America.

For those decisions that shape the permissible policies and practices in school desegregation, the preeminent emphasis should be directed to the improvement of teaching and learning in the schools. Resources should be allocated in direct proportion to the degree of student need. The highest priority should be given to the establishment of programs and services aimed at the alleviation of situations where socioeconomic factors and academic deficiencies combine to present the most demanding challenges to the skills of educators. Systemwide intervention programs and services should be aimed at the prevention and remediation of cumulative deficiencies in the acquisition of basic reading and math skills (*Milliken* v. *Bradley*, 1977).

The concept of multicultural education should be promoted. The American culture should be viewed as a conglomeration of the diverse life styles of all the groups who have helped to build America. The study of black and Hispanic history and culture should be incorporated into the regular curriculums of all schools. Any honors program or program for gifted and talented students should comprise a representative

number of minority students and the admissions criteria and procedures for recruitment and selection of students should be consistent with the principle of equal educational opportunity.

Continuous professional development programs should be established for school personnel to enable them to cope more effectively with the sociological and educational challenges inherent in school desegregation. Policies determining how federal and state funds are applied to reinforce a commitment to equal educational opportunity and a quality education for all students should be publicly stated. Equal educational opportunity and equal employment opportunity must be treated as companion components of school desegregation. The policy that either black or white students can serve as the minority student population for the purposes of desegregation should be clearly established. The burdens of required disruptions and dislocations should be equitably distributed among white, brown, and black students (*Kelley* v. *Metro Board of Education*, 1980). When busing is proposed, the right of choice must be given to minority parents.

A system-wide evaluation program directed toward the determination of the effectiveness of instructional programs should be established and the results of evaluation for planning and policy determinations applied. A comprehensive

program of counseling and career guidance for repairing the effects of past discrimination and for responding to the pressures and needs of a pluralistic and highly technological society should be established. Structures for community relations at the local, regional, and central levels should be provided, reflecting the racial composition of the school system and offering parents direct access to the decision-making process as it pertains to policy planning and program development and implementation.

Black children have a constitutional right to attend desegregated public schools, whether or not their parents elect to exercise this right. But the rigid adherence to racial-balance plans that ignores the importance of black history and culture, pays little attention to the quality of education, imposes excessive burdens on minority students, or denies minority parents some choice amounts to a denial of equal educational opportunity. Speaking for a growing number of minority parents, a black school superintendent says: "If you can have quality education and racial mixing, good. But if you cannot have both, I will take quality education" (statement made in a telephone interview with Ulysses Byas, Superintendent of Schools in Roosevelt, N.Y., in June 1981 and printed in Scott, 1983).

REFERENCES

Bell, D.A., (1981). *Shades of Brown.* New York: Columbia University Press.

Jones, L., (1979). *From Brown to Boston: The desegregation struggle.* New Jersey: The Scarecrow Press, Inc.

Kelley v. Metro Board of Education of Nashville, 409 U.S. 1001 (1980). From memorandum opinion issued by Judge Thomas A. Wiseman, Jr., of the U.S. District Court for the Middle District in Tennessee.

Kirp, D.L., (1976, November) Race, politics, and the courts: School desegregation in San Francisco, *Harvard Educational Review,* 572-611.

Miller, V., (February, 1979). The emergent pattern of integration, *Educational Leadership.*

Milliken v. Bradley, 433 U.S. 267. L Ed. 2d. 745, 97 S. Ct. 2749 (1977).

Scott, H.J., (1983, Winter). Beyond racial balance remedies: School desegregation for the 1980s, *New York University Education Quarterly, 14* (2), 13–21.

Scott, H.J. (1981, October). *Perspectives on desegregation of predominantly black school systems,* presented at the National Conference on Educational Issues, New York City.

U.S. Commission on Civil Rights. (1977, February). *Statement on metropolitan school desegregation.* Washington, DC.

Equity and Excellence: An Emerging Trend in the Desegregation of Schools

LAMAR P. MILLER
J. THEODORE REPA

INTRODUCTION

The issue of race equity and educational excellence must be put into historical perspective if we are to chart the meaning of equal educational opportunity for the ensuing decade. The examination of progress in desegregation over the past thirty years reveals a mixed bag insofar as success in achieving equality in educational opportunity is concerned. Then and now the arguments for and against the strategy of desegregation to achieve equality hinge on the issue of race. Almost everyone will agree that closing the educational gap between whites and minorities is crucial to the achievement of a sound and just society, and again almost everyone will agree that while some progress has been made, the goal of achieving equality of opportunity has not been realized. The controversy thirty years after the *Brown* decision is not the goal, but the means to achieve the goal of equality and quality in education.

The question of means is complicated by a rapidly changing demographic scene in our major cities, described by Orfield (1983) in his report on school desegregation patterns in the states, large cities, and metropolitan areas from 1968 to 1980. Orfield's report indicated that southern and border states led the nation in desegregation of schools, that segregation of black students was increasing in the Northeast, and that there has been a serious increase in the segregation of Hispanic students in all regions of the United States. At the same time, there has been improvement in the quality of education of blacks. There has been gradual increase in overall enrollment, retention, and graduation of blacks in the last decade (Price-Curtiss, 1981). However, while the trends have been somewhat positive, there is a major achievement gap between minorities and whites that continues to exist (Coleman et al., 1966 and Jencks, 1972). These issues have set the stage for recent arguments regarding what policies we should follow.

One of the critics of current school desegregation efforts, Derrick Bell, argues "we should have learned by now that, in the absence of shockingly overt racial discrimination, constitutional protections alone will not be read as authorizing an effective remedy for blacks when that remedy threatens the status of middle and upper class whites" (1983). Bell raises the issue, thought to be decided by the 1954 decision, about whether "equalization of funding and facilities and proportional representation in educational policy making" are better ways of achieving quality education as well as equal educational opportunity for minorities. Bell's position is a return to the *Plessy* v. *Ferguson* (1896) decision, in which the Court ruled that racial separation in public facilities was constitutional so long as the separate facilities were equal. It must be remembered that four years after the *Plessy* decision, black schools fell far behind white schools because of the differences in expenditures (Miller, 1982). Similarly, there is no assurance that Bell's proposals would prevent the quality of education in the resulting separate black schools from declining in a similar manner, given that the balance of economic power remains with the majority. The Supreme Court reached a similar conclusion in the *Brown* decision in 1954 when it ruled that separate but equal facilities are inherently unequal. Bell's main point is that desegregation via *Brown* has not provided the quality education for minorities that they deserve. We agree. But returning to *Plessy* v. *Ferguson* is not the answer. Bell's position only exacerbates the problem.

Given our position that desegregation is the preferable means to achieving equal educational opportunity, the question

LAMAR P. MILLER is Professor of Education, and Executive Director, the Metropolitan Center for Educational Research, Development, and Training, School of Education, Health, Nursing, and the Arts Professions, New York University.

J. THEODORE REPA is Associate Professor of Organization and Administrative Studies and Associate Director of the Metropolitan Center for Educational Research, Development, and Training, School of Education, Health, Nursing, and Arts Professions, New York University.

remains: Why has desegregation not led to higher achievement levels among blacks in schools? The answer we wish to explore is that desegregation, until recently, has not emphasized the process of education that leads to gains in achievement and better quality. Courts and consent decrees were much more concerned with moving children than they were with creating excellence in schools in a desegregated setting.

Scherer and Slawski's (1979) view of desegregation clarifies the meaning of this contention. They, too, believe that school desegregation should be viewed as a "process" rather than as an "event." The perspective of school desegregation as an "event" involves the racial mixing of students and is approached as a straightforward, lockstep procedure concerned only with racial balance. Alternatively, the perspective of school desegregation as a "process" focuses on how students should be educated as well as where they receive that education.

The problem since the Brown decision is that desegregation has not consistently focused on the process of achieving quality. Instead, school desegregation efforts have emanated from three different value positions (King, 1977). These value orientations are summarized here:

- The desegregation-oriented view holds that efforts should be directed toward desegregating schools by reassigning students.

- The integration-oriented view holds that efforts should be directed toward desegregation and toward enabling schools to overcome the postdesegregation problems of racial inequality and isolation.

- The equal educational opportunity orientation holds that efforts should be directed toward eliminating any negative effects of desegregation by providing quality education to all students.

While these orientations are not mutually exclusive, most desegregation activities have focused on reassigning students and enabling schools to overcome the effects of racial isolation. The reason that more progress has not been made in improving both the quality and integration of schools is that there has not been an equal opportunity orientation that focuses on improving the educational system.

From the above discussion, our position on equality and quality education becomes apparent. Equality must be viewed in the context of King's equal educational opportunity value orientation. Equality refers to the equitable distribution of resources, depending on need, that will produce a quality education for all students. Quality education focuses on ensuring that students achieve commensurately with their ability. This position is in accord with Salomone's (in press) conclusion that the courts have come full circle to focus desegregation efforts both on means and ends when attempting to achieve equal educational opportunity.

While previously the courts and the federal government have been instrumental in opening up educational opportunity, there has been growing concern, particularly among those currently involved in education at the federal level, that the move toward educational equity has brought with it a move away from educational excellence. Many feel that the de-emphasis on meritocracy brought about by efforts to increase equity is leading to mediocrity or worse. Everything from discipline problems in the schools to the decreasing scores on the Scholastic Aptitude Tests have been attributed to the search for educational equity.

The concern about the quality of education is certainly legitimate and is shared by educators, parents, and the general public. No one is against a quality education. A quality education is not, however, in conflict with an equitable education. Indeed, equity and inequity affect all students and educational equity, rather than being the antithesis of quality education, is an important part of it.

Courts have viewed desegregation in the broader context of a process that leads to a quality education. The Milliken II (1977) Supreme Court decision is a case in point. Specifically, the Supreme Court said that when a Federal Court is fashioning a remedy:

1. The remedy must be related to the condition alleged to offend the Constitution.

2. The decree "must indeed be remedial in nature, that is, it must be designed as nearly as possible" to restore the victims of discriminatory conduct to the position they would have occupied in the absence of such conduct (Milliken II, the Court quoting from Milliken I).

3. The court "must take into account the interest of state and local authorities in managing their own affairs, consistent with the Constitution" (Milliken II).

Von Euler and Parham (1978) have characterized this decision as a landmark U.S. Supreme Court judicial precedent because it addresses educational concerns in the context of school desegregation and provides a legal framework upon which current desegregation efforts can be built. Thus, armed with legal clout, desegregation efforts can go beyond the limited goal of reducing minority-group isolation to address the broader issues of quality education.

Buffalo, New York, is probably the best example of a school district that has achieved the twin goals of eliminating racial isolation and creating a high-quality education program. The Buffalo program combines court-ordered busing with magnet schools; it has made Buffalo, which is 47 percent black, a national model for school desegregation. Test scores are up substantially, white flight has been insignificant, more than 1,500 white students have left private schools to return to public schools in the last five years, and community support is strong and growing. Other school districts that used a voluntary model, such as Memphis, Tampa, and Seattle, have also had success by using desegregation as an opportunity to upgrade the public schools. Mobilization of popular support for the effort followed.

A Matter of Choice

The emerging trend in desegregation in the eighties is a concern more with how students are educated than where students are educated. This does not mean that schools have overlooked or should overlook the need to eliminate racially identifiable schools. But a primary objective in many states and school districts is to ensure that schools—and especially urban schools—are effective for the most vulnerable students.

Our experience with school districts suggests developing strategies that achieve the objective of equity, while providing parental choice in school selection. A number of individuals and educational leaders around the country have become excited about the potential of programs that allow parents to choose schools that will best meet the individual needs of their children. Albeit there are those who are dubious about the effects of choice because of the possibility of creating selective schools. Clearly, there is a danger of creating selective schools where admittance is based on questionable tests of merit. If choice of school is going to be used as a desegregation tool, then admission should be based on interest so that all children have an opportunity to attend a particular school. By limiting choice, however, we have created new inequities, as those who can afford alternatives to public education simply choose not to enroll their children. According to Charles Glenn (1985), choice is eliminated only for the poor.

In desegregated settings, the opportunity for parents to select from among different kinds of schools is a response to the diversity of beliefs about how children should be educated. Moreover, a number of educational leaders in places like Lowell, Massachusetts; Cincinnati, Ohio; Milwaukee, Wisconsin; Minneapolis, Minnesota; and Buffalo, New York, believe that excellent schools do not all have to be the same. Consider schools like Boston Latin in Massachusetts, the Bronx High School of Science and the La Guardia School of Music and the Arts in New York City.

The notion of choice as part of educational strategy is particularly well suited for schools in urban settings. Glenn (1985) points out that "whether parents feel that a school is congruent with their own beliefs and attitudes, as well as their aspirations for their children, has much to do with whether the children are successful. If this is true, (and much research suggests it is), then it is particularly important with respect to those poor and minority students whose success is in question."

Schools that provide a special focus and accept students based on interest in certain subject areas can stimulate improved achievement and improved behavior. Equally important is the motivation to attend such schools because they are special. Parents' interest in what a school has to offer and their desire to have their children attend create a spirit of community and a sense of responsibility on the part of the school. All parents want quality education for their children and most parents respond favorably if they have a choice in selecting that education.

In addressing a process to achieve quality education in a desegregation setting, it seems prudent to begin with those components we are most familiar with: school organization, curriculum, instructional practices, assessment of students, the staff, and in-service training. All schools are concerned with these components of education. However, they have a special meaning when viewed in the context of desegregation because of the added dimensions of personal and human interaction. Our discussion of the activities that form the basis for a process approach to desegregation reflect the special meaning of these components.

School Organization

A recent trend in school desegregation is to organize schools around subject areas that will "attract" students and therefore lead to greater racial balance. These so-called magnet schools have proliferated during the last decade to a point where in 1983, there were over 1,000 magnets in more than 130 of the largest urban school districts (Blank, Dentler, Baltzell, & Chabotar, 1983). The models for magnet schools came from such well-known specialty schools as Boston Latin School in Boston, Massachusetts, and Bronx High School of Science in New York City, where entrance was secured based primarily on test results. About twenty years ago, entrance to new types of magnet schools based upon interest in the performing arts, mathematics, or science was introduced. This trend was expanded, particularly by northern urban districts, to include other types of organizational themes. Examples are schools in which the curricula focus on computer science, business, law, humanities, and foreign languages, as well as different types of schools (open, fundamental, alternative, and traditional). The general idea was that school districts would develop optional magnets of high academic quality that would reflect the interests of the students and parents. By locating these schools in areas that would increase the racial diversity of the student body, these school districts could achieve the twin objectives of improving the quality of education and voluntarily desegregating their schools.

The federal government provided major support for magnet school efforts in 1976 with an amendment to the Emergency School Aid Act (ESAA). This legislation provided grants to support desegregation through magnet schools. This support has been replaced by Title VII of the Education for Economic Security Act, Public Law 98-377, which authorizes the Magnet Schools Assistance Program. The support is consistent with the Reagan Administration's position on desegregation of schools: "Our remedial program has as its centerpiece special magnet schools and other curriculum enhancement programs that provide educational incentives to all children in the public school system" (see Reynolds' contribution, pp. 47–50). Magnet schools are seen by the Administration as a way of avoiding "forced" busing to achieve desegregation.

Although the research on the outcomes of magnet schools is still somewhat sketchy, certain trends can be inferred from the literature. Students who do attend magnet schools tend to score somewhat better on standard tests and have fewer absences and suspensions than do comparable students who do not attend magnet schools (Weber, McBee, & Lyles, 1983; Blank, Dentler, Baltzell & Chabotar, 1983; Alkin, 1983; and Bortin, 1982). Whether magnet schools caused these results or attracted students with these characteristics cannot be determined from the design of these studies.

Magnet schools can also have significant impact on reducing district-wide segregation under certain conditions, including strong commitment and effective implementation of a district-wide plan (Blank, Dentler, Baltzell, & Chabotar, 1983). However, totally voluntary plans where the magnet is located in a formerly all-minority school have difficulty attracting whites (Royster, Baltzell, & Simmons, 1979; Fleming, Blank, Dentler, & Baltzell, 1983; and Larson, 1980). Thus, the evidence does not support the Administration's position that voluntary magnet schools will desegregate all schools. In Buffalo, where magnet schools have been successfully used to improve and desegregate their entire system, assignment to magnets was based on a complex admissions system that was only partially voluntary. Minority and nonminority students enter separate pools where they are randomly selected, one from each pool, in order to maintain racial balance. Busing students to schools was part of the court order but seems not to be an issue in the district as long as quality programs are at the end of the bus ride.

A key to the success of any magnet is the principal, hardly a surprising finding given the effective school literature (Blank, Dentler, Baltzell & Chabotar, 1983). A principal needs to be a curriculum leader as well as a successful manager. However, the principal will not succeed without strong district leadership and school board commitment to the magnet school policy.

Available evidence also indicates that magnet school per-pupil costs are slightly higher than nonmagnet alternatives. Blank, Dentler, Baltzell & Chabotar (1983) found per-student costs for magnet programs to average approximately 200 dollars more than for nonmagnet programs. This cost declined to 59 dollars as more experience with magnet schools became available.

Lastly, magnet schools are more successful when there is active community involvement in program planning, design, instruction, and support (Blank, Dentler,

...

Baltzell, & Chabotar, 1983). This involvement tends to decrease opposition to the desegregation efforts and also leads to increased community confidence in public education.

Thus, the research evidence on magnet schools suggests that they are effective in improving the quality of the school and of desegregation if the assignment is carefully developed and monitored. Effective magnet schools require excellent principals, strong support from the central administration, and active participation by parents and community in planning, implementation, and evaluation of the schools. Magnet schools will cost slightly more than nonmagnet schools, but the added cost needs to be balanced against the twin gains of higher achievement and desegregation.

The Curriculum

The curriculum needed to achieve an equitable, quality education should, first of all, be representative of the full range of knowledge and content that allows students to function within our rapidly growing technological society and, secondly, should be representative of the cultural and ethnic diversity of this society. The basic skills necessary for survival are evolving with the advance of technology. The Task Force on Education for Economic Growth (1983) has called for a broadening of the definition of these skills that would reach beyond reading, computation, and writing mechanics to include the "learning-to-read" skills of analyzing, problem solving, reasoning, and conceptualizing. Decision making, social participation, and personal interaction are additional skills educators consider essential for effective participation in our society (Banks, 1982).

There are many aspects of the social and personal interaction between teacher and student and student and student that do not pertain, in a strict sense, to the acquisition of skills and knowledge that typically form the content of a curriculum. The varieties of interaction include those of motivating, persuading, and the establishing of attitudes and values. Much attention has been given to intervention strategies directed at changing basic cognitive processes, while the affective domain, which may be considerably more plastic and malleable, has been overlooked. Cognitive function may be more susceptible to change by affective, not cognitive intervention. Indeed, it appears that the strength of a curriculum depends on the way it integrates the affective and cognitive domains.

Students may be able to develop a qualitatively higher level of functioning because they are motivated to apply whatever skills and potential they have to a task. Considering it another way, if the social interaction and strategies provide the motivation needed to become involved and the aspiration level is high enough, the affective process may induce changes in the cognitive process. The tendency in most programs has been to separate affective and cognitive domains from each other. Yet the two cannot be separated; they are so integrally related that it makes no sense to talk about one as distinct from the other or to develop programs that do not relate the two.

However, it is not enough to develop such heightened skills in and of themselves. It is also imperative that educators align the skill development process of students with an increased sensitivity to and appreciation of the diversity of humanity. Therefore, we believe that a multicultural education is synonymous with an equitable, quality education.

Multicultural education has been defined by Cortes (1979) as "the process of preparing young people to live constructively and sensitively in a multicultural nation and on an increasingly interdependent, constantly shrinking planet." Banks names as a primary goal of a multicultural education the education of students "...so that they will acquire knowledge about a range of cultural groups and develop the attitudes, skills and abilities needed to function at some level of competency within many cultural environments" (1979b). Sagar and Schofield (1979) claim that a multicultural educational environment has three important functions: (1) it assists the staff and students in a multiracial and/or multiethnic school to recognize the diversity of the student body; (2) it assists students in defining and deciphering their experiences in interracial and/or interethnic settings; and (3) it can help to create a school climate of mutual acceptance and appreciation. Banks (1979a) has identified a fourth important function of a multiethnic curriculum: that of creating a school climate that facilitates minority pupils' search for a sense of identity and self-worth.

Multicultural education is a logical adjunct of desegregated schools. It provides a mode through which schools can move from a superficial mixing of people and cultures to true integration, with its concomitant interpersonal, intergroup, intercultural, and international understanding. In order to achieve this vision, schools must develop a well-conceived, well-coordinated, fully integrated multicultural approach to education. In such an approach, multicultural education cannot be viewed as enrichment. It is not an elective. It is not an extra. Multicultural education is basic to all facets of the educational process because learning to relate to human beings, learning to understand human and group similarities and differences, learning to address intercultural issues, and learning to cooperate across cultural, ethnic, racial, and national lines are basic to our future. Cultural and ethnic materials such as music and books on minority history can help to make a curriculum multiethnic, but they do not ensure that the curriculum will be integrated (Forehand & Ragosta, 1976).

Thus, the curriculum must emphasize the acquisition of basic affective and cognitive skills, which will lead to increased learning. In addition, the curriculum must reflect the diversity in a multicultural setting if a true quality education is to be achieved.

Instructional Practices— Cooperative Learning and Computer-Assisted Instruction

During the past decade, there have been a large number of research studies that focus on the possible effects of a strategy known as cooperative learning. Cooperative learning is a grouping technique whereby majority and minority students work together to improve academic achievement. This student team learning concept is based on research that demonstrates that heterogeneous teams made up of low and high performers and boys and girls of different racial or ethnic backgrounds can be a success in the classroom as well as on the athletic field. Researchers find that black and Hispanic students improve performance, attitudes toward school, and (in desegregated settings) attitudes toward others when learning activities are cooperative in nature (Slavin, 1980).

Specific successful cooperative learning techniques include Group Investigation (Sharan, 1980), which involves intergroup competition based on intergroup cooperation; Jigsaw (Aronson, Blaney, Stephan, Sikes, & Snapp, 1978), which is a structured peer tutoring program for heterogeneous students; and Teams-Games-Tournaments and Student Teams-Achievement Divisions, both developed at Johns Hopkins University (Slavin, 1978, 1980). Slavin (1979) has described how to structure cooperative interaction among students. In multiracial learning teams, "students work together to learn academic material. Individual quiz scores on the material are combined to form a team score, the most successful teams gaining recognition" (Slavin, 1979). Slavin and his colleagues discovered improved racial attitudes and behaviors and learning in the classrooms they studied that employed student team learning groups.

Crain, Mahard, and Narot (1982) present a second instructional practice option currently under evaluation: individualization of curriculum through computerized instruction. This allows matching of the student to the curriculum and provides immediate feedback to the student. Their study of this technique was limited because the instructional use of computers was not widely institutionalized when they were gathering data for their research. They did find, however, that the use of electronic media for instruction was a practice that was widespread and one that had positive effects on achievement—if the available equipment was handled by an audiovisual expert who could assist in the proper use of the media. They believe the higher student achievement found in schools with such media is attributable to increased student involvement not present in most other kinds of class work.

The goal of quality instructional practice is to match the students to the curriculum in order to maximize academic achievement and provide opportunities for positive interracial contact (Forehand & Ragosta, 1976). It is important to stress that various strategies may be implemented to achieve this goal and a variety of learning situations can be considered within a particular setting. For example, MacKenzie (1983) cites an instance of a school district mixing strategies in the following way: instruction was carried out with the whole class at grade level and with small groups at a student's individual level. Whatever instructional strategies are implemented by a school to enhance the quality of education, they should increase academic achievement and encourage interracial contact.

Assessment of Students

The issue of quality education, which has been raised by the struggle to integrate the public schools, leads us to examine an issue of vital importance for students. Educational and psychological testing is still one of the most controversial and complex issues for school officials because of its effect on minority children. Miller

(1974) has identified the major problems as: (1) the disparities in standardized test scores between black and white youth (2) the intense interest in whether desegregation has a positive effect on achievement scores of all students, and (3) the appropriateness of grouping by ability.

The way in which a testing program is conducted is critical to the school. Equal treatment in a desegregated school cannot be accomplished if the testing program makes invidious comparisons of groups and if classrooms are organized on the basis of test results. Testing can and should be used as a diagnostic and prescriptive tool for teaching and learning and as a management tool to help keep schools on target in terms of achievement. However, evaluation procedures must avoid labeling, sorting, and tracking. If testing programs or other screening devices encourage the emergence of segregated classrooms within desegregated schools, the chances of integration are remote.

In the final analysis, the function of assessment and the impact of testing on students are still not clearly understood. The controversies and problems revolve around state education competency tests, standardized tests versus criterion-referenced tests, and the notion that schools should be held accountable for student learning and achievement.

The Staff

One of the most important factors to consider when discussing quality education is the quality and effectiveness of the educational staff. The curriculum we recommend for a quality education is representative of the ethnic diversity of our society. Likewise, we believe that the educational staffs in our schools should represent this diversity as well.

Research supports the notion that teaching staffs are more effective when they are desegregated. Minority students in schools with desegregated teaching staffs are less likely to face discriminatory behavior, will have higher staff expectations for their performance, are less likely to face discrimination through assignment to ability groups and in the grades they receive, and are less likely to be alienated from school (Hawley et al., 1981). The national desegregation experts with whom Hawley and his staff conducted interviews stressed the importance of having desegregated staffs in order to provide role models for minority students. Forehand and Ragosta (1976) emphasized the importance of having a

desegregated staff, particularly as a positive race relations model for all students to emulate. An integrated staff whose minority members have positions of status and prestige equal to majority staff will provide a model for equality.

In-Service Training

An important way to improve educational quality is to improve the effectiveness of the educational staff. Continuous well-planned and well-implemented staff development programs are the means through which staff quality and effectiveness can be improved. Research studies that attempt to identify the key components of effective schools indicate that staff development focusing on teachers' expectations, teaching strategies, classroom management, and instructional practices is a key ingredient in promoting school success (MacKenzie, 1983; Hawley et al., 1981).

Researchers and practitioners agree that, while in-service training is important for teachers, administrators, school boards, and all supporting staff (Orfield, 1975; Forehand & Ragosta, 1976; and Porter, 1979), teachers are the group who have the greatest need for in-service training. They face the demands of teaching children in classes that are heterogeneously grouped, of teaching children who may have been subject to substandard teaching, and of identifying the kinds of changes that must be made in schools.

In general, the goals of general in-service training and "desegregation-specific" in-service training are the same. These can be placed in the categories of improving student achievement, interpersonal relationships, classroom management and discipline techniques, and "stimulating curricular innovation" (Hawley et al., 1981). Specifically, as a result of desegregated settings, Hawley calls for training related to (1) instructional methods that will improve achievement, particularly minority achievement, in classrooms that have become more heterogeneous (for example, techniques for cooperative learning, small-group or individual instruction, team teaching); (2) reevaluating curricula and development and teaching of multiethnic and multicultural curricula; (3) increasing self-awareness of race-related attitudes and behavior vital to improving student relations; (4) dealing with classroom behavior; and (5) ways to promote parent involvement in schools (see Hawley et al, Vol. I, 1981).

King, Carney, and Strasz (1980) identified strategies for improving race relations and fostering an atmosphere for equal educational opportunity that were perceived by school and community representatives as effective. Based on their interpretations of interview and survey data and the integration of these data with relevant literature of desegregation, the authors proposed that there should be a heavy emphasis on multicultural education as well as on the content area subjects. In-service education must be continuous and reflect both of these aims to promote excellence in education.

Summary

We have emphasized that desegregation is preferable to segregation in achieving an equitable, quality education. The desegregation movement should have three focal points:

- The reduction in minority group student isolation

- The prevention of racial inequality in desegregated schools

- The provision of quality education to all students

Unfortunately, racial composition rather than the desegregation process that leads to quality often has been emphasized. We have indicated that this occurs because observers and participants in desegregation characterize the phenomenon as an event rather than a process. However, the emerging trend is to shift desegregation efforts to the tripartite focus just listed. The process of an equitable, quality education requires (1) a school organization that allows some choice by parents and students about the programs they wish to take, (2) an appropriate curriculum that provides both the necessary skills and a multicultural emphasis appropriate to achieving educational excellence, (3) instruction practices that provide for interracial cooperative experiences on an equal status basis, (4) a varied staff that has achieved excellence in administering a school and teaching a diverse student body and has high expectations for all students, (5) testing procedures that assist teachers in correctly diagnosing and evaluating students in order to maximize learning, and (6) pre-service and in-service training to maintain excellence and to meet the instructional needs of all students.

The trend toward school improvement through desegregation is a healthy development in education. In the last decade, we have learned how to improve education and provide equality of opportunity at the same time. Refinements of the process are needed and the process needs to be adapted to each district, but we need to apply the lessons of successful experiences to those areas, particularly in urban settings, that are still in trouble.

REFERENCES

Alkin, M. C. (1983, April). *Magnet school programs evaluation: assessing a desegregation effort.* Paper presented at the annual meeting of the American Educational Research Association, Montreal, Quebec.

Aronson, E., Blaney, N., Stephan, C., Sikes, J. & Snapp, M. (1978). *The jigsaw classroom.* Beverly Hills, CA: Sage Publications.

Banks, J. A. (1979a). Shaping the future of multicultural education, *The Journal of Negro Education, 48*(3), 237-252.

Banks, J. A. (1979b). *Teaching strategies for ethnic studies* (2nd ed.) Boston: Allyn and Bacon.

Banks, J. A. (1982). Educating minority youth: An inventory of current theory, *Education and Urban Society, 15*(1), 88-103.

Bell, D. (1983). Learning from our losses: Is school desegregation still feasible in the 1980's? *Phi Delta Kappan, 64*(8), 572-575.

Blank, R. K., Dentler, R. A., Baltzell, D.C. & Chabotar, K. (1983). *Survey of magnet schools: Analyzing a model for quality integrated education.* Chicago: James Lowry and Associates.

Borton, B. H. (1982). *Magnet school program: evaluation report 1980-81.* Milwaukee, WI: Milwaukee Public Schools

Brown v. Board of Education of Topeka, 347 U.S. 483 (1954).

Coleman, J. S., Campbell, E. O., Hobson, C. J., McPartland, J., Mood, A. M., Weinfield, D. & York, R.L. (1966). *Equality of educational opportunity.* Washington, DC: U.S. Government Printing Office.

Cortes, C. (1979, July). *From desegregated schools to integrated education.* Paper presented at the Urban Educational National Conference, Milwaukee, WI.

Crain, R. L., Mahard, R. & Narot, R. (1982). *Making desegregation work.* Cambridge, MA: Balinger Publishing Company.

Fleming, D. S., Blank, R. K., Dentler, R. A. & Baltzell, D. C. (1983). *Survey of magnet schools, interim report.* Chicago: J. H. Lowry and Associates.

Forehand, G. & Ragosta, M. (1976). *A handbook for integrated schooling.* Princeton, NJ: Educational Testing Service.

Glenn, C. (1985). *Equity, choice and effective urban education: a focus on schools* (Publication No. 13988-195-3-85). Quincy, MA: Massachusetts Department of Education, Bureau of Equal Educational Opportunity.

Hawley, W. D. (1982). Effective educational strategies for desegregated schools. *Peabody Journal of Education, 59*(4), 209-233.

Hawley, W., Crain, R. L., Rossell, C. H., Fernandez, R. R., Schofield, J.W., Smylie, M. A., Tompkins, R., Trent, W. T. & Zlotkin, M. S. (1981). *Assessment of current knowledge about the effectiveness of school desegregation strategies* (Vol. 1, pp. 144-167). Nashville, TN: Center for Education and Human Development Policy, Institute for Public Policy Studies.

Jencks, C. (Ed.) (1972). *Inequality: A reassessment of the effects of family and schooling in America.* New York: Basic Books.

King, N. J. (Ed.). (1977). *Title IV of the Civil Rights Act of 1964: Expansion of program responsibilities* (R-2136-HEW). Los Angeles, CA: The Rand Corporation.

King, N. J., Carney, M. & Strasz, C. (1980). *Staff development programs in desegregated settings* (R-2539-NIE). Los Angeles, CA: The Rand Corporation.

Larson, J. C. (1980). *Tacoma Park magnet school evaluation: Part I.* Rockville, MD: Montgomery County Public Schools.

REFERENCES

MacKenzie, D. E. (1983). Research for school improvement: An appraisal of some recent trends. *Educational Researcher, 12*(4), 5-18.

Miller, L. P. (Ed.). (1974). *The testing of black students: A symposium.* Englewood Cliffs, NJ: Prentice-Hall.

Miller, L. P. (1982). Black education. In H. E. Mitzel (Ed.). *Encyclopedia of Educational Research* (5th ed.). (pp. 211-219). New York: The Free Press.

Milliken v. Bradley, 433 U.S. 267 (1977).

Orfield, G. (1975). How to make desegregation work: The adaptation of schools to their newly-integrated student bodies. *Law and Contemporary Problems, 39*(2), 314-340.

Orfield, G. (1983). *School desegregation patterns in the states, large cities and metropolitan areas, 1968-1980. A report to the Subcommittee on Civil and Constitutional Rights of the Committee on the Judiciary of the U.S. House of Representatives.* Washington, DC: Joint Center for Political Studies.

Plessy v. Ferguson, 163 U.S. 537 (1896).

Porter, J. (1979). *A policy statement on urban school desegregation.* Denver, CO: National Project and Task Force on Desegregation Strategies.

Price-Curtiss, W. (1981). Black progress towards educational equity. *Educational Leadership, 38*(4), 277-280.

Royster, E. C., Baltzell, F. C. & Simmons, F. C. (1979). *Study of the Emergency School Aid Act magnet school program.* Cambridge, MA: Abt Associates.

Sagar, H. A. & Schofield, J. W. (1979). Integrating the desegregated school: Perspectives, practices and possibilities. In M. L. Wax (Ed.), *When schools are desegregated: Problems and possibilities for students, educators, parents and the community.* New York: Academic Press.

Salomone, R. C. (in press). *Public policy and the law: Legal precedents and prospects for equity in education.* New York: New York University, Coalition for Equity.

Scherer, J. & Slawski, E. J. (1979). Coping with desegregation: Individual strategies and organizational compliance. In M. L. Wax (ed.), *When schools are desegregated: Problems and possibilities for students, educators, parents and the community.* New York: Academic Press.

Sharan, S. (1980). Cooperative learning in small groups: Recent methods and effects on achievement, attitudes, and ethnic relations. *Review of Educational Research, 50,* 241-271.

Slavin, R. (1978). Student teams and comparisons among equals: Effects on academic performance and student attitudes. *Journal of Educational Psychology, 7,* 532-538.

Slavin, R. (1979). Integrating the desegregated classroom: Action speaks louder than words. *Educational Leadership 36*(5), 322-324.

Slavin, R. (1980). Cooperative learning. *Review of Educational Research, 50,* 315-342.

The Task Force on Education for Growth. (1983). *Action for excellence.* Denver, CO: Education Commission of the States.

Von Euler, M. & Parham, D. L. (1978). *The citizen's guide to school desegregation law.* Washington, DC: National Institute of Education.

Weber, L. J., McBee, J. K. & Lyles, J. H. (1983, April). *An evaluation of fundamental schools.* Paper presented at the annual meeting of the American Educational Research Association, Montreal, Quebec.

PART III
Legal Perspectives

Featured Address

Desegregation: Challenges and Responsibilities

ROBERT L. CARTER

On May 17, 1954, the United States Supreme Court outlawed racial segregation in the nation's public schools. The basic thrust of the *Brown* decision was that an integrated setting was essential to the delivery of equal educational opportunities (*Brown* v. *Board of Education*, 1954).

Almost the entire country applauded *Brown*. There was resistance to the decision in the parts of the South. But even there, opposition to the principle it enunciated was not uniform, though *Brown* had doomed the dual school system that had often been touted as basic to the maintenance of southern values and culture. *Brown* is one of the peaks of American jurisprudence because in stating the guarantee of equality as fundamental to our basic law, it expresses the loftiest values in our society. In assuming that the system could move more or less routinely, in conformity with the highest ethical considerations, the decision uplifts the spirit for it depicts us as we like to view ourselves. The *Brown* decision eased, for the moment at least, deep felt fears of an irreconcilable division in our society along racial lines. As a hortatory appeal to conscience, *Brown* remains a historic statement in American law.

However, in the area of our interest and concerns, that is education, *Brown* has not fared so well. Few dispute the black child's right to equal education, yet more black children are attending all-black or virtually all-black schools than was true before the *Brown* decision.

Although the pre-*Brown* black and white dual school system is no longer with us, in the urban North and West and now in the desegregated urban South, the neighborhood schools policy has produced and perpetuated black-white school separation as effectively as did the dual school system. Because of this policy, racial segregation has increased in the past thirty years. By and large, black students are now concentrated in a small number of large urban school districts across the country where they constitute a majority of the school population. In 1980, two-thirds of the students in the nation's ten largest districts were minorities, and according to a University of Chicago study, that ratio is rising steadily. Segregation has been eased or eliminated in many parts of the south, but severe school segregation now occurs in the northern and southern cities that have the highest percentages of minority children. For black and Hispanic students in these cities, all-minority schools are still the norm. For example, in Illinois in the 1980–81 school term, 68 percent of the black students attended schools where at least 90 percent of the students were members of minority groups. The same profile exists in Michigan, New York, New Jersey, Virginia, Washington, D.C., and Pennsylvania because most of the black and Hispanic public school students in each of these states are concentrated in that state's largest school district.

While there is no intradistrict disparity between predominantly black and predominantly white schools in per-pupil expenditures, as was true under the dual school system, one of the chief consequences of the neighborhood school policy has been that the schools reflect the socioeconomic characteristics of the neighborhoods they serve. The result is schools of high and low quality with a direct correlation between the quality of the educational product and the socioeconomic status of the neighborhood served. In the classroom, the neighborhood school policy mirrors the socioeconomic and racial stratification characteristics of the residential patterns of the community. Unfortunately, this pattern of school organization throughout urban America denies poor blacks access to equal educational opportunities almost as effectively as they were denied under the dual school system of the South. Today, black children are receiving segregated and unequal education.

While in the 1950s and early 1960s some protested that this inequality was not true in the urban North, professional educators

HONORABLE ROBERT L. CARTER is Judge, United States District Court for the Southern District of New York. As counsel of the National Association for the Advancement of Colored People, he argued the Brown v. *Board of Education* case.

are now conceding that where school organization is superimposed on patterns of residential segregation, the schools for the black poor are not producing quality education on a par with schools for middle-class whites.

In 1955, the New York City Board of Education, which had been assuring the public that quality education was being offered in schools of high black and Hispanic concentration equal to that offered in schools serving white middle-class areas, was prodded into authorizing a study by the Public Education Association to settle the question. That study revealed what common sense had long perceived—the schools of black and Puerto Rican majorities were not equal in educational quality to schools of white middle-class concentration. The study compared the schools on the basis of composite scores made on standardized citywide achievement tests. This study showed that majority black–Hispanic schools were roughly one half a year behind the predominantly white middle-class schools in the three Rs at the fourth grade, one and a half years behind at the sixth grade, and a staggering two and a half years behind at the eighth grade. Some ten years later, a new survey revealed that there had been no substantial change. Moreover, this bleak phenomenon is not limited to New York City, but is typical of all school systems where de facto segregation is operative. While I am certain none of this is new and certainly should not be a surprise to any of you in attendance at this conference, I remind you of it because educators, particularly those in public education, seem to have selective recall about unpleasant facts of this kind and do not want to face up to the harsh reality implied by such data.

Not long ago, an uneducated man could rise to fame and fortune in the United States through the use of ingenuity and industry. While these instances have been rare, such occurrences have helped further and perpetuate an American myth that each individual was in full control of his fate, that with determination and will an American man (I don't believe women were embraced in this legend) could find his way to the moon. Today, few hold that belief. We know in 1984 that this is pure fantasy. We now live in a highly mechanized society where economic success is functionally related to education. Our economy has become largely service-oriented, and increasing reliance on sophisticated computer technology in the business community requires knowledge obtainable only through a fairly rigorous academic program. To put it more precisely perhaps, the gateway to a skilled job is a thorough education in rudimentary academics—the higher the skill, the greater the necessary academic grasp. Thus, today, as never before, education is the key to employability, and meaningful employment is the passport to the bounty of our society. Indeed, there is growing concern as to whether our educational system is strong enough to continue to develop the intelligence and skills to enable us to remain competitive throughout the world in an era where computer technology will be dominant.

Because of the very real correlation between academic skills and employment, and income and anti-social conduct, a good education is virtually indispensable for all Americans. Education has traditionally been the avenue of upward mobility in American life and as such is perhaps a more urgent necessity for blacks than for whites. Blacks have made vast strides in the last thirty years in catching up with the general population in terms of literacy, years of completed schooling, and college attendance. Still, the system of financial rewards based on education for blacks differs from the one operative for whites. For example, the most recent data reveal that in families headed by high school graduates, 48 percent of the blacks as compared to 26 percent of the whites have incomes under 15,000 dollars. In families where the head of household has completed four years of college, 9 percent of the blacks as compared to 21 percent of the whites have incomes of 50,000 dollars or more. Indeed, the income distribution among black families whose heads of household completed four years of college parallels the income distribution of white families headed by high school graduates. Because of this wide disparity in rewards, a good education is essential to black survival. The demand for equal educational opportunities is now so economically necessary that it can be classified as one of the "basic" civil rights.

Moreover, education also bears a close relationship to the noneconomic needs of a democratic society. Without it there can be no intelligent use of the franchise and reliance cannot be placed on the first amendment to ensure effective public influence on decision-making processes. When the United States Supreme Court decided Brown v. Board of Education, it described education as necessary to the maintenance of a democratic society and as a requisite for personal success.

There is substantial agreement that a racially integrated education, as opposed to a segregated one, has certain identifiable characteristics that are more consistent with the underlying philosophies and principles of this society. Integration educates white and black students equally in the fundamental of racial tolerance and understanding. Learning to live interracially is, or in a democracy should be, a vital component in every student's experience.

I quote from a speech by Senator Charles Sumner on the Senate floor in 1872 in which he gave his reasons for favoring integrated education and opposing separate schools for black children.

The senator said:

The child is not trained in the way he should go; for he is trained under the ban of inequality. How can he grow up to the stature of equal citizenship? He is pinched and dwarfed while the stigma of color is stamped upon him...

Nor is separation without evil to the whites. The prejudice of color is nursed when it should be stifled...the school itself must practice the lesson [of equality]. Children learn by example more than by precept. How precious the example which teaches that all are equal in rights. But this can be only where all commingle in the common school as in common citizenship...There should be no separate school. It is not enough that all should be taught alike; they must all be taught together...nor can they receive equal quantities of knowledge in the same way, except at the common school.

Our educators should be constructing a bridge based on the democratic and constitutional principles connecting whites and blacks and designed to lead the two races, starting with young children, to a harmonious, peaceful, civilized existence. That bridge should be a plan for equal educational opportunities for all in an integrated, unitary public school system, with school officials affirmatively seeking in good faith and with dedication ways to make the plan work. Unhappily few public school authorities have viewed this as their ultimate responsibility.

Post-*Brown* pressure for desegregation in northern communities began as early as 1955. The elimination of racial concentration was proposed through school pairings, redrawing of attendance lines, site selection with the object of improving integration, busing, the development of magnet schools, and merging of school districts. There were even proposals that schools be located on a campus setting and all children would attend schools on this campus. This would, of course, have made desegregation easy. Most of these proposals were practicable but few northern school districts would accept them because they departed from the neighborhood school even though adherence to that policy kept segregation firmly entrenched. Nor were there meaningful steps taken to upgrade academic levels in the predominately black and Hispanic schools.

Thus, civil rights lawyers turned to the courts. At first the courts were not sympathetic, but gradually some successes were achieved. Over the last decade, the courts rather than school administrators have been in the forefront of the effort to fashion viable remedies to alleviate the racial isolation of nonwhite minority school children in northern communities and to eliminate the educational deficiencies that plague the schools those children attend. Public school authorities, instead of aiding these efforts or offering solutions of their own, have generally reacted with suspicion and hostility.

We all profess to accept the value of integrated education and to favor equal education for all, but resistance to the implementation of programs to achieve these goals has been fierce and unrelenting. Resistance has centered on busing—indeed, in almost every election year, Congress tacks a rider on legislation in order to bar the use of federal funds for busing to achieve integration. White parents are convinced that the quality of their children's education will suffer once the schools are integrated. No studies that I know have established that integration lowers the quality of education. Indeed, some studies have revealed the contrary. Nonetheless, whites have fled from central cities to the suburbs seeking better schooling for their children, and most of those who remain have taken their children out of the public schools.

Few professional educators have provided needed leadership to secure public acceptance of school integration as a desired goal in public education. They have excused their outright resistance to desegregation efforts and their timidity about proposing solutions to ease racial isolation by voicing concern about white flight. Though white flight is a problem, courageous leadership from educational authorities might calm the fears and concerns of middle-class families and keep them in school systems containing sizable minority populations. Unfortunately, the negative approach of public school authorities to school integration has legitimated white as well as black middle-class desertion of urban public school systems.

School authorities are prone to attribute the failure of predominantly black schools to keep children at grade level in the three Rs to causes over which the public school has no control: socioeconomic factors, incidents of family life, the child's background, deprivations and disabilities. This thesis places no responsibility on poor school administration, inadequate or indifferent teaching performance, or racist perceptions and expectations. Acceptance of the thesis that educational deprivations are the product of social-class factors means that since these educational deficiencies are predetermined by class, there is little hope of the black underclass ever achieving equal educational opportunity.

The quality and distribution of public education depends in great part on political power. Since the white middle class holds the dominant and controlling political power, it is able to corner for itself a disproportionate share of available educational resources, thus ensuring the perpetuation of its dominant authority. This analysis may not provide much optimism about poor blacks securing equal educational opportunity. There is a great difference, however, between focusing on the privileges and prerogatives of power as the link to educational deprivation, rather than on the personal weakness of the black child, for then one may conclude that much of the fault lies in the unequal distribution of educational resources rather than in the innate character of the black poor.

Two Supreme Court decisions have dealt a heavy blow to hopes of either achieving full integration of inner-city school systems through metropolitan school districting or of securing equal funding for school districts with a majority of poor black and Hispanic pupils. By requiring state governments to assume full responsibility for all educational expenditures, the Court held that there is no constitutional requirement that largely white school districts surrounding the central city be merged with city school districts to achieve integration. In the second case, the Court upheld the traditional state educational funding formula where the state provides a minimum basic funding floor for public schools. Local school districts supplement these state funds from taxes raised in the various school districts. This formula has produced wide disparities in per-pupil expenditures between affluent white suburban districts and districts populated by poor black and Hispanic children.

Brown has not been successful in securing an integrated education for black and Hispanic children. The fight for school integration and for quality education for black children coupled with the failure of educators to deal successfully with the problem has revealed serious weaknesses in the public school system as a whole. The recent report of the National Commission on Excellence in Education, entitled *A Nation at Risk: The Imperatives for Education Reform,* stated, "If an unfriendly foreign power had attempted to impose on Americans the mediocre educational performance that exists today, we might well have viewed it as an act of war. As it is we have allowed it to happen to ourselves."

Public education has been put on the defensive. Sparked perhaps by this report, there appears to be a growing nationwide recognition of the need to upgrade public education. Blacks have been demanding principal and teacher accountability measured by the academic mastery the children achieve. This concept is basic to the general educational reforms now being proposed. Steps are being taken throughout the country to infuse greater academic rigor into the classroom and to raise the standards for certifying teachers. Some school districts are establishing educational objectives that must be met at each grade. Some are seeking to raise teachers' salaries, but to tie the increases to performance yardsticks. These proposals all focus on developing systems that turn out children who can demonstrate that they have reached a certain acceptable level of academic achievement. Some states seem ready to provide funds and controls to ensure a satisfactory statewide public educational system, thereby voluntarily assuming the responsibility for eliminating interdistrict disparities in per-pupil expenditures—a responsibility the Supreme Court refuses to impose. The irony is that some of the proposals now being favored to improve the academic quality of the public school system as a whole were rejected as unworkable when they were suggested as a means to improve the quality of education in predominantly minority schools.

The picture does not lack bright spots, however. Blacks have made some educational gains in the thirty-year span since 1954. Overall, between 1960 and 1981, black males made gains of 4.4 years of schooling completed compared to a gain of

1.9 years for white males. Black females showed gains of 3.5 years of completed schooling compared to a 1.3 year gain among white females. Thus, the 1981 median level of schooling for both black males and females was above 12 years, and the gap in schooling between blacks and whites was only a half a year. And between 1980 and 1981, the median years of schooling completed increased slightly for blacks (1 percent) and stayed the same for whites.

Illiteracy for blacks has also dropped dramatically. In 1959, for persons between fourteen and forty-five years of age, 63 per thousand blacks as compared to 13 per thousand whites were illiterate. By 1979 the figure had dropped to seven per thousand for blacks and four per thousand for whites. Thus in 1959, 50 more blacks per thousand were illiterate than whites. By 1979 that gap had closed to three.

Since 1968 the dropout rate for blacks has decreased while remaining relatively constant for whites—in 1968 the dropout rate among fourteen to twenty-four year olds was 21.6 percent for blacks and 11.9 percent for whites. By 1981 the black dropout rate had fallen to 15.4 percent while the white dropout rate had been slightly lowered to 11.3 percent. Thus the gap between the two groups was 4.1 percent in 1979.

The figures for college enrollment cause concern. In 1970, 260 per thousand black high school graduates enrolled in college. By 1975 the rate had increased to 320 per thousand, about equal to the white rate. Unhappily, the 1981 figure for blacks had dropped to 280 per thousand and the white rate had moved to 330.

Integrated education or even equal educational opportunities in the separate schools remains beyond the reach of most poor black and Hispanic children today. The extent and depth of racism is so pervasive that its force alone is undoubtedly responsible for *Brown's* failure to achieve educational remediation for black children. Let me give you an example that crystallizes the problem.

You have all probably heard of the experiment done some years ago by a Harvard professor, then at the University of California, in which he told a group of teachers that certain of their students were bright and others not so bright. This was, you may recall, an arbitrary classification made by the professor, who had no idea about the intellectual capacity of any of these children. The teachers accepted his designation as an established fact. The

teachers proceeded to give the children designated "bright" their full attention and wasted little time with those designated "not so bright"—indeed they dismissed the latter as dullards. Some years later, two professors tried a similar experiment in multiracial classrooms in Illinois. They told the teachers—who were white—that some white children were gifted and some black children were gifted and some in both groups were slow learners. The results will probably surprise you. Both groups of white children received better treatment and more attention than either black group. But the gifted black children were treated worst—criticized constantly and dealt with more harshly than the others. It is even more depressing that the white teachers involved reacted uniformly and some were young.

The basic insights these studies afford as to the real nature of the race problem in this country were not perceived in 1954 and in many places are not understood even today. We felt in 1954 that racial segregation was the basic evil and we welcomed *Brown* because it seemed to rid us of this problem in one easy stroke. However, what makes the race problem so intractable is white supremacy: it must be conquered before the racial problems that plague us are resolved. *Brown* is important because it made the real problem more visible than it had been before.

This country has taken white supremacy so much for granted that it may be difficult to understand the stress I place on it. After all, the country is predominantly white, and nothing is wrong with white supremacy, one could say, as long as nonwhite minorities are accorded their rights. However, nonwhite minorities will not be fully granted their rights unless white supremacy is dealt with, because white supremacy refuses to accept the notion of white–black equality or the right of blacks to equal access and an equal share. Whites are determined to have the best and the most, and whites believe that blacks are entitled to and satisfied with less. And when, as now, limited resources may mean that black access results in white denial, a solution becomes even more problematic. No dominant group in history has ever been known to relinquish its prerogatives of power and privilege voluntarily. Moreover, the problem becomes magnified almost beyond redress because, as Louis Harris states in the *Anguish of Change* (1973), blacks and whites do not like each other as groups.

Brown has contributed to the visibility, if not the intensification of this group disaffection. The sedateness and ritualistic protocol

that used to mark racial encounters have been replaced with cacophony, rudeness, and open disdain. Fear and unease on the part of whites have always been there but masked by fantasy and a refusal to face the truth. Blacks have always been resentful. Scratch a black skin and you will uncover antiwhite feelings, and the deeper you probe, the more you expose the vehemence of these sentiments. Before *Brown*, these feelings were masked and kept under control. Black inferiority is a fact of life in America—an inferiority imposed by the majority—but before *Brown*, this imposed inferiority was accepted by both groups as manifesting the theoretical truth of innate inferiority.

Brown changed all that, at least for blacks, and altered the psychological pattern of race relations. By mandating equality for blacks as constitutionally guaranteed, at least in all the public reaches of American life, *Brown* revolutionized race relations in this country. Heretofore, being black had been a mark of oppression—a curse. After *Brown*, being a "Negro" went out of fashion. Negroes became black. Since they were equal under the law to whites, blacks could accept their blackness, their physical differences from whites, without hurt or shame. Blacks were able to free themselves of a heavy burden. They could feel better about themselves.

Blacks have now become convinced that they alone must control their own destiny. They have little faith in white institutions or that any white-controlled instrumentality will fully support their continuing drive for equal rights. This alienation and dissatisfaction has intensified over the past four years. There will be no solution to this critical problem as long as blacks and whites live in isolated communities and attend separate schools in their formative years. Integrated education should be a high priority on the national agenda.

However, in the near future, integration certainly will not be achieved in large city school districts, where housing segregation has created large black and Hispanic ghettos. Moreover, there is no will to deal with these troublesome demographic factors to achieve integration. In these districts, it is essential to find the means to uplift the level of educational quality in the inner-city schools.

This task is not easy, but at least we now know that success, sometimes spectacular success, can be achieved. Schools in low socioeconomic and racially isolated settings can match and even exceed national norms. We also know that principals with whole schools and particular teachers in individual classrooms are able to secure high achievement among students year after year. What has not been mastered is a successful method of packaging these successes so that they can be reproduced on a mass scale.

Integration should be the goal of all American public school systems. School administrators should seek to achieve it because it is right and because it promises to remove the racial divisions that have plagued us for so long. Where full and complete integration cannot be achieved, affirmative programs should be fostered to alleviate racial isolation to the greatest extent possible and to produce high-quality education in minority schools. The objective of the professional public educator should be to devise the means to provide and ensure meaningful integration in the public school system and quality education throughout. That goal should be embraced with enthusiasm and pursued with vigor. The stakes are high. Our future may depend on the extent to which this responsibility is accepted as the ultimate obligation of public school authorities.

REFERENCES

Brown v. Board of Education of Topeka, 347 U.S. 483 (1954).

Center for the Study of Social Policy. (1983). A dream deferred: Economic status of black Americans. Pamphlet.

Harris, L. (1973). *The anguish of change.* New York: Norton.

Legal Perspectives and the Future of Desegregation

JULIUS L. CHAMBERS

In reflecting on school desegregation over the past thirty years, perhaps one should begin by noting that many of the arguments advanced today by those who seek to impede desegregation are similar to those used by opponents of *Brown* v. *Board of Education* (1954) and its implementation. One wonders why we continue to give credence to arguments many of us thought had been effectively rejected years ago. One is reminded of the admonition of Alexander Bickel, constitutional scholar and Yale law professor, who wrote that sustained opposition to desegregation may eventually prevail (Bickel, 1962).

Yet, it is true that times have changed since *Brown*. People's attitudes have changed as have the resources available and the issues being addressed. Today, no one questions, at least publicly, the right of black students to equal educational opportunities. The question more likely to be debated is the extent of the states' obligation to ensure that right.

Attitudes have changed. Advocates of desegregation are more informed regarding their rights. They insist, rightfully, on more than just the mixing of black and white students. Black and white parents, in voicing their concerns, are more aware of the meaning and implications of desegregation programs. At the same time, opponents seek to use, without explanation or analysis, the sometimes uneven results in desegregated school systems to argue for more limited desegregation.

Resources have changed. The army of lawyers and funds that were available to promote desegregation in the past, though never fully adequate, have decreased sharply. Of necessity, private attorneys have had to turn to more remunerative practices. Public interest law firms, such as the NAACP Legal Defense Fund, have had to divert already limited resources to other areas. The previous support from the U.S. Department of Justice has, particularly during the past four years, turned into active opposition. Many who sincerely desire desegregated education are left without adequate legal support.

Issues have changed. In the early stages of the implementation of *Brown*, the issue was clear: to end the total, or almost total, exclusion of black students and teachers from various public schools. Even as we progressed from *Brown* in 1954 to a unanimous Supreme Court decision in *Swann* v. *Charlotte-Mecklenburg Board of Education* in 1971, we were still dealing with practices and policies that effectively excluded black students and teachers from some schools. However, as we achieved some success with respect to exclusion, other issues arose and multiplied—many not as clear-cut. Some examples follow:

■ To what extent must a school system affirmatively mix students by race in order to discharge its responsibility?

■ Is assigning students according to race and by percentage consistent with the Constitution?

■ What factors in addition to race should a court consider in devising and ordering desegregation plans?

■ What about the racial composition of individual classes? The qualifications and attitudes of teachers and administrators? The types and quality of educational programs offered? The funds provided for individual schools; their comparison with other schools in the system; and comparisons with other school systems?

■ Is interdistrict relief appropriate or desirable?

■ What has been the effect of prior discrimination on the achievement levels of black students?

■ Are students being taught what they need to know in order to enter future job markets?

In short, the issues are more numerous, more complex, and much more expensive to address. Additionally, the courts are less receptive to establishing new grounds for substantive liability or relief. Today, before

JULIUS L. CHAMBERS is Director-Counsel, National Association for the Advancement of Colored People Legal Defense and Educational Fund, Inc.

undertaking school desegregation litigation, one must consider carefully the facts of each case and must have very specific remedies in mind.

I have been and remain an ardent advocate of school desegregation. I have had the opportunity to observe how changing a school system can change a whole community. State-imposed segregation has disappeared from virtually all walks of life in Charlotte, North Carolina, where I spent twenty years practicing civil rights law.

The Charlotte-Mecklenburg school system has become, I believe, the most desegregated system in the nation. While some race-related problems remain, desegregation has benefited not only the school system, but the community and all its citizens. Schools can and do affect the whole community. When the Supreme Court unanimously upheld court-ordered busing in Charlotte-Mecklenburg in its 1971 decision in *Swann*, Chief Justice Warren Burger said that school desegregation cases were limited in their ability to affect areas other than education. In light of the experience of Charlotte-Mecklenburg, I question that observation.

With these thoughts in mind, I would like to suggest several areas of consideration for future school desegregation litigation.

First, how do we deal with efforts by the Justice Department that would overturn legally established principles governing relief? The department challenges the appropriateness of traditional remedies even where *de jure* segregation has been established. It contends that some remedies require direct proof of intentional segregation. This is contrary to three Supreme Court decisions: *Keyes* v. *School Board of Denver* (1973), which shifted the burden of proof from complainants to defendant school officials once segregative intent was proved in a significant part of a school district; and *Dayton Board of Education* v. *Brinkman* (1977), *Columbus Board of Education* v. *Penick* (1978), the latter of which found that the failure of intentionally segregated school systems to take effective steps to desegregate constituted proof of continuing discrimination.

In the future, as we develop remedies in desegregation cases, we must address practices that have a disproportionately negative impact on blacks whether or not it can be shown that these practices are intentional. Because of limitations imposed by the Supreme Court in *Washington* v. *Davis*, which changed the standard of proof in discrimination cases from "effect" to "intent," it will be necessary to find factual

situations in both northern and southern school districts that will fit standards established in other Supreme Court cases such as *Keyes*.

Unless we take the initiative in this area, it will become more and more difficult to establish liability in desegregation cases. In several recent cases, federal district courts and courts of appeals have imposed practically impossible standards of proof of intentional discrimination, ignoring intentional acts that have obviously discriminatory consequences.

The limited relief for desegregation that the Justice Department advocates now in Nashville, East Baton Rouge, Norfolk, Charleston, Chicago, and Bakersfield should be challenged. The desegregation plans supported by the Justice Department in these school districts could reinstate the status that existed before or immediately following *Brown*.

This is the case in Norfolk, where the NAACP Legal Defense Fund represents black school children (*Riddick* v. *School Board of the City of Norfolk*, 1984). The district court sanctioned the effort of the Norfolk school board to reinstate neighborhood schools and the LDF appealed. The Justice Department entered the case on the side of the school board. A decision is pending in the Fourth Circuit Court of Appeals. If the position of the school board and the Justice Department prevails, other desegregated school systems may follow suit. The results will be devastating. With the encouragement and active support of the federal government, many of these systems will revert to their pre-*Brown* status.

A second area that must be considered in future litigation is the need for interdistrict relief. Here, even the Supreme Court has ignored history and the natural consequences of state practices. In *Milliken* v. *Bradley*, known as *Milliken I*, the court reviewed a desegregation plan covering public schools in Detroit and adjoining suburbs. It held that a plan that crossed school district lines could not be ordered without proof that violations in one district had significant segregative effect in another district. In other words, there could be no interdistrict relief without proof of intentional interdistrict violations.

Contrast this with the ruling in *Rogers* v. *Lodge* (1982), a case dealing with voting rights violations, in which the Court sanctioned reliance on circumstantial evidence that certain practices lead naturally to discrimination. Clearly, this is a different standard of proof than that demanded by

the Court in school desegregation cases.

Is there a legally justifiable basis for treating school cases differently from voting rights cases? Has the Supreme Court chosen to ignore the substantial role that states play in the operation of public schools? Is the Court sanctioning, in the name of strict construction, racially segregated schools in St. Louis, Detroit, and many other school districts? By its indulgence in school cases, is the Court not keeping communities, housing, public services, and jobs segregated?

A third issue, one which we have only recently begun to address, is the question of what goes on within desegregated schools. Segregation of students within classes through tracking or grouping programs; the absence of bilingual educational programs; disciplinary or other policies that isolate minority students; behavior and attitudes of teachers and administrators; and the quality of educational programs all must be examined to determine if desegregation plans are effective.

Fourth, we have to deal with the fact that, even after completing public school, many minority students are ill-equipped for today's labor market. For example, vocational programs in secondary schools and in junior and community colleges do not meet the needs of minority students. We must challenge discrimination in curricula and in the quality of programs offered to minority students.

Fifth, there is the need to challenge the federal government's contention that federal district courts have no further supervisory jurisdiction over school systems once desegregation plans are in effect. The government finds support for its position in *Swann* v. *Charlotte-Mecklenburg Board of Education*, where the Court indicated that a time would come when racial imbalances might be the result of demographic changes and not intentional segregation. It is a misreading of *Swann* to claim that this finding prevents a district court from revising a defective plan or one that is not being implemented fairly or effectively. School districts should not be absolved of liability or permitted to continue discriminatory practices simply because black children are attending previously all-white schools. District courts must retain jurisdiction to ensure that segregation is eliminated "root and branch."

Sixth, we must remember that desegregation of faculties and school administration is a vital part of any integration plan. In at least three cases, the Supreme Court has noted that the extent of desegregation among school personnel is one index for measuring the general level of integration desired by school officials (*U.S.* v. *Montgomery County; Swann* v. *Charlotte-Mecklenburg Board of Education*; and *Keyes* v. *Denver School Board*). Today, there are serious problems regarding education and certification of black teachers and administrators. Until these problems are solved they will have continuing adverse effects on school desegregation. Current and future litigation should be designed not only to eliminate discrimination in education jobs, but to ensure that blacks are available and qualified for employment in educational systems.

Finally, we see today a growing number of predominantly black urban areas with low tax bases and inadequate funds to support quality public education. In *San Antonio* v. *Rodriguez*, the Supreme Court dealt with one aspect of this problem. *Rodriguez* challenged school-funding practices that had resulted in unequal spending among schools within a district and between school districts. The Court held that a mere showing of unequal spending was not a violation of the equal protection clause of the Fourteenth Amendment. Decisions such as those rendered in *Rodriguez* and in *Milliken I*, if left unchallenged, will accelerate the growth of isolated, inadequately funded black school districts surrounded by white school districts with

more funds and substantially more resources. It is the future business of the NAACP Legal Defense Fund to respond to these rulings and to provide a legal basis for relief.

We seek to develop a challenge to *Rodriguez* that will demonstrate unequal funding based on racial bias or adverse impact based solely on race. We are exploring the possibility of bringing such a challenge in Richmond, Virginia, by emphasizing the role historical discrimination has played in unequal spending in public schools.

The second part to *Milliken* v. *Bradley* (1977), known as *Milliken II*, addressed the special problems experienced by intentionally segregated black schools or school districts. The Supreme Court allowed the district court to determine what additional remedies besides interdistrict relief were appropriate for overcoming the adverse effects of past discrimination. These included a requirement that the state provide additional funds and remedial programs for Detroit's public school children. The Legal Defense Fund has been bringing cases to implement the principles established in *Milliken II*.

Nonetheless, available remedies are insufficient to offset totally the effects of past discrimination. We need a new legal theory. Perhaps it can be established that economic status is a protected classification under the Fourteenth Amendment. Relative to public education, this approach would benefit blacks because of their disproportionate representation at and below the poverty level.

In closing, I will touch briefly on the problem of desegregation in higher education, which warrants a separate discussion. Assaults on affirmative action and the serious difficulties faced by predominantly black or all-black institutions of higher learning remain a priority for the NAACP Legal Defense Fund. The U.S. Department of Education's current position is to provide (1) limited enforcement of Title VI of the Civil Rights Act of 1964 and other statutes and regulations that prohibit discrimination in the allocation and spending of federal funds; (2) limited support for black institutions; and (3) challenges to affirmative-action plans.

We are continuing efforts to define what constitutes effective desegregation in higher education, to enhance black colleges and universities, and to expand and defend the legal framework that supports affirmative action.

Despite the challenges and the setbacks, I remain optimistic that we will continue to make progress in desegregating public education. When we consider the value of desegregation to black students and their parents, and to the country as a whole, the effort is worth the price.

REFERENCES

Bickel, A. (1962). *The least dangerous branch. The Supreme Court at the bar of politics.* New York, N.Y.: Irvington.

Brown v. Board of Education of Topeka, 347 U.S. 483 (1954).

Columbus Board of Education v. Penick, 439 U.S. 1348 (1978).

Dayton Board of Education v. Brinkman, 443 U.S. 526 (1977).

Keyes v. School Board of Denver, 413 U.S. 189 (1973).

Milliken v. Bradley, 418 U.S. 717 (1974).

Milliken v. Bradley, 433 U.S. 267 (1977).

Riddick v. School Board of the City of Norfolk, F. Supp. (1 Va. 1984) Civil Action No. 84–1815, 4th Circuit (appeal pending).

Rogers v. Lodge, 459 U.S. 613 (1982).

San Antonio v. Rodriguez, 411 U.S. 1 (1973).

Swann v. Charlotte-Mecklenburg Board of Education, 402 U.S. 1 (1971).

U.S. v. Montgomery County, 395 U.S. 225 (1969).

Washington v. Davis, 426 U.S. 229 (1976).

Participation by Social Scientists in Litigation Regarding School Desegregation:

Past Contributions and Future Opportunities

STUART W. COOK

Social scientists have participated in litigation related to desegregation in a number of ways. I would like to sketch these briefly and indicate some ways in which social scientists might be useful in the future. Let me begin with an overview of what I shall be discussing.

Our involvement began in the late 1940s and early 1950s when social scientists, led by Kenneth Clark, brought to the attention of the federal courts and eventually to the Supreme Court what we knew at the time about the consequences for children of government-enforced segregation. This was the period in which the NAACP was bringing to a head its challenge to the "separate but equal" doctrine on which school segregation was based. Our involvement at that time peaked in 1954, when the Supreme Court's *Brown* v. *Board of Education* decision held segregation of the public schools to be unconstitutional. According to the second *Brown* decision delivered in 1955, segregation was to be terminated "with all deliberate speed." What was being prohibited was the busing of black children away from their neighborhood schools to more distant, segregated schools.

For the next decade and a half, little desegregation took place. Then, two developments brought a renewed attack on segregation that again involved social scientists. One of these was that the Supreme Court, which in 1955 had ordered desegregation "with all deliberate speed,"

changed its directive to "terminate dual school systems at once." The other was the realization that sending children to neighborhood schools was producing very little desegregation because decades of school segregation had produced neighborhood residential segregation with children attending segregated schools.

This situation led to challenges to the type of school segregation that was based on acts of government in the past. In such cases, legal counsel faced the task of showing that past actions that had produced current segregation reflected official segregative intent even though no official record of this was available. Social science theory was often employed to support this interpretation.

Two subsequent developments initiated the need for a third phase of contributions by social scientists. The first was the observation that after desegregation had been accomplished, powerful social forces might bring about resegregation. Could this be checked, and if so, how? The second development was the evolution of a judicial position that the damage of segregation could not be remedied simply by reassigning children to desegregated schools. Rather, as victims of past discrimination, it was determined that these children had to be compensated by educational programs that would go beyond the simple removal of segregation. What kinds of programs would be most effective?

Let me return, now, to the late 1940s. I recall a personal experience in 1948 that, although it seemed insignificant at the time, has since acquired a certain amount of nostalgia for me. A black youth had been denied admission to the University of Oklahoma Law School on the basis of race. I had gone to testify at the hearing on his suit for admission. My co-witness was a young black sociologist, Robert Weaver. We were excused by the court as having nothing of relevance to say. Reporters caught a symbolic picture of the two of us descending the courthouse stairs on the way home. As some of you know, Weaver went on to become secretary of the Department of Housing and Urban Development. I am certain that the judge excused us on grounds of judicial principle, but I have often wondered whether he ever learned that he had evicted a future member of the U.S. Cabinet.

Eventually, desegregation litigation focused on secondary schools and the prosegregation decisions in five of these cases were appealed to the Supreme Court. The Court consolidated four of the five under the joint title, *Brown* v. *Board of Education*

STUART W. COOK is Professor Emeritus, Department of Psychology, Institute of Behavioral Science, University of Colorado. With Kenneth Clark and Isidor Chein, Dr. Cook prepared the Social Science Statement for the plaintiffs in the *Brown* case.

of Topeka. In each of these cases, the plaintiffs argued that government-enforced segregation of public schools deprived black children of equal educational opportunity, even if tangible school facilities were equal. Cast in constitutional terms, the parents of these children were arguing that a "separate but equal" education deprived them of their rights to equal protection of the law under the Fourteenth Amendment.

Prior to the Court hearing, social scientists, under Dr. Clark's leadership, prepared a review of evidence and theory relevant to the effects of segregation on black children, titled "The Effects of Segregation and the Consequences of Desegregation: A Social Science Statement" (*Brown* v. *Board of Education*, 1954). It began with an examination of the effects of segregation, prejudice, and discrimination, and their social concomitants (such as poor housing, disrupted family life, and other substandard living conditions) on black children. The "Social Science Statement" asserted that, in the course of their development, segregated children learn from their environment that they belong to a group with an inferior status in American society. They react to this knowledge with a sense of humiliation and feelings of inferiority, and often entertain the possibility that they are, in fact, worthy of second-class treatment. This, in turn, leads to self-hatred and rejection of their own racial group.

The statement revealed that another consequence of the awareness of inferior social status was a lowering of personal ambition that is reflected, for example, in a depression of educational aspirations. Such effects "impair the ability of the child to profit from the educational opportunities provided him." The "Social Science Statement" also noted that white children derived an unjustified and inflated sense of their status because of the prevailing attitude in society of white superiority.

Studies cited showed that from the earliest school years, children are aware of status differences between whites and blacks. Government-enforced segregation was said to be a major contributor to this awareness for two reasons: (1) enforced segregation results from the decision of the majority group without the consent of the segregated group, and is commonly so perceived; and (2) historically, segregated patterns in the United States were developed on the assumption of inferiority of blacks dating back to slavery days.

Whether the Court was influenced by the "Social Science Statement" in the *Brown* decision (1954) is uncertain. Some observ-

ers have seen a relation between the statement and the most famous passage from the Court's Opinion: "To separate them [blacks] from others of similar age and qualifications solely because of their race generates a feeling of inferiority as to their status in the community that may affect their hearts and minds in a way unlikely ever to be undone." Another passage in the Opinion bears strong resemblance to wording in the statement:

Segregation of white and colored children in public schools has a detrimental effect upon the colored children. The impact is greater when it has the sanction of the law; for the policy of separating the races is usually interpreted as denoting the inferiority of the Negro group. A sense of inferiority affects the motivation of a child to learn. Segregation with the sanction of law, therefore, has a tendency to retard the educational and mental development of Negro children and to deprive them of some of the benefits they would receive in a racially integrated school system. Whatever may have been the extent of psychological knowledge at the time of Plessy v. Ferguson, this finding is amply supported by modern authority.

As a footnote to this passage, the Opinion listed seven social science references that the "Social Science Statement" had also cited.

On the other hand, analysis of the events surrounding the Court's decision has persuaded others that the "Social Science Statement" served a quite different function. According to this analysis, the justices knew that segregated schools were favored by a large majority of the population. They were worried about the possibility that a decision to desegregate would not be accepted, so they used the evidence of the "Social Science Statement" to appeal to the conscience of the nation for support.

As I noted earlier, very little desegregation took place in the decade following the Supreme Court decision. In 1964, ten years after the first *Brown* decision, a study of the eleven Confederate states showed that 99 percent of black students were still in segregated schools. There were two reasons for this. One was that the Court's order to desegregate the schools "with all deliberate speed" provided the lower courts with a very vague guideline for enforcement. It proved relatively easy for school districts to seem to comply with the order while they were in fact evading it. The other was the interrelation of school segregation

and residential segregation. In residentially segregated urban areas, simply assigning pupils to their neighborhood schools without regard to race did not desegregate them.

With respect to the "all deliberate speed" guideline, here is a case where social scientists might be tempted to say, "I told you so." In 1955, the Supreme Court had held a second hearing on the *Brown* school desegregation cases (*Brown* v. *Board of Education*, 1955). The purpose was to make additional rulings regarding implementation of the 1954 decision. Dr. Kenneth Clark had gathered social science evidence clearly indicating that painful social change occurs with least opposition when behavior change rather than attitude change is emphasized, when a specific date is set for the change to occur, when all involved are required to change at the same time, and when authorities make clear their intent to support the change firmly and unhesitatingly. The NAACP counsel presented this view to the Court. Why did the Court reject it?

A psychological interpretation goes something like this. As I said earlier, the Court knew that the great majority of the nation favored residential segregation. Moreover, the justices knew that President Eisenhower and a majority of Congress either opposed desegregation or favored gradual implementation of it. They had to consider whether, in that climate, their desegregation decision was enforceable. Could they risk a rejection that would endanger the nation's basic commitment to judicial interpretation of the Constitution? Ordering implementation "with all deliberate speed" was their compromise. They saw it as giving the nation time to get used to the idea that segregation had to go.

Then, in 1964, something happened to change the climate in which the Supreme Court was operating. In 1963, President Kennedy had proposed an extensive Civil Rights Act and, in 1964, President Lyndon Johnson engineered it through a hesitant Congress. Under that act, the Justice Department filed more than 500 school desegregation suits. The Department of Health, Education, and Welfare threatened more than 600 school districts with the loss of financial aid if they did not desegregate. In the new climate, the Supreme Court took two major steps. First, in decisions announced in 1968 (*Green* v. *County School Board of New Kent County*) and 1969 (*Alexander* v. *Holmes County Board of Education*), it replaced its guideline of "all deliberate speed" with a new one that said, desegregate "today," "at once" and defined these words as not permitting any delay. Second, the Supreme Court formulated an additional guideline in response to the realization that the judicial remedy of assigning black children to their neighborhood schools was a corrective for official segregation only if the neighborhoods were residentially desegregated. The Court stated that where past official actions were responsible for presently segregated schools, the violations might be corrected by steps in addition to, or other than, directing school boards to send all children to their neighborhood schools. These steps, the Court said, might include transporting students to desegregated schools by bus (Swann v. Charlotte-Mecklenburg Board of Education, 1971).

Following this guideline in states previously segregated by law was not difficult. In such states, actions such as building new schools in the path of expanding white or black populations, or assigning black teachers only to predominantly black populations, had obviously been carried out with the then lawful intent to facilitate segregation. In 1971 (Swann v. Charlotte-Mecklenburg Board of Education), in accordance with the new guidelines, the first of a series of southern cities was ordered to desegregate even though this required students to attend schools away from their home neighborhoods. The situation was not clear, however, in states that had not had segregation laws. Here, one found a wide spectrum of cases. At one extreme were school districts that had had explicit segregation policies. At the other extreme were districts for whom there was no record of such policies, but in which segregation was equally clear-cut.

In the former cases, where the record documented that segregation had been augmented by such acts as the location of new school buildings, pupil assignment plans, concentration of black teachers in black schools, or by government subsidies of housing, the courts have ordered desegregation with little hesitation. However, at the other extreme, where similar historical acts can be identified but no record of segregative intent can be uncovered, judgments of federal courts have varied. The reason for this has been the difficulty in deciding whether segregative intent can be inferred when the evidence is limited to the past behavior of school boards and other government agencies. Courts must always consider an alternative interpretation of the origin of segregated schools, one that explains school segregation as a necessary consequence of residential seg-

regation, which, in turn, might have been a consequence of factors in which government was not involved, such as racial differences in economic status, preferences of ethnic groups for self-segregation, and private—but not public—discrimination in housing.

The courts' guideline for inferring intent is that it is reasonable to assume that people intend the natural, probable, and foreseeable consequences of their actions. Foreseeable by whom is not made explicit. However, let's suppose that that bridge is crossed, and segregative intent is established, as it often is. What then? At this point, yet another guideline is needed, because the extent of a remedy ordered by the court must be justified in terms of the extent of the damage caused by official—as distinct from private—discrimination. This calls for a judgment by the court of how much current segregation results from historical acts over and above that which might have existed without such acts. The Supreme Court has tagged this excess with the label, "incremental segregative effect" (Dayton Board of Education v. Brinkman, 1977).

When dealing with school segregation that involves such inferences and estimates, legal counsel, perhaps in desperation, have again turned to social scientists. Let me give you an example from my own experience. I was involved in a case that arose in a midwestern city. There was little to go on in the historical record, and, understandably, the district court and the appeals court came to different conclusions. The appeals court discerned foreseeable segregative consequences in the school district's actions, while the district court did not. The Supreme Court agreed with the appeals court that official actions in the past had had segregative intent, but faulted both lower courts for not being more clear about the incremental segregative effect of these actions. (U.S. v. School District of Omaha, 1977).

I entered the picture at this point. The hearing began with a rehash of the evidence regarding the past actions of the school board and housing officials that might have contributed to school segregation. It continued with the testimony of two expert witnesses for the school board to the effect that school segregation in the community was due to private attitudes and behavior that had no basis in governmental actions. I presented a fairly standard theory of the determinants of social attitudes and social behavior. With appropriate qualifications that obviously tested the patience of the presiding judge, I also indicated the

relevance of this theory to the case under consideration. As an aside I should note that whether generalized theories are in fact applicable in specific communities is, of course, the responsibility of the courts to decide.

My testimony emphasized three points. First, the actions that people take lead others to make assumptions about their related social attitudes. Thus, if prominent public figures take actions that support segregation, observers assume they favor segregation, regardless of whether they do. This, of course, is only a restatement of what social scientists call motivational attribution. Second, an important source of influence on the social attitudes of average citizens is their perception of the social attitudes of respected community figures. Thus, if as a result of their actions, members of school boards and other leaders of local government are perceived to favor segregated social arrangements, average citizens tend to believe that such arrangements are proper and should be continued. This is simply an exemplification of prestige as a source of influence on attitudes and behavior. Third, children's attitudes toward social policies are strongly influenced by the social arrangements that prevail in the society in which they grow up. Hence, in an area where official acts have contributed to segregated social arrangements, children will absorb from their experience with these arrangements an unthinking endorsement of them. They will carry this over into adulthood as attitudes favoring continued segregation.

All of this adds up to a potentially pervasive impact of official actions on the development and maintenance of both residential and school segregation in the community. In discussing its decision to order a systemwide desegregation plan, the district court indicated that it found this interpretation to be persuasive.

What I have been discussing up to now is the process of determining whether violations of the Constitution have been involved in the development of segregated public schools—and, if so, how much. The other side of the story has to do with the remedy for such violations once the courts have ruled that they have occurred. In this area, social scientists have been less helpful than they could have been—and still could be in the future.

Until just a few years ago, 1977 to be exact, the courts sought two objectives in their remedies for segregation. One was to desegregate the students; in other words, to get minority and majority children into the same schools. The other was to desegregate the school environments; that is, to ensure that schools attended by students provided an environment that would not perpetuate the effects of segregation.

Desegregating students has been approached in two ways. One was by some form of pupil reassignment that might involve pairing or clustering primarily black with primarily white schools and sending all the children in some grades to one school and those in the remaining grades to the other school. Or it might entail transporting students to schools in such a way that each school approximated the minority–majority proportion in the district. The second approach has been to use a voluntary enrollment plan, which in recent years has usually involved magnet schools. Sometimes mandatory pupil reassignment and voluntary enrollment plans have been combined, giving students a choice of either going where assigned or electing to attend the magnet school. Sometimes, but not always, the racial composition of the magnet schools has been controlled.

Desegregating school environments has evolved more slowly. While still not uniform, it frequently includes desegregating administrative personnel and teaching faculty, training teachers to understand and handle the special needs of children from different backgrounds, and introducing multicultural curricula.

In 1977, the Supreme Court took the major step of authorizing a third category of desegregating remedies. In one of its two rulings on desegregating in the City of Detroit, the Court put it this way: "Pupil assignment alone does not automatically remedy the impact of previous, unlawful educational isolation. The consequences linger, and can be dealt with only by independent measures" (*Milliken* v. *Bradley II*, 1977).

As examples, the Court endorsed mandatory support for remedial reading, bias-free testing, and counseling programs. In decisions in other cities, courts have added multicultural curriculum materials and human relations programs. An interesting sidelight points to another implication of this development. Having found the State of Michigan to be partly responsible for the origins of Detroit's segregation, the court of appeals ordered the state to pay half of a 50-million-dollar bill for new vocational programs and almost 6 million dollars annually for other compensatory education programs.

The implications of this development are obvious. In the sometimes colorful lan-

guage of the Supreme Court, the objective of desegregation remedies was to eliminate the "vestiges" of segregation, "root and branch" (*Green* v. *County School Board of New Kent County*, 1968). To achieve this objective, the Court now said it was necessary to restore the victims of discrimination to the positions in society that they would have occupied in the absence of discrimination. As time has passed, the courts have broadened their view of how this might be accomplished. Stimulated by recommendations of educators and social scientists, district court judges have incorporated aspects of these recommendations in their desegregation orders. When defendants who must implement these orders—often by instituting costly programs of remedial education—decide instead to appeal to higher courts to reverse the district court, judicial decisions are made that have implications not only for the specific appellant but also for other school systems. In this process, broader conceptions of compensatory remedies for the negative consequences of desegregation have gradually evolved.

This picture of the many-sided approach to remedying the impact of segregation brings us to three questions that should be of particular interest to social scientists. Given the fact that students are to be desegregated, which approaches are most effective? Given the fact that school environments are to be made supportive of desegregated students, which components of such environments really make a difference? Given the fact that compensatory educational programs may be ordered by courts, which ones should receive highest priority?

Unfortunately, for the most part, the answers to such questions are not available. It isn't that we have neglected to study the outcomes of desegregation. On the contrary, more than a hundred such studies have been done. Rather, the difficulty is that the outcomes of desegregation have been assessed with little attention to the type of desegregation plan employed or the community conditions under which it was carried out. This is not said in criticism. I believe it simply reflects our ignorance of the kind of information that might have been more helpful to the courts.

Before addressing studies that may offer guidance to desegregation plans and compensatory education, let me briefly review the rather inconclusive studies of the overall impact of desegregation, especially how it affects black student achievement. (For a more detailed discussion of the evidence

on this topic, see S.W. Cook, 1984. The 1954 Social Science Statement and school desegregation: A reply to Gerard. *American Psychologist, 39*, 819–832.)

Since 1975 there have been five major reviews of studies on the effects of desegregation on school achievement. Two of the reviewers came to the conclusion that the studies were inconclusive; they judged that the results neither provided evidence that desegregation enhanced the school achievement of minority children, nor showed that it failed to do so. A third reviewer concluded that, of the thirty-four studies he felt were worth consideration, one-fourth showed greater achievement under desegregation, while the remainder showed either mixed or no effects. The fourth and fifth reviewers concentrated on studies of planned desegregation. Both concluded that approximately 60 percent of the studies of planned desegregation found greater achievement among minority students in desegregated schools. Almost all of these studies had assessed outcomes after one year of desegregation.

To the extent that the five reviewers included different studies in their reviews, the differences in their conclusions are understandable. The conditions under which desegregation has been carried out have varied from racial tension and hostility to consideration and friendliness. The fact that researchers found different outcomes for the students involved is not surprising.

Within the last several years a new method of summarizing the results of a group of studies has been developed. In the traditional method, there was a tendency to count noses. Studies in which there were big differences, either positive or negative, between the experimental conditions and the control conditions were counted in the same manner as those in which there were small differences. Moreover, there was a tendency to disregard studies showing no difference. The new method, called *meta-analysis*, produces a single figure that represents the average difference across all studies between the effects of the two things being compared—in our case, segregation and desegregation. This average is called *effect size*. There is a statistical procedure for determining if this effect size is reliably different from zero.

Three meta-analytic reviews have been done by individual investigators (Crain & Mahard, 1982; Krol, 1978; Wortman & Bryant, 1985). Another set of reviews, based on a selected group of nineteen studies, has been carried out by a panel of four experts under the auspices of the National Institute of Education (NIE) (T.D. Cook, 1983). Each of the separately conducted meta-analytic reviews reached the conclusion that the achievement of black children under desegregation was significantly greater than that under segregation. Their estimates on the size of the difference varied from one month to three months in grade-equivalent terms. Remember that most studies evaluate achievement gain after one year of desegregation. Hence, even a one-month advantage in achievement gain is large enough to be of practical meaning. The meta-analyses by the NIE panel essentially confirmed those of the individual investigators, although the effect they found was limited to reading skill.

Many students of desegregation have noted that a more meaningful assessment of its effects would span an educational career rather than a single year. However, since so few studies have followed the achievement of students under desegregation for more than a year, it has not been possible to get evidence on the duration question. Nevertheless, many observers have speculated that duration of exposure to desegregation would make a difference. The information now available on the question comes from a new direction. It does not constitute proof, but I find it very impressive and very suggestive. For some years a national assessment of educational progress, based on a national probability sample of secondary school students, has been conducted. Approximately 2,500 children in several selected age groups are given achievement tests at four- or five-year intervals. Exactly the same tests are used from one occasion to the next. For example, in 1971, approximately 2,500 thirteen-year olds were given reading and mathematics tests. In 1975, another group of approximately 2,500 thirteen-year-olds took the same tests. In 1980, still another sample of thirteen-year-olds was tested. This made it possible to compare achievement in reading, for example, of thirteen-year-olds over the decade of the 1970s. Professor Lyle Jones, the director of the Thurstone Psychometric Laboratory at the University of North Carolina, compared the performance of white students and black students during this period. He found that there had been no change in the performance of white students. However, the performance of black students had improved dramatically. The black–white achievement gap in reading had been cut in half. The comparisons in math are not as dramatic, but they, too, are impressive.

Professor Jones proposed that the most likely interpretation of these findings is that they reflect the growing proportion of thirteen-year-olds who have been in desegregated schools throughout their school careers (Jones, 1984).

Against this background, let me mention two types of studies whose results might influence court-ordered desegregation plans, either in their choice among alternative desegregation approaches or in the content of compensatory education programs.

The first type of study is relevant to one aspect of the pupil reassignment approach to student desegregation. Courts have often felt uncertain about transporting younger children away from their neighborhood schools, particularly those in kindergarten and first and second grades. In the mid-1970s, two reviewers of the school achievement literature called attention to the possibility that children who began desegregation at kindergarten or first or second grade might be showing more benefit from the experience than those who were desegregated later (St. John, 1975; Weinberg, 1977). Neither had very much evidence to work with, and little attention was paid to their observations. A few years later, however, a research team was able to locate many additional studies and found among them twenty-three that included students beginning desegregation at kindergarten or first grade (Crain & Mahard, 1982). In these twenty-three studies, the research investigators found forty-five separate comparisons of the achievement gains of groups of black students who had been desegregated and groups of black students who were still segregated. In forty of these comparisons, the desegregated students showed greater achievement gain. The researchers then conducted a meta-analytic review of the same studies and found that the average advantage of the desegregated over the segregated students was three months in grade-equivalent terms. They found the gain to be significantly larger than that for students who began desegregation in the upper elementary, junior high, or high school grades.

The second type of study suggests an additional form of compensatory education. These studies began with the knowledge that individuals in groups cooperating to achieve a joint goal help one another and are more motivated to achieve success than individuals working alone. Task interdependence of this sort was found to increase mutual respect and liking across, as well as within, racial groups. In the early 1970s,

these principles were adapted to school classrooms in the form of interracial learning teams where assignments are given to teams rather than to individual students. Such assignments might call for all members of a team to learn a particular computational procedure. Or, they might require the team to produce a group report involving a division of labor. Commendation and rewards are given for group achievement rather than individual achievement— although quarterly and semester grades are given to individuals.

Fifteen experiments on the effects of this procedure on academic achievement have been conducted in desegregated schools in the last ten years. In eleven of these experiments, there was a significantly greater gain in achievement by students working in interracial teams than by students in classrooms with the same racial composition taught by traditional methods where teachers relate to individual students. In four of the experiments, the investigators found no difference in performance.

This same classroom procedure has other desired effects as well. Experiments have shown that it almost always produces friendlier race relations, as well as higher self-esteem among minority children. The atmosphere in classrooms organized in this way is markedly more businesslike.

The group teaching method has been tried out in more than 1,500 schools and has been approved for dissemination by the Department of Education. It is easy for teachers to learn and many become enthusiastic about it. It would make a valuable component of a compensatory program.

My final comments have to do with two additional roles for social scientists in future desegregation litigation. They are necessitated by three major developments of the past ten to fifteen years. The first of the three is the rapid increase in residential segregation in our large urban areas. As you know, this is largely a result of migration to the suburbs by the white middle class. While this migration has been under way for the last three decades, it has accelerated in the past decade and a half. Its magnitude is striking. Instances in which the enrollment of white students in city schools drops by one-third in a five-year period are not uncommon. Demographers can specify many of the reasons why this is happening. Most agree that the much discussed "white flight" from school desegregation is a relatively trivial part of the phenomenon, one that is largely limited to the first desegregation year.

Specialists in the study of urban migration have summarized the causes of suburbanization as follows (Taeuber & Wilson, 1978):

Massive suburbanization of the white population is a fundamental factor of twentieth-century social change. It has been spurred by numerous governmental actions, often in ways not fully anticipated. At the federal level, public housing, slum clearance, highway construction, urban renewal, transformation of residential mortgage markets, public assistance regulations, facility location, and other programs, together with pervasive racial discrimination in the conduct of each, all contributed to shaping the current urban crisis and its racial dimensions. State and local governmental actions similarly contributed.

Other authorities (Farley & Wurdock, 1977) have described the impact of school desegregation in this context:

In large cities where many of the students were Black, the incremental loss of Whites associated with substantial integration frequently equalled about one year's normal loss of Whites. That is, during the year of integration the loss of Whites was about twice as great as expected in the absence of integration. White reactions to desegregation are quite similar in metropolitan school districts and those which are limited to a specific central city. It is inappropriate to conclude, however, that school integration is the major cause of declining White enrollments in central cities. Demographic data demonstrates that even if no schools were integrated, most cities would lose a substantial number of the White students annually.

The second development is a potential road-block to further progress in disengaging school desegregation from the growing residential segregation. Ten years ago, in the first of its two decisions regarding Detroit, the Supreme Court concluded that it had no constitutional justification for ordering suburban school districts to join the city school district in a metropolitan desegregation program (*Milliken v. Bradley*, 1974). This meant that desegregation had to be limited to the largely black, city-only school district, a restriction that led the appeals court to say, in apparent despair, that it had no suggestions for the district court about how desegregation might be meaningfully accomplished.

The third development is a growing emphasis on combining mandatory pupil reassignment approaches to desegregation with freedom of choice approaches. The latter, as I noted earlier, take the form of magnet schools. Prior to 1974, magnet schools had been used mainly as an alternative to other desegregation approaches rather than as one component of a desegregation plan. Under those circumstances, they produced very little desegregation. In contrast, a national survey completed a year ago indicated that of the 138 school districts now employing magnet schools, 73 percent do so in the context of a court-ordered desegregation plan (Blank, Dentler, Baltzell, & Chabotar, 1983).

The net effect of these three developments, it seems to me, is to create urgent needs for assistance from social scientists with the school desegregation problems of the large cities. One such need relates to future litigation regarding the fixing of governmental responsibiliy for the development of metropolitan segregation. The Supreme Court decision separating suburban districts from involvement in Detroit's desegregation was the result of a five to four vote. One member of the five-justice majority discussed a number of considerations that might justify case-by-case exceptions to the Detroit ruling. One of these would be to show partial responsibility of state education and housing agencies for the interrelationship of city and suburban segregation. The facts documenting this responsibility are available in state records. What is missing is a clear, theoretically sound exposition linking the data to people's housing decisions.

The second future contribution would be for social scientists to study ways of enhancing the effectiveness of magnet schools. The survey I mentioned makes it clear that among the 65 percent of magnet schools whose admissions procedures ensure a full representation of all ethnic and racial minorities in their student bodies, there is considerable variation on two outcome criteria: (1) academic achievement and (2) positive race relations. The report suggests reasons for the variation and makes it clear that there is a need for research on innovative improvements. Case studies report that the more effective magnet schools have reattracted white students from private schools and suburban areas that presumably cannot duplicate the magnet schools' theme-related educational offerings. The strength of this effect remains to be determined. It may be that research could point the way to enhancing it.

In conclusion, I believe that the record documents a series of useful contributions by social scientists to the task of eliminating the effects of ethnic and racial discrimination in education. The combination of law and social science constitutes a powerful tool with which to complete that task in the future.

REFERENCES

Alexander v. Holmes County Board of Education, 369 U.S. 19 (1969).

Blank, R.K., Dentler, R.A., Baltzell, D.C., & Chabotar, K. (1983). *Survey of magnet schools: Analyzing a model for quality integrated education.* Chicago: James Lowry and Associates.

Brown v. Board of Education of Topeka, 347 U.S. 483 (1954). (*See also* Appendix to Appellants' Briefs—The effects of segregation and consequences of desegregation: A social science statement).

Brown v. Board of Education of Topeka, 349 U.S. 294 (1955).

Cook, S.W. (1984). The 1954 Social Science Statement and school desegregation: A reply to Gerard. *American Psychologist, 39,* 819–832.

Cook, T.D. (1983). *Critical examination of meta-analysis of school desegregation and the academic achievement gains of black children* (Report to National Institute of Education). Evanston, IL: Northwestern University.

Crain, R.L. & Mahard, R.E. (1982). *Desegregation plans that raise black achievement: A review of the research.* Santa Monica, CA: Rand Corp.

Dayton Board of Education v. Brinkman, 433 U.S. 406, 420 (1977).

Farley, R. & Wurdock, C. (1977, March). *Can governmental policies integrate public schools?* Ann Arbor, MI: Population Studies Center, The University of Michigan (Mimeo).

Green v. County School Board of New Kent County, 391 U.S. 430 (1968).

Jones, L.V. (1984). White–black achievement differences: The narrowing gap. *American Psychologist 39,* 1207-1213.

Krol, R.A. (1978). A meta-analysis of comparative research on the effects of desegregation on academic achievement. *Dissertation Abstracts International, 39,* 6011, (University Microfilms No. 7907962).

Milliken v. Bradley, 418 U.S. 717 (1974).

Milliken v. Bradley, 443 U.S. 267 (1977).

St. John, N. (1975). *School desegregation: Outcomes for children.* New York: Wiley.

Swann v. Charlotte-Mecklenburg Board of Education, 402 U.S. 1,767-8, 769, 772 (1971).

Taeuber, K.E. & Wilson, F.D. (1978, January). *The demographic impact of school desegregation policy.* Institute for Research on Poverty Discussion Papers (#478-78). Madison, WI: University of Wisconsin–Madison.

U.S. v. School District of Omaha, 433 U.S. 667, 670 (1977).

Weinberg, M. (1977). *Minority students: A research appraisal.* Washington, DC: National Institute of Education.

Wortman, P.M. & Bryant, F.B. (1985). School desegregation and black achievement. *Sociological Methods and Research, 13,* 289-324.

Legal Perspectives and the Vision of America

NORMAN REDLICH

It would be presumptuous of me to address the legal perspective on issues of school desegregation, particularly in the presence of so many who have been directly involved in waging these legal battles. I would, however, like to give you the viewpoint of someone who has been a little more than peripherally involved in these issues—and in other civil rights and civil liberties issues as well—in order to place *Brown* (1954) in perspective.

I would like to go back thirty-seven years to my own first personal involvement with civil rights issues from the legal perspective. In my last year at Williams College, in Williamstown, Massachusetts, I was editor of the school newspaper. A black student came to me and said, "Do you know that in Williamstown a black student cannot get his hair cut?" I found this hard to believe in a small New England town that saw itself as part of the liberal community.

The two of us went down to the barber shop, where in those days one could get a haircut for fifty cents. The barber turned to the student who was with me and said, "For you, it's going to be $3.50." We left, rather shaken. I drove to the nearest town that had a lawyer, North Adams, four miles away. I wandered along the main street looking at the second floor signs of the buildings—that's where lawyers always work in small towns. Finally, I located one and walked in and said, "There must be a law…"

Indeed there was a law. Massachusetts had a civil rights act, passed after the Civil War, forbidding discrimination in places of public accommodation. It provided for a civil suit that entitled the plaintiff to a $50 recovery. This was not a small sum of money when the law was enacted, nor was it in 1947. So I asked the lawyers to bring a law suit. The case made the front page of the *New York Times*, and we brought in a lawyer from the NAACP in Boston. It became a major issue in the community, as you might expect.

I discovered some interesting things. First, I discovered that there were many black working people living in Williamstown, Massachusetts. On the morning of the trial, the court room was filled with black people who were concerned with this issue. I also learned the depth of the intense reaction from whites in the community who felt that outside agitators were creating this problem. The judge who heard this case was a Democrat plunked down in northwestern Massachusetts by Governor Curley as a slap in the face to the Republicans, who dominated the western part of the state.

I was editor of the college newspaper and was working in my office preparing to be a witness. The judge called me and said, "I'm hearing this case today."

And I said, "I know that."

"I'll hear the facts," he said, "and I'll apply the law. But I want you to know that I'm behind you one hundred percent. When I

moved to this town these SOBs wouldn't give me a place to live because I was Jewish, and I've been waiting for five years to get even with them. Now they'll never forget this day."

So much for the impartial majesty of the law!

Indeed they didn't forget. After listening to testimony, he went back to the Magna Carta, the Declaration of Independence, the United Nations Charter, and, of course, ruled for the plaintiff. We all walked out feeling great. But the final outcome of the case was somewhat disappointing. We won the case, and I thought we had achieved great social change—indeed, the case inspired me to become a lawyer. However, the case was followed by one disappointment after another: the barbers' union paid for the legal defense of the barber and a year later nothing had changed in Williamstown, because it never occurred to us to involve the black community, to try to organize people to get their hair cut immediately following the trial. A great deal might have happened if we had organized promptly.

I learned then the lesson we are still learning today, that while the legal perspective is essential, the political battle must be waged; and indeed legal victories often

---

NORMAN REDLICH is Dean and Judge Edward Weinfeld Professor of Law, New York University School of Law.

help with the political struggle. There are many examples of this need for joint legal and political action today. The women's rights movement won court victories for reproductive freedom in the 1970s but underestimated the intensity and importance of the political battle. Another example is in the area of separation between church and state. A few years ago people believed that the church–state issue was settled—all the legal victories had been won. We've learned, to our dismay, that this is not true. In the relationship between law and politics, the need for community action is essential to achieve the goals sought in litigation. One type of action cannot proceed without the other.

In the pursuit of racial justice, we have moved beyond the issues of thirty years ago, but at the same time, we sense concern and pessimism. This concern is not confined to racial matters. It is with the essence of the American vision. I know of no country on earth that has tried to achieve true racial equality and true religious diversity through constitutional principles. One is unique to this country—separation of church and state. The other has a unique meaning in this country—equal protection of the law.

I believe we are threatened today with a very different vision, the vision of a fundamentally uniform society. President Reagan's house on the hill—which he loves to talk about—is predominantly occupied by white people who share the same values and religious persuasion. The President's fervent religious supporters envision a racially and religiously uniform society—white and Christian—where differences may be toler-

ated, but only through the sufferance of the majority.

I believe that the issue of racial equality and religious diversity are inseparable. Those who inhabit the "Bob Jones" world will not accept a racially diverse or a religiously pluralistic society. In their minds pluralism and diversity are twin evils. They have a vision of an America that never existed—an America they are trying to create through legal and political means. Those of us who share a different dream, who recognize that the United States embodies a unique experiment in the history of the world, a society of racial and religious diversity, believe that this other vision must be fought vigorously. The threat to diversity is greater today than at any other time in this century.

This conference deals with matters of school desegregation, and Julius Chambers has outlined far better than I could the legal issues lying before us. I think his analysis is right to the point. I would like simply to emphasize a few issues.

First, we ought not to be talking in terms of "betrayed" hopes. *Brown* was a great achievement and much of its promise has been fulfilled, at least as the issues were perceived in 1954. There has been significant legal work involving many people in this room and at this table. For the most part, the legal framework that developed the post-*Brown* desegregation cases is still in place. The principles established in those cases have been cut back in places, but they're still there. The Supreme Court has not yet abandoned them.

Secondly, even when limitations have been imposed—most importantly, geo-

graphic limitations as in the Detroit busing case (*Milliken* v. *Bradley*, 1974)—advancement can occur. There are many legal issues that can be weighed within that context. It is not a matter of relitigating that case, but trying to work around it and through the cracks that are created. Another significant issue facing us is the question of what I call the temporal limits, such as those involved in the issue coming up in Norfolk (*Riddick* v. *School Board of Norfolk*, 1984), where, in a city that was previously segregated, the school board seeks to have the busing remedy removed on grounds that a unitary system now exists. What happens five, ten, fifteen years down the road when it is alleged that the court order has been complied with, busing has been implemented, and it is alleged that the original evil of segregation no longer exists. It may become necessary to prove intentional segregation all over again, this time without the history that led to the initial decree. There are legal strategies that can be developed to deal with this problem. One does not have to accept the idea that the court's jurisdiction is over. In cases such as these, where there has been an original finding of intentional segregation, changes in school district lines or pupil school assignments should not be permitted to decrease the integration of the system.

There is a serious present threat to the goal of racial and religious diversity—the themes that concern us today. The history of our country teaches us that it is difficult, perhaps impossible, to achieve racial justice except in an open, diverse, and free society.

REFERENCES

Brown v. Board of Education of Topeka, 347 U.S. 483 (1954).

Milliken v. Bradley, 418 U.S. 717 (1974).

Riddick v. School Board of the City of Norfolk, F. Supp. (1 Va. 1984) Civil Action No. 84–1815, 4th Circuit (Appeal Pending).

PART IV

Reactions to the Conference

School Desegregation— The Real Stakes

MICHAEL H. SUSSMAN

Thirty years after *Brown*, the central premise of that case has been vindicated, but in an odd way. Separate is unequal in our society not merely as an objective matter, but because we perceive separate as unequal. White Americans who have not had contact with black Americans, who shun black Americans, and who seek to set up walls barring the entry of blacks truly believe that Blacks are unequal. And the perpetuation of separateness through social institutions merely confirms and perpetuates this perception. It often does so in the young, who are vulnerable to such impressions and without the capacity to see the truth.

If one looks at the ten most populous American cities today, one still sees rampant segregation of housing patterns and schools. New York, Chicago, Los Angeles, Houston, Detroit, Miami, Atlanta, Baltimore, Philadelphia, and St. Louis all have a vast preponderance of their students in segregated schools. Each city is surrounded by predominantly white suburban areas that, with the exception of St. Louis, educate their children separately. Indeed, millions of students are being educated today without the opportunity of contact with members of other races and a chance to develop insights about people of other races on their own.

Those who observe "white flight" emphasize the obvious—that whites who have created or condoned the creation of a segregated society will now exercise their constitutional right to choose a private school or their equally fundamental right to change residence rather than "subject" their children to integration. The critical question is not whether "white flight" exists, but how it affects the possibility of a fully integrated society.

Fear is at the heart of racism; racism itself pardons separation as the only manner by which the majority can divorce itself from the pernicious effects of the feared minority. Mistreatment stems from the majority's lack of caring for a minority that it fears. The only way to break this cycle is through contact.

Often critics of desegregated school systems point to the violence exhibited by students in such schools. Others argue that intergroup relations have not radically improved as a consequence of integration. Still others claim that promoting the social goal of interracial understanding is not the function of schools. All of these arguments are wrongheaded, but they are rarely attacked head-on.

First, young people will exhibit violent tendencies in some small number whatever the race of their classmates. That such violence continues after integration is no argument against integration. It merely indicates that integration does not cure violence. Second, we cannot expect groups that have been separated for generations and have developed negative images and stereotypes of each other to come together in one minute or one week and forge a trouble-free environment. An environment characterized by cooperation is a consequence, not a precondition, of integration. A dialectic process of social change must unfold, but it can begin only when all the players are accounted for and in attendance. It cannot begin when we have dual school systems.

Finally, our schools are supposed to serve the important functions of assimilation and acculturation. These are social functions that go beyond the three *R*s. Today, with our teeming multi-ethnic society, we cannot overemphasize the role of the school system as a place where children from different social and racial groups can meet and get to know one another as human beings. How else can the society overcome the isolation of groups and the sense of polarization that now grips many of our urban areas?

Today, the separateness in our big city school systems symbolizes exactly what dual school systems represented in the South in the 1940s—the desire of the majority culture not to associate with the minority. This strong desire for separateness strongly determines both housing

MICHAEL H. SUSSMAN is Assistant General Counsel, National Association for the Advancement of Colored People Special Contribution Fund.

and schooling patterns. Parents control the social contacts their children may have and thus substantially determine their children's ability to form new social attitudes based on stimuli more immediate and personal than television sit coms.

What is most troubling today is not the fact that the Civil Rights Division champions, most proudly, the cause of white males and opposes almost all effective remedial devices that could assist minorities. It is not that so many white Americans continue to harbor feelings of racial hatred and act, when the opportunity permits, out of such instincts.

More troubling are lack of contact between children of opposite races and the absence of an organized and mobilized force clamoring for racial integration as one of our best hopes for the future. Where racial integration has been given a fair opportunity to work— in Austin or Charlotte or Seattle or Cleveland or Buffalo or Columbus—it has proven exciting and, indeed, revolutionary for entire school systems. But in too many places, demographics and choices made by people acting out of emotion, not reason, have precluded integration. Those of us who believe in integration as a critical social form, as the best test of the meaning of this democracy, need to be concerned about the business of building a political climate that sets this achievement as a central goal. If we are not, those who have never

had contact with other races and who bring to the discussion ignorance and fear will command the discussion and the attendant social policies.

Finally, we must pose this question to our adversaries: If not integration, then what? Blacks may choose to believe that a separatist future bodes better for black children than does involvement in the broader society. This is a choice each black American must make. But, as a white person, and I address myself primarily to whites, I believe we have no choice. Consistent with the ideals of this society, we must accept and welcome blacks into the mainstream of American society. Given the value we place on individuals, we cannot reject any black person based on fear of blacks as a group. We cannot prejudge any child based on the status of his or her mother or father. We must accept the fact that the history we created—of racial slavery and forced separation of black families—has had social and economic effects. We cannot, without being entirely blind, believe that the gap between whites and blacks is anything other than the aggregated consequence of generations of overt discrimination and exclusion. We must admit that while such exclusion precluded black advancement, many of us and our families "made it" at the expense of those being held back. We cannot act as if each generation has created from scratch its own place under the sun. We must

realize that the longer we allow substandard housing and poverty to increase and the longer we postpone the development of effective social programs to help people out of these conditions, the longer we must resign ourselves to an increasingly hostile underclass. As we are the products of the opportunities provided, others are the equally understandable products of the opportunities denied them.

All these lessons must be learned before whites can actually help create an integrated America. These lessons must not only be learned, they must be externalized through the creation of social forms. Otherwise, nothing will change. Desegregated schools represent society's commitment to a different future. Desegregation is not the natural result of housing patterns. It is imposed on patterns we acknowledge were created intentionally to keep people apart.

The future is now in our schools. Where schools continue to be segregated, the past and present forge an iron shield against the sword of the future. Children are denied the chance to live differently than their parents whose racist choices will dominate the future. We must do better.

The <u>Brown</u> Plus Thirty Conference: A Personal View

CORA WATKINS

The *Brown* Plus Thirty Conference on desegregation was both inspiring and disquieting. As a member of the "baby boom" generation, I was too young to remember the passage of the 1954 *Brown* decision. Still as one who maintains some recollection of the Little Rock incident, and who participated in the demands for more black teachers and black history at the high school and college level, it was enjoyable to see that there were so many eloquent and knowledgeable black lawyers and other black professionals involved in the landmark Supreme Court mandate. On the other hand, to hear Kenneth Clark explain that New York City, in particular, and New York State, as a whole, are more segregated now than during the period of the *Brown* case, or to hear repeatedly that many of the gains of the civil rights movement are currently under siege, suggested a dim future and was quite disturbing.

However, what was most disturbing was the apparent underlying struggle between two differing ideological perspectives—nationalism versus integration. According to Harold Cruse, author of *The Crisis of the Negro Intellectual* (1967), this has been a longstanding historical problem that has partly contributed to the failure of black leadership. Of course, the theme of integration was dominant at the conference due to the focus on *Brown* v. *Board of Education* (1954).

Presenters included Kenneth Clark,

whose life has virtually been devoted to integration efforts through research, writing, and other activities; and Beverly Cole, representing the NAACP, a major civil rights organization that set the *Brown* case into motion, employing lawyers and others to remove the legal barriers toward equal educational opportunities not only in education but also in other areas of the lives of black people throughout the United States. Also defending and attempting to provide factual data on the value of desegregation as a worthwhile goal were social scientists Robert Crain, Willis Hawley, Gary Orfield, and respected researchers in the area.

Throughout the conference, and within the discussion groups, questions were continually raised regarding the viability of desegregation as an effective strategy in the education of black children. The questions included the following: What happens when geographic and population factors cause desegregation to become virtually impossible? Is "mixing children" still our goal? What are the priorities and where does the focus on quality education fall on the list? Are we implying that all black schools are inferior and always have been? If so, what about the black colleges that educated and graduated many of the conference participants themselves? Addressing these issues on a practical basis was Nelvia Brady, Assistant Superintendent of Chicago Public Schools. She is presently in the midst of attempting to implement a new

desegregation plan that she described as "not designed to ensure black/white interaction," but rather to provide quality educational programs. Superintendent Constance Clayton of Philadelphia included in her presentation a number of questions regarding the viability and practicality of making desegregation the main objective of a school system. Her own "modified" desegregation plan consisted of a standardized curriculum, clearly defined goals, high expectations, and parent involvement. Superintendent Clayton concluded her remarks by stating, "we cannot afford to be trapped by history," possibly suggesting that desegregation may not be a goal to seek in the future. Finally, Hugh Scott directly challenged the goal of desegregation for all black children and charged that the purpose of *Brown* was to provide black children with the right of choice, that racially desegregated schools are not the only model, and that school desegregation has resulted in the imposition of an educational environment in which the "cure" is almost as destructive as the "disease." Although it should be stated clearly that from some of his other writing, for example, "Beyond Racial Balance Remedies: School Desegregation for the 1980s" (1983), Hugh Scott is

CORA WATKINS is Assistant in Education Integration, Office of Non-Public Schools, Civil Rights and Intercultural Relations, New York State Education Department.

not against the mandate of *Brown*. He is against the way *Brown* is implemented; desegregation strategies ignore the important issue of quality education for black students.

The positions taken throughout the conference appeared to lean toward either the integrationist perspective or the nationalist perspective. This, according to Cruse, has been a historical problem among black leadership. He writes: "Negro leadership has usually been caught up in the unresolved conflict between group needs and individual needs, economic nationalism and economic integration. On the social level it comes out as nationalism vs. integration, separatism vs. inter-racialism, black vs. white, etc." (Cruse, 1967).

Although Cruse's analysis begins with the Negro intellectual of the 1920s during the Harlem Renaissance and continues through to the Black Power movement of the 1960s, the main ideological perspectives and struggles he outlines are still very much applicable today and are useful as a framework for a review of the perspectives provided at the conference, omitting the left-wing view that he also develops. Cruse approaches the issue of black leadership from the political, economic, and social standpoints; a similar approach can be taken for the single issue of education/desegregation. It is clear that Clark (although he appears weary of the struggle), Cole, the three social scientists, and several of the other panelists are proponents of making desegregation the priority issue. On the other hand, Scott, Brady,

Clayton, and others wish to pay equal attention to the negative effects desegregation can have on black children when they are forced into an alien environment.

Again Cruse's perspective is applicable when he calls for creative solutions that will ultimately provide leadership to the masses of blacks and other children of color suffering from the lack of effective policy and action. Should one study the condition of black youth in the public schools, one would undoubtedly find (1) pockets of racial isolation, particularly in the northern urban centers, where desegregation would be very difficult to implement (Timberlake, 1984); (2) racial isolation that does not necessarily only refer to the black/white populations but to the increasing racial isolation of Hispanics, as stated by one social scientist (Castellanos, 1980; Ascher, 1982); (3) suburban areas with small minority populations that often maintain schools, classes, and/or programs which have a disproportionately large number of minority students and have problems such as high suspension rates, low expectations and low achievement (Scott, 1976); and (4) excellent all-black schools (Bond, 1972).

In essence, black, Hispanic, Native-American and other children of color find themselves in many different situations and a nationalistic or an integrationist viewpoint alone will not serve the needs of all. Therefore, a creative solution that first considers the historical analysis of education for blacks in this country and desegregation in general is needed along with an open and critical dialogue. A creative solution that

encompasses the variety of situations and deals with the realities of desegregation for most children is essential. Such a solution would relieve the suffering of those children who find themselves in the minority and experience the effects of misunderstanding, alienation, and vestiges of racism. This solution would recognize the geographic circumstances where desegregation is not feasible, yet racial isolation still exists. This solution would allow the implementation of desegregation with equal status, power, and consideration given to all racial/ethnic groups involved in the process; no one group would bear a disproportionate burden of the desegregation goal.

If black leadership does not move toward this aim, then thirty years later another group of blacks and whites will be called to assemble and reassess the 1954 *Brown* decision, and other young blacks searching for direction and avenues in which to channel their energy will again experience frustration and a degree of confusion. Cruse states it clearly: "The farther the Negro gets from his historical antecedents in time, the more tenuous become his conceptual ties, the emptier his social conceptions, the more superficial his visions. His one great and present hope is to know and understand his Afro-American history in the United States more profoundly. Failing that, and failing to create a new synthesis and a social theory of action, he will suffer the historical fate described by the philosopher who warned that 'Those who cannot remember the past are condemned to repeat it.'" (Cruse, 1967)

REFERENCES

Ascher, C. (1982, March). *Desegregation as an equal educational opportunity strategy for Hispanics*. (ERIC/CUE Fact Sheet No. 10) New York: ERIC.

Bond, H. M. (1972). *Black American scholars: Study of their beginnings*. Detroit: Balamp Publishing.

Brown v. Board of Education of Topeka, 347 U.S. 483 (1954).

Castellanos, D. (1980, Fall). Desegregation of Hispanics and its implications: A critical issue for the 1980's. *Progress: A report of desegregation trends in the states*.

Cruse, H. (1967). *The crisis of the Negro intellectual: An historical analysis of the failure of black leadership*. New York: William Morrow & Company.

Scott, H.J. (1983). Beyond racial balance remedies: School desegregation for the 1980s. *New York University Education Quarterly, 14* (2), 15.

Timberlake, C. (1984, May). A historical perspective of school desegregation. *The Crisis*, pp. 26–29.

Where Next?

LEONARD B. STEVENS

Where next? Thirty years after the Supreme Court found no place for racial segregation in public education, a decade after school desegregation came North, with unfinished business and progress equally visible, with black children still trailing white children in the test-score race, with Hispanics and Asians adding culture and language to the desegregation equation, with schools in the political limelight, desegregation under political assault, and excellence more attractive than equity, is the nation now about to turn from desegregating the schools and turn instead toward the making of effective schools, however racially isolated they may be, on the modish ground that pursuit of quality is more feasible and more practical than continued pursuit of desegregation? It seems possible. The times favor precisely this reorientation. Indeed, the coalitions, bipartisan and biracial, could easily be formed. And yet this prospect, however more popular than the more arduous goal of continued desegregation, is deeply troubling.

At one level, it is troubling because it implies a number of things that are not true. Namely:

■ That desegregation need be or should be no longer pursued because it has accomplished all that can be accomplished or because it has failed. Neither is true. The data show amply how much racial isolation remains—and also pinpoint where it can be undone. Similarly, the data document beyond debate the large amount of segregation that has been dismantled—not, really, in the thirty years since *Brown*, but only in the twenty years since the mid-sixties when the new policy began to have effect.

■ That desegregation has excluded the matter of school quality, focusing exclusively on the racial composition of classrooms. Such is not the case. The desegregationist who is indifferent toward the quality of desegregated schools is a rare commodity. Integration and good instruction are equally desirable and highly compatible—quite obviously so. The very notion that desegregation exposes "second generation" problems in instruction, discipline, finance, community relations, staffing, and other quality-related areas—problems to identify and address—emerged from the southern experience with desegregation, and has had wide influence there and elsewhere. In the North, the incorporation of educational objectives in desegregation plans became a legal and administrative principle, starting with Detroit, extending to Boston and Cleveland, and rippling beyond to lesser-known places.

■ That desegregation results are inevitably slow and imperfect, and future progress is even more problematic. Not so. The history is quite clear: Desegregation works well where and when it is expected to work, is rooted in planning, and is tended with leadership. Which is to say that results and pace are determined by the talent of implementors in the schools, not by limitations of the goal.

Looking to the future, the prospect of a turning away from desegregation is more troubling. Either racially separate schools are inherently unequal, or they are not. Either the hearts and minds of children are susceptible to lasting damage as a result of segregated education, or the Supreme Court was wrongheaded to so conclude. The Court did not distinguish between superior and inferior separate schools—it spoke simply of separate schools. The passage of thirty years may change the politics of race, but not this principle. If separateness is acceptable when instruction is made effective, then separate but equal has been rehabilitated as a plank of public policy—and educational equity hangs on the never-yet-demonstrated capacity of school boards and school administrators to operate racially separate schools that are demonstrably equal in everything from budgets to teacher expectations. So much of the social dynamic of contemporary America—well beyond education—

LEONARD B. STEVENS is Director of the Office on School Monitoring and Community Relations, Cleveland, Ohio.

depends on the unequivocal declaration that separate is inherently unequal, that to stand this principle on its head or to bend it out of recognizable shape would have incalculable effects.

Without doubt, schools that are all black can be just as effective cognitively as schools that are all white. Indeed, there is no reason that black schools cannot exceed white schools in achievement levels, test scores, competency measures, retention rates, parent satisfaction, and academic reputation. The reality, however, is that the graduates of black schools are minorities in an American culture shaped and dominated by a majority whose children, if not educated in integrated schools, are educated in white schools. A second reality, unfortunately, is that in the majority's psyche are embedded racial attitudes conditioned by many generations of tradition and instruction, including the instinct that white is superior to black on all matters, great and small. One product of separate but educationally equal schools would be a majority educated exclusively in majority schools and as a result conditioned to believe, consciously or otherwise, in its inherent superiority. This majority would inevitably perceive blacks as second-class not for objective reasons of education, occupation, intelligence, earning power, or talent, but because of their blackness. Too little is made of the ameliorative effect of school desegregation on the racial attitudes of white children; too little concern is expressed for the socializing loss to white children that would occur if desegregation is halted in its tracks or redefined as not requiring the presence of white and black children in common classrooms.

Curiously, the radical ideal of desegregated public schools has come to appear antiquated in only thirty years. Is the appearance valid or mistaken? Are school desegregation and school excellence competitive or collaborative? Is it even possible to return the schools to their pre-1954 character, altering only (for the better) the quality of the black schools? Or has so much happened in the demographics of the cities (blacker), the suburbs (richer), and the Hispanic population (larger) that separate but equal applied now to the schools would yield a future nation with racial divisions so sharp and of such great magnitude as to defy practical remedy? For a diverse nation with high aspirations for social equity and openness, and also a demonstrated capacity to discriminate invidiously, where does wise public-policy ground lie?

For perhaps the balance of this decade, expedient answers may satisfy, even prevail. For the future, though, expediency is unworthy of the awesome consequences of choosing separate but equal schools, considering that the schools have become the nation's best institution for breaching racial walls, however imperfectly, to a substantial degree. No other institution causes so much contact across the races for so many Americans of such a young age and for so many years. How we respond at this time to the challenge of continued desegregation of schools—driven by expedience or by ideal, focused on the present or the future—may prove to be far more important than most of us now think, perhaps as important to a future generation as was Madison's response to the question of federalism to our generation and all its predecessors.

Seattle's Reaction to the Proceedings of the Brown Plus Thirty Conference

MICHAEL W. HOGE

Our primary message is that school improvement *and* desegregation must both continue to be primary goals for our nation's schools. We do not believe that improving schools alone is enough to prepare our students to live and work in our society; nor do we believe that desegregation alone is enough to assure high-quality education for minority youth. Both goals must continue to be vigorously pursued. The pursuit of one does not imply the abandonment of the other; in fact, the pursuit of both is necessary to achieve either.

We believe that Seattle's story can be instructive to those who despair of achieving both improved education for minority youth and desegregation: *It is possible,* and we must not give up.

The Seattle School District instituted a systemwide desegregation plan in the fall of 1978. Adoption of the plan followed fifteen years of unsuccessful attempts to desegregate Seattle's school system using all possible voluntary methods—from voluntary transfers with free transportation to an extensive magnet schools program. Between 1963, when voluntary desegregation efforts began, and 1977, the last year before the Seattle Plan, racial imbalance grew steadily worse. The number of segregated schools and the degree of segregation within schools increased. Moreover, minority students bore a greatly disproportionate share of the burden of movement, since few whites volunteered.

The Seattle School Board and community leaders have had a long-term commitment to school desegregation. When it became apparent that the best voluntary efforts possible were not capable of desegregating Seattle's schools, a local consensus formed to desegregate without court intervention. Local business, religious, and political leaders and civil rights organizations jointly urged the Seattle School Board to implement a locally developed and controlled desegregation plan without court direction. The school board responded by (1) adopting a definition of racial imbalance (minority enrollment at any school more than 20 percent above the district-wide minority percentage); (2) requiring that desegregation occur through *educationally sound* strategies; and (3) initiating a six-month process of citizen planning activities, which culminated in December 1977 with the adoption of the Seattle Plan for elimination of racial imbalance. Local media have been strongly supportive of Seattle's effort to maintain local control of this issue.

The Seattle Plan relies on roughly equal numbers of mandatory and voluntary student reassignments to accomplish desegregation of the schools. Where voluntary strategies appear incapable of achieving desegregation, elementary schools are desegregated by joining together the populations of two or three neighborhoods in "pairs" or "triads." For example, students from two neighborhoods are paired and

attend school together, first in grades 1–3 at one site then in grades 4–6 at the other site. Thus, students are assigned on the basis of their neighborhood and not individually on the basis of race. Students brought together in the elementary grades remain together at the secondary level. Neighborhood students stay together throughout their school careers if they so choose, and students have predictability and stability in their assignments—factors that Seattle citizens indicated were important in any desegregation plan. Equity of movement is a key feature of the plan—roughly equal numbers of minority and majority students participate. Parents and students have the opportunity to select voluntary alternatives to their initial fixed assignments, which has no doubt enhanced community acceptance of the plan. Educational options include both program content and teaching-style alternatives.

Mandatory desegregation is more cost-effective than voluntary. Voluntary desegregation transportation costs over two times as much per student as mandatory, because scattered student movement is less efficient than transporting entire neighborhoods. Enhanced program content and staffing at magnet schools are additional expenses of voluntary programs. In spite of the drastic decline in federal desegregation

MICHAEL W. HOGE is General Counsel, Seattle Public Schools.

aid and the tremendous uncertainties of school finance generally in Washington State, Seattle will attempt to preserve the important voluntary features of its plan.

The Seattle Plan has successfully desegregated Seattle's schools, and educational quality has been enhanced. All students now have the opportunity for a multi-ethnic education, which Seattle citizens believe is essential to preparation for life in this pluralistic society. There have been no adverse educational effects. Achievement scores have been rising in the past several years; most notably, there appears to be a solid trend of fewer students scoring in the lower three stanines. Achievement gains in the pairs and triads appear slightly greater than in other district schools. We expect to continue to see achievement gains in the next few years as a result of the district's concentration in the past few years on effective schools, firm and consistent discipline, and basic skills. These organizational emphases have been possible as a result of the stability created by implementing a plan without the uncertainty and energy drain of lengthy court proceedings.

The Seattle Plan has not had a harmful effect on white enrollment. Before the plan, enrollment had fallen steadily from nearly 100,000 (over 85 percent white) in 1963 to under 60,000 (65 percent white) in 1977. In the first three years of the Seattle Plan, the proportion of white students in the district declined roughly 3 percent per year, the

same rate as in the three years before the plan. Had it not been for the influx of thousands of Asian immigrant students, the drop in the proportion of white students in 1980–81 and 1981–82 would have been closer to 1 percent, as it has been in each of the last three years. And it appears that school desegregation has played a part in slowing, and even reversing, the trend toward greater residential segregation in some portions of the city.

Seattle has adjusted peacefully to desegregated schools. At the last local property-tax levy election, a record rate of voter approval—roughly 85 percent—was achieved. And in all recent school board elections, pro-Seattle Plan candidates have defeated anti-Seattle Plan candidates. Several efforts to stop the plan, including a statewide initiative and recent legislative action, have been resisted successfully by the school board in the courts.

In spring 1981, after a lengthy process of citizen involvement, the Seattle School Board adopted a three-year plan of school closures and complementary changes in the desegregation plan. Following a similar process, a three-year plan for 1984–87 was adopted in spring of 1984.

Seattle is now prepared to make further progress. The city council and school board have jointly adopted goals calling for coordinated action to encourage residential integration, and the school board and superintendent have recently initiated contacts

with other area governmental agencies and realtors to pursue joint action. With cooperation of the city, the school district, housing officials, and others, Seattle should be able to reduce the need for mandatory student assignments over the long term.

We believe the Seattle experience demonstrates how proper planning and responsible leadership can produce school desegregation that is successful educationally and successful in stabilizing a city school system.

PART V

Summary of
Conference

Editor's Summary

In summarizing the proceedings of the *Brown* Plus Thirty Conference, we were impressed with both the presenters' and conferees' depth of understanding of the issues regarding desegregation. We expected those individuals who participated in the 1954 case to give us an historical view of desegregation, but they provided a great deal more. Their insights concerning the thirty-year struggle are profound, and they point the way to future solutions and recommendations. Equally impressive were the contributions of school administrators, researchers, attorneys, and technical-assistance experts, who pointed to convincing evidence of successful desegregation efforts and analyzed the strengths and weaknesses of past and present desegregation activities.

Clearly, desegregation remains a complex and controversial social issue, as is epitomized by the current anti-desegregation mood in the country led principally by the current Administration. The pessimistic mood of the country regarding desegregation has caused many of those involved to overlook some remarkable changes that have taken place; this negative atmosphere has also reduced our opportunities to take advantage of the knowledge and experience gained over the last thirty years. We believe that these proceedings help place desegregation in a proper perspective, thus benefiting future desegregation efforts; hence, we offer this summary.

PAST AND PRESENT DILEMMAS

Samuel Proctor set the tone of the conference by noting that the 1954 *Brown* decision "called for a level of community in America that had been unknown, unanticipated, and unaccepted in the larger society." The Court placed schools in contraposition to society, which gave rise to a persistent resistance, since 1954, to the Court's order. Kenneth Clark expressed the sentiments of the conferees when he said, "Racism in American democracy continues." That the position of the 1954 Supreme Court has not prevailed is a reflection of the pervasiveness of racism in America.

In regard to desegregation, present-day conditions in the schools are clear. The center of gravity of the struggle to desegregate public schools has moved from the southern states to northern urban communities. There are more children in absolute numbers and by percentage in racially segregated schools in urban areas than there were at the time of the *Brown* decision (1954). According to Gary Orfield, "the seventeen southern and border states have shown the most dramatic changes since the Supreme Court ruled out 'freedom of choice' desegregation in 1968 and approved the use of busing in 1971." However, there is also a recent trend toward resegregation in these states due to the growth of segregated residential patterns. Outside the South, desegregation has been accomplished primarily in places where there have been major court orders. The most dramatic increases in segregation have occurred in large urban centers in states like California, Texas, Illinois, Florida, and New York. Over the years, however, in both the North and South, the courts have been in the forefront to alleviate racial isolation in the schools.

Since the courts have played a major role in the implementation of *Brown*, it was also crucial to examine the role of the federal government in desegregation. Ultimately, the implementation of *Brown* is a power question. As Samuel Proctor stated, "It is a moral issue; it is a professional challenge. But in the final analysis...[it] resolve[s] into a simple power question: Who can cause it to happen and who can prevent it." In the past, the progress made in desegregating school districts was in part the result of strong support from the federal government. The position of the present Administration was articulated by Assistant Attorney General for Civil Rights William Bradford Reynolds, who said, "Our focus is no longer on the mandatory transportation feature, but rather on voluntary student-transfer techniques.... Our remedial program has as its centerpiece special magnet schools and other curriculum enhancement programs that provide educational incentives to all children in the system."

Many participants at the conference were strongly opposed to Reynolds' views. Beverly Cole of the NAACP and Julius Chambers of the Legal Defense Fund were among those who argued that the current national Administration has not only refused to endorse desegregation laws and court orders, it has actively challenged them. Others noted that the Administration argues that busing does not work at a time when busing is being used successfully in desegregation plans. Moreover, LaMar Miller and Theodore Repa and Willis Hawley argued that the evidence does not support the Administration's position that voluntary magnet schools will desegregate all schools. Places such as Buffalo have magnet schools, but their plans include mandatory busing. Busing, in fact, appears not to be an issue as long as there is a quality education program at the end of the bus ride.

Presenters and participants challenged the Administration's views on other counts. They argued that the Administration has continually ignored its constitutional obligation to implement, through the Department of Education and the Department of Justice, a vigorous and effective enforcement program in the area of desegregation based on relevant civil rights laws and court orders. It has also persistently refused to release civil rights data on students and faculty in public schools.

Another issue discussed at the conference was what Hawley called "the false promise of separate but equal." Recently, an increasing number of minority leaders (blacks in particular) and whites who had once advocated desegregation seem to be calling for a retreat from desegregation in favor of strengthening minority schools. Their point of view grows out of the evidence obtained from studies on more effective schools mainly in minority urban areas and the fact that the Brown case focused essentially on racial imbalance. Several participants, including Derrick Bell, Hugh Scott, and Nelvia Brady raised the issue of whether equalization of funding and facilities and proportional representation in educational policymaking wouldn't be better ways to achieve quality education and educational opportunity for minorities. Clearly, we know a lot more about improving student achievement than we ever did, and we know that we can attain significant improvements in schools that are racially isolated. But as Hawley stated, "It is one thing to assert that we can do better than we have in educating children in predominantly minority schools and another to say that racially separate schools are likely to be more effective than racially desegregated schools."

Most participants agreed that with some notable exceptions, desegregation via Brown has not provided the quality education for minorities that they deserve. To return to separate but equal schools, however, is not the answer, according to Hawley and Miller and Repa. They argue that in order for separate but equal schools to work, minority schools would have to receive the resources of society without discrimination and in ways that acknowledge that quality education for students from low-income families (for various reasons) requires larger resources than quality education for children from more affluent backgrounds. Given that the balance of economic power lies with the white majority, it is unlikely that minority schools would receive adequate resources.

Turning to the legal perspectives of Brown, Chambers pointed out that "many of the arguments advanced today by those who seek to impede desegregation are similar to those used by opponents of Brown" in 1954. Yet it is also true that times have changed since Brown. People's attitudes have changed, as have the resources available and the issues being addressed. Attitudes have changed in that advocates of desegregation are more informed regarding their rights, and they insist, rightfully, on more than just the mixing of students. Their opponents, on the other hand, seek to use, without explanation, the sometimes uneven results in desegregation systems to argue for more limited desegregation. Resources for desegregation efforts have changed in that the army of lawyers and the funds available in the past have decreased sharply. Issues have changed from a focus on practices and policies that excluded black students and teachers from some schools to issues that are not as clear-cut.

The following issues are some examples: To what extent must a school system affirmatively mix students by race in order to discharge its responsibility? Is assigning students according to race and by percentage consistent with the Constitution? What factors in addition to race should a court consider in devising and ordering desegregation plans? What about the racial composition of individual classes; the qualifications and attitudes of teachers and administrators; the types and quality of educational programs offered; the funds provided for individual schools and their comparison with other schools in the system and other school systems? Is interdistrict relief appropriate or desirable? What is the effect of prior discrimination on the achievement levels of minority students? Are students being taught what they need to know in order to enter future job markets?

In short, the issues of desegregation today are more numerous, more complex, and much more expensive to address. Additionally, the courts are less receptive to establishing new grounds for substantive liability or relief. Today, before undertaking school desegregation litigation, we must consider carefully the facts of each case and must have very specific remedies in mind.

The legal perspectives on desegregation to a great extent depend on answers to social science questions. In 1954, social scientists led by Clark brought to the attention of the courts what was known about the effects of enforced segregation on children. Over the past thirty years, social scientists have been involved in every phase of desegregation litigation. According to Stuart Cook, social science theory was often used to support the interpretation that past actions which have produced current segregation reflected official segregative intent, even though no official record of this was available. And perhaps the most recent involvement of social scientists was in support of the position that the damage of segregation could not be remedied simply by reassigning children to desegregated schools. Rather as victims of past discrimination, it was determined by the courts that these children had to be compensated by educational programs which would go beyond the simple removal of segregation.

Cook has reviewed studies of the overall impact of desegregation, which he claims are inconclusive, and then suggests studies

that may offer guidance to the courts and to compensatory education. He suggests that a combination of law and social science constitutes a powerful tool with which to complete the task of desegregating public schools.

While the need to combine law and social science is highly important, Norman Redlich points out that joint legal and political action is essential in winning the battle for racial justice. For lawyers and social scientists to achieve the goals of desegregation litigation, political action is necessary. As Redlich says, "One type of action [legal or political] cannot proceed without the other."

Redlich admonished the *Brown* conference participants for talking in terms of "betrayed" hopes. *Brown* was a great achievement and much of its promise has been fulfilled, at least as the issues were perceived in 1954. For the most part, the legal framework of the post-*Brown* desegregation cases is still in place. The principles established in those cases have been cut back in certain areas, but they are still valid. The Supreme Court has not yet abandoned them.

Redlich is among those who addressed the question of when and under what circumstances a school district under court order is entitled to a judicial declaration of unitariness, thereby releasing it from the courts' jurisdiction. This issue was also raised by Reynolds, who urged the federal courts to release their hold on school districts that have long been in compliance with comprehensive decrees. Reynolds reported that the Justice Department had urged the Court not to measure unitariness in terms of racial balance throughout the school system in the Denver case (*Keyes* v. *School Board of Denver*, 1973). The Justice Department argued that even if some schools in the system, because of factors beyond the school boards' control, such as demographic shifts, may never have attained (or even if attained, continued to maintain) the precise racial percentages for student enrollment contemplated in the court-ordered plan, a declaration of unitariness should follow.

Chambers rejected the Justice Department argument. He said, "there is the need to challenge the federal government's contention that federal district courts have no further supervisory jurisdiction over school systems once desegregation plans are in effect. The government finds support for its position in *Swann* v. *Charlotte-Mecklenburg*, where the Court indicated that a time would come when racial imbalances might

be the result of demographic changes and not intentional segregation." According to Chambers, "It is a misreading of *Swann* to claim that this finding prevents a district court from revising a defective plan or one that is not being implemented fairly or effectively. School districts should not be absolved of liability or permitted to continue discriminatory practices simply because black children are attending previously all-white schools. District courts must retain jurisdiction to ensure that segregation is eliminated 'root and branch.'"

In these proceedings, the relationship between desegregation and quality education is a major theme. Despite their frustrations, pessimism, and sometimes anger, participants and presenters focused on questions regarding improving the quality of education in desegregated settings. There was also grave concern for the improvement of education in those large city school districts where it is unlikely that schools will be desegregated in the near future. Robert Carter described the paradox of the *Brown* decision. He noted that "*Brown* is one of the peaks of American jurisprudence because in stating the guarantee of equality as fundamental to our basic law, it expresses the loftiest values in our society....However, in the area of...education, *Brown* has not fared so well." But Carter also acknowledged that in thirty years, desegregation has produced some achievements. Both Robert Carter and Robert Crain pointed out how education had improved for minority students in the past two decades, as shown by higher scores on achievement tests, more years of schooling completed, and a decrease in illiteracy. Crain noted that desegregation must receive much of the credit for the improvement in blacks' test scores. While these achievements are notable, almost all of the presenters pointed to the continuing disparities between minority and majority youngsters' performances in the nation's school systems. As Carter put it, "Because of the very real correlation between academic skills and employment, and income and antisocial conduct, a good education is virtually indispensable for all Americans."

Carter's words became more significant as other presenters described the conditions in the public schools with respect to quality education and desegregation. Constance Clayton, superintendent of the Philadelphia public schools, suggested that quality education, effective schools, and desegregation are not ends in themselves. They are means to enable each child to develop to his or her full potential. As a result, the Philadelphia desegregation plan is based on excellence and equity. She urged more concern for distinguishing means from ends, a greater appreciation for the constraints found in urban environments, and a greater sensitivity to parents.

Nelvia Brady described the Chicago desegregation plan, which dealt with the reality of an urban school system that is 80-percent minority. Unlike many other plans, Chicago's focus is on equity of access, equity of process, and equity of outcome. Minority schools can be quality schools, according to Brady. She suggests that racial balance must be rejected as an isolated goal if we are to achieve the practical tasks of desegregating large urban school districts in the 1980s.

The picture of desegregation in Philadelphia and Chicago is quite different from that in Buffalo, Seattle, Austin, and Charlotte Mecklenburg. Buffalo, a city where 50 percent of the students are minority children, has been called a model desegregated school system. Buffalo School Superintendent Eugene Reville has described desegregation as the best thing that ever happened to Buffalo. The Buffalo plan incorporates three phases over a ten-year period. It features the development of a quality education program that includes such innovative techniques as early childhood centers, high parent involvement, and magnet schools. There has been no disruption, no violence, no white flight during the Buffalo desegregation effort.

The Buffalo plan is based on the insistence of the school's attorney, Aubrey McCutchen, that no remedy would be effective unless both minority and majority children benefited from better education. McCutchen asserted that if the violation (segregation) deprived minority children of privilege and preference, then the remedy must ensure that minority children would have privilege and preference. Eugene Reville placed the Buffalo experience in perspective by suggesting that if a school system is found guilty of segregating its schools, it undoubtedly has more than a trace of the racism that provoked the court order and that this racism certainly infects the community. The entire school system must establish as a first priority the banishment of this infection. In-service training programs, biracial committees, other creative programs, and parental involvement must focus on this unfinished task. The result will be an educational experience for children that is second to none, namely, a truly integrated educational system.

EMERGING TRENDS FOR THE 1980S AND 1990S

As we close this summary, Hawley's list of the most significant lessons learned from thirty years of desegregation bears repeating:

- Americans, both the beneficiaries and victims of the ways power and privilege are distributed, are much more committed to and capable of sustaining social differences than we like to believe.

- Myths, perpetrated by all sides, are more influential in shaping public policy and collective action than facts and (more or less) objective analysis.

- Despite widespread support for the principle of desegregation and our national disdain for government coercion, very little desegregation will occur if voluntary choice is the primary means we use to reduce racial isolation.

- School desegregation is an effective way to achieve a more integrated society, and there is no other way to achieve social integration that even approximates its real and potential efficacy.

- The notion of "separate but equal" schools is a fantasy that will not die.

- We can effectively pursue the goals of equity and excellence but to do so will require major changes in the way we organize and operate our schools.

The inclusion of quality education components in desegregation plans is the most important emerging trend. There is no necessary trade-off between equity and educational excellence. One without the other is insufficient. There are challenges for schools who seek to develop programs that focus on equity and excellence, and these challenges will require fundamental changes in the way schools function.

The process of an equitable quality education requires (1) a school organization that allows some choice by parents and students about the programs that are offered, (2) an appropriate curriculum that provides both the necessary skills and multicultural emphasis appropriate to achieving educational excellence, (3) instructional practices that provide for interracial cooperative experiences on an equal status basis, (4) a varied staff that has achieved excellence in administering a school and teaching a diverse student body and has high expectations for all students, (5) testing procedures that help teachers cor-

rectly diagnose and evaluate students in order to maximize learning, (6) pre-service and in-service training to maintain excellence and to meet the instructional needs of all students, (7) parent involvement that focuses on assisting students as well as shared governance, (8) adapting to and using student diversity as a strategy for improving performance and behavior, and (9) the maintenance of order through practices that promote a school environment that is conducive to learning.

Throughout these proceedings there has been a common theme, which Hawley states well: "It has been and will be much harder to achieve desegregation than any advocate of desegregation would have believed a few years ago. Indeed, one might marvel at the progress given the realities of this nation. But it is also clear that future successes may be even harder to achieve and that there may be fewer people of all races willing to pay the price." But Redlich responds by saying, "The history of our country teaches us that it is difficult, perhaps impossible, to achieve racial justice except in an open, diverse, and free society."

LaMar P. Miller

List of Participants

BROWN PLUS THIRTY
CONFERENCE

September 11–14, 1984
Penta Hotel
New York City

Mickie Agrait
Conciliator
Community Relations Service
U.S. Department of Justice
New York, NY

Coessie Alexander
Administrative Assistant
Community Relations Service
U.S. Department of Justice
New York, NY

Gail Allmon
Administrative Assistant to the Superintendent
Parkway School District
Chesterfield, MO

Joan Arnold
Assistant Commissioner
Office of Non-Public Schools, Civil Rights and
    Intercultural Relations
New York State Education Department
Albany, NY

Carol Ascher
Research Specialist
ERIC Clearinghouse on Urban Education
Columbia University
New York, NY

Dr. Joseph P. Atkins
Assistant Superintendent
Jefferson County Public Schools
Louisville, KY

Thomas Atkins
General Counsel
NAACP
Brooklyn, New York

Dr. Leonard C. Beckum
Far West Laboratory for Educational
    Research and Development
San Francisco, CA

James Blaine
OEEO
New Jersey State Department of Education
Trenton, NJ

Dr. Boyd Bosma
Human and Civil Rights Specialist
National Education Association
Washington, DC

Dr. John Brademas
President
New York University
New York, NY

JoAnne Bradley
Dean
Downstate Medical Center
Brooklyn, NY

Dr. Nelvia M. Brady
Associate Superintendent
Chicago Public Schools
Chicago, IL

Dr. Roy W. Browning, Jr.
Assistant Superintendent
Student Support Services and Staff Development
Topeka Public Schools
Topeka, KS

Robert A. Burnham
Dean
School of Education, Health,
    Nursing, and Arts Professions
New York University
New York, NY

Dr. Eugene L. Cain
Assistant Superintendent
Michigan Department of Education
Lansing, MI

Liz Calvin
Director, Technical Assistance
Missouri Department of Elementary and
    Secondary Education
Jefferson City, MO

Norma Cantu
Educational Director
Mexican American Legal Defense
    and Educational Fund
San Francisco, CA

Emanuel G. Carr
EED Director
District of Columbia Schools
Washington, DC

Honorable Robert L. Carter
U.S. District Court
Foley Square
New York, NY

Charles Cassidy
Office of Non-Public Schools, Civil
    Rights and Intercultural Relations
New York State Education Department
Albany, NY

Norman J. Chachkin
Deputy Director
Lawyers' Committee for Civil Rights
    Under Law
Washington, DC

Julius Levonne Chambers
Director/Counsel
NAACP Legal Defense and Educational
    Fund Inc.
New York, NY

Roland E. Charpentier
Magnet School Planning Coordinator
Worcester Public Schools
Worcester, MA

Dr. Kenneth Clark
Clark Phipps Clark Harris Inc,
New York, NY

Dr. Constance E. Clayton
Superintendent of Public Schools
Board of Education
Philadelphia, PA

Judith Coburn
Occupational Education, Civil Rights Unit
New York State Education Department
Albany, NY

Eleanor Cocalis
OEEO
New Jersey State Department of Education
Trenton, NJ

Dr. Beverly Cole
Education Director
NAACP
Brooklyn, NY

Dr. Robert Crain
Johns Hopkins University
Center for Organization of Schools
Baltimore, MD

Claire Cunningham
Associate Director, Legal Council of Chief State
    School Officers
Resource Center on Educational Equity
Washington, D.C.

Ora A. Curry
Associate
New York State Education Department
New York, NY

Earl S. Davis
Director
Afro-American Affairs
New York University
New York, NY

John De Sane
OEEO
New Jersey Department of Education
Trenton, NJ

Robert E. Diaz
Deputy Director
Office of Legal Services
New York City Board of Education
Brooklyn, NY

Dr. Harriet Doss Willis
Assistant Commissioner
New Jersey Department of Education
Trenton, NJ

Dr. Ogle B. Duff
University of Pittsburgh
Office of Research
Pittsburgh, PA

Dr. Richard Dyksterhuis
Consultant
Department of Integration and Special Programs
Seattle, WA

H. Wilson Eaves
Superintendent of Schools
Rockville Centre Union Free School District
Rockville Centre, NY

Dr. Edgar Epps
Department of Education
University of Chicago
Chicago, IL

Mary Ann Etu
Supervisor
Office of Non-Public Schools, Civil Rights and
    Intercultural Relations
New York State Education Department
Albany, NY

Dr. Mary Lee Fitzgerald
Superintendent of Schools
Board of Education
Montclair, NJ

Dr. Gordon Foster
Director, RDAC
University of Miami
Coral Gables, FL

Dr. Olivia P. Frost
Vice President
NAACP Mid Manhattan
New York, NY

Jane M. Goodson
Coordinator
Staff Development and Training
State Department of Education
Jackson, MS

Fletcher Graves
Conciliator
Community Relations Service
U.S. Department of Justice
New York, NY

Charlene Green
Supervisor, Chapter II
Indianapolis Public Schools
Indianapolis, IN

Floyd M. Hammack
Associate Professor
Educational Sociology and Higher Education
New York University
New York, NY

Chris Hansen
Special Litigation Counsel
ACLU
New York, NY

Dr. John Harris
Professor, Educational Administration
Indiana University
Indianapolis, IN

Edward Harshaw
Affirmative Action Officer
Community Relations Service
U.S. Department of Justice
City of Wildwood, NJ

Willis Hawley
Dean, Peabody College
Vanderbilt University
Nashville, TN

Charles B. Hayes
Professor
Educational Administration
New York University
New York, NY

James Heck
Director of School Integration
Buffalo Public Schools
Buffalo, NY

Cheryl Brown Henderson
Brown and Brown Associates
Topeka, KS

Jeanne Heningburg
Director of Human Relations
Montclair Board of Education
Montclair, NJ

Charles Henson
Attorney
Topeka Public Schools
Topeka, KS

Frederick Hill
Unit Head
Office of Equal Opportunity
New York City Board of Education
Brooklyn, NY

Michael W. Hoge
General Counsel
Seattle School District
Seattle, WA

Stephanie Hughes
Coordinator, Multicultural Education
Norwalk Public Schools
Norwalk, CT

Marilyn A. Hulme
Coordinator, Regional Materials
    Sex Desegregation Assistance Center
Consortium for Educational Equity
Rutgers University
New Brunswick, NJ

Robert Immoor
Psychologist
Coram Elementary School
Middle Island, NY

Dr. Donald G. Jacobs
National Director
National Council of Churches
Office of the Black Churches
New York, NY

Spencer Jennings
Office of Non-Public Schools, Civil
    Rights and Intercultural Relations
New York State Education Department
Albany, NY

Jon Johnson
Conciliator
Community Relations Service
U.S. Department of Justice
New York, NY

Dr. Joseph E. Johnson
Superintendent of Schools
Red Clay Consolidated School District
Wilmington, DE

Timothy Johnson
Conciliator
Community Relations Service
U.S. Department of Justice
New York, NY

Ernie Jones
Senior Conciliator
Community Relations Service
U.S. Department of Justice
Atlanta, GA

Honorable Nathaniel Jones
U.S. Court of Appeals
Cincinnati, OH

Tommie C. Jones
Regional Director
Community Relations Service
U.S. Department of Justice
New York, NY

Nancy Kiefer
Midwest Center
Kansas State University
Department of Administration and Foundations
Manhattan, KS

Dr. Everett C. Lattimore
Assistant Superintendent
Plainfield Board of Education
Plainfield, NJ

Dr. Rebecca Lubetkin
Director
SDAC
Consortium for Educational Equity
Rutgers University
New Brunswick, NJ

Vernon Manley
Deputy Director
The Neighborhood Stabilization Program
Commission on Human Rights
New York, NY

Elizabeth C. Marion
Coordinator
Essex County Vocational Schools
East Orange, NJ

Beverly Martin
Affirmative Action
Personnel Administration, Ithaca City Public
    Schools
Ithaca, NY

James McClendon
Associate
Office of Non-Public Schools, Civil Rights
    and Intercultural Relations
New York State Education Department
Albany, NY

Dr. Aubrey McCutcheon
Attorney at Law
Detroit, MI

Walter Milman
City School District of Newburgh
Newburgh, NY

Dr. Thomas Minter
Dean of Education
Herbert Lehman College
City University of New York
Bronx, NY

Michael Moon
Equity Specialist
Office of Non-Public Schools, Civil Rights and
    Intercultural Relations
New York State Education Department
Albany, NY

Dr. Charles Moody
School of Education
University of Michigan at Ann Arbor
Ann Arbor, MI

Thelma Moore
Assistant Superintendent
Parkway School District
Chesterfield, MO

Steven Obus
Assistant U.S. Attorney
U.S. Attorney's Office
Southern District
New York, NY

Dr. Gary Orfield
Professor of Political Science
University of Chicago
Chicago, IL

Earnest L. Palmer
Superintendent
Perry County Board of Education
Marion, AL

Dr. Nancy Peck
RDAC
University of Miami
Coral Gables, FL

Robert L. Pegues Jr.
Superintendent of Schools
Warren City Schools
Warren, OH

Edward Porter
Assistant Superintendent for Curriculum and
    Instruction
Middle Island School District
Middle Island, NY

Dr. Samuel Proctor
Professor of Education
Rutgers University
Graduate School of Education
New Brunswick, NJ

Dr. Charles Rankin
Director
Midwest Center
Kansas State University
Department of Administration and Foundations
Manhattan, KS

Barbara Rapoport
Associate, Educational Integration
New York State Education Department
New York, NY

Dean Norman Redlich
New York University Law School
New York, NY

Dr. Eugene R. Reville
Superintendent
Buffalo Public Schools
Buffalo, NY

William Bradford Reynolds
Assistant Attorney General
Civil Rights Division
U.S. Department of Justice
Washington, D.C.

Victor Risso
Senior Conciliator
Community Relations Service
U.S. Department of Justice
New York, NY

Stephanie Robinson
Director of Education
National Urban League
New York, NY

Rae Roeder
OEEO
New Jersey Department of Education
Trenton, NJ

Sandra Priest Rose
Reading Reform Foundation
New York, NY

Dr. Howard E. Row
Assistant to State Superintendent
Delaware State Department of Public Instruction
Desegregation Advisory Committee
Dover, DE

Marjorie Rush
Director of Civil Rights and Intercultural Relations
Office of Non-Public Schools, Civil Rights, and
    Intercultural Relations
New York State Education Department
Albany, NY

Dr. Hugh Scott
Dean, Division of Programs in Education
Hunter College
New York, NY

Ruby Shaw
Assistant Superintendent for Human Relations
Norwalk Public Schools
Norwalk, CT

Ralph Sloan
Superintendent
Board of Education
Norwalk, CT

Dr. Karen Smith
Director of Integration and Human Relations
Yonkers School District
Yonkers, NY

Linda Brown Smith
Brown and Brown Associates
Topeka, KS

Marcellus Smith
OEEO
New Jersey Department of Education
Trenton, NJ

Dr. Leonard Stevens
Director
Office of School Monitoring and Community
   Relations
Cleveland, OH

Paul G. Strollo
Director, Magnet Schools
Rochester City School District
Rochester, NY

Michael H. Sussman
Assistant General Counsel
NAACP Special Contributions Fund
Brooklyn, NY

Nida Thomas
OEEO
New Jersey Department of Education
Trenton, NJ

Luz Torres
Training Coordinator
Office of Equal Opportunity
New York City Board of Education
Brooklyn, NY

Dr. Lee Ann Truesdale
Professor
Special Education Program
Queens College
Flushing, NY

Leon Trusty
OEEO
New Jersey Department of Education
Trenton, NJ

Lynette Tucker
Director
Office of Equal Opportunity
New York City Board of Education
Brooklyn, NY

Benjamin Turner
Director
Kent State Center for Educational Development
   & Strategic Services (KEDS)
Kent State University
Research and Sponsored Programs
Kent, OH

Betty E. Veal
Assistant Superintendent for Instruction
Montclair Public Schools
Montclair, NJ

Gay Wainwright
Associate
New York State Education Department
New York, NY

Evelyn Hull Warner
President
Ambler NAACP
No. Wales, PA

Dr. Frank Warnock
Coordinator
National Origin Desegregation Project
State Department of Education
Jackson, MS

Cora Watkins
Assistant in Educational Integration
Office of Non-Public Schools, Civil
   Rights and Intercultural Relations
New York State Education Department
Albany, NY

Dr. Bruce Williams
Deputy Director, Social Science Program
Rockefeller Foundation
New York, NY

Dr. Collin Williams
Director, Integration and Special Programs
Seattle Public Schools
Seattle, WA

Dr. Peyton Williams Jr.
Associate State Superintendent of Schools
Georgia Department of Education
Office of State Schools and Special Services
Atlanta, GA

Dr. Reginald Wilson
American Council on Education
Washington, DC

Karl Wittman
Occupational Education Civil Rights
Coordinating Unit
New York State Education Department
Albany, NY

Ronald Woo
Assistant Director
Office of Equal Opportunity
New York City Board of Education
Brooklyn, NY

Metro Center

EXECUTIVE COUNCIL

Vincent Clephas
Chairman
Director of Public Affairs
Philip Morris, Inc.

Martha B. Bernard

Peggi Drum
Project Manager
Communications Program Development
J.C. Penney Co., Inc.

Gordon Marshall, Esquire
Graubard, Moskovitz, McGoldrick, Dannett &
    Horowitz

Arthur Nitzburg

Billie M. Oliver
Public Affairs
Manhattan Division
Con Edison

Sandra Priest Rose
Trustee
Reading Reform Foundation

David Fred Roth

Marie Scott
Executive Search Consultant
Federated Department Stores

Ernest McD. Skinner
Past President
Urban Bankers Coalition

Anita Soto
Community Relations Manager
New York Telephone Co.

Michael Varriano
Staff Assistant
Equal Opportunity Programs
    Coordinator
IBM®

ADVISORY BOARD

Michael C. Clendenin
Assistant Vice-President
New York Telephone Co.

Beverly Cole
Director of Education
National Association for the Advancement of
    Colored People

Lloyd M. Cooke

Jeanne Frankl
Director
Public Education Association

Gerald Freeborne
Deputy Commissioner
Office of Elementary, Secondary
    and Continuing Education

Angelo Gonzales
Executive Director
ASPIRA of New York, Inc.

Elizabeth H. Graham
Director
Division of Day Care
New York City Department of Health

David R. Jones
Executive Director
New York City Youth Bureau

Georgia McMurray
General Director
Community Service Society

Harriet Michel
Executive Director
New York Urban League

Nathan Quinones
Chancellor
New York City Board of Education

Charles W. Rudiger
Assistant to the President
Dowling College

Albert Shanker
President
United Federation of Teachers

Arnold Webb
Assistant Commissioner for Educational
    Programs
New Jersey Department of Education

Rachel T. Weddington
Professor of Education
Queens College

ADVISORY BOARD EX-OFFICIO MEMBERS

Robert Burnham
Dean
SEHNAP
New York University

James H. Finkelstein
Director of Research and Development
SEHNAP
New York University

Arnold Spinner,
Associate Dean
SEHNAP
New York University

LaMar P. Miller
Executive Director
Metro Center
New York University